OLD GIMLET EYE

OLD GIMLET EYE

THE ADVENTURES OF SMEDLEY D. BUTLER

BY

LOWELL THOMAS

Soldier Press
2018

Old Gimlet Eye The Adventures of Smedley D. Butler by Lowell Thomas. Annotated edition © copyright Soldier Press.

Published by Soldier Press, Los Angeles.

FIRST PRINTING, 2018.

ISBN: 9781728963006.

CONTENTS

Foreword 9

  An Opening Salute 9

Chapter I..11

  Sixteen and with the Marines...11

Chapter II...16

  Remembering the Maine..16

Chapter III 24

  A Full-Fledged Marine 24

Chapter IV..27

  Marking Time in the Philippines 27

Chapter V...34

  Off to China to Fight the Boxers 34

Chapter VI..40

  A Hot Time in Tientsin 40

Chapter VII...47

  On to Peking 47

Chapter VIII 55

  "Those Damn Knapsacks"..55

Chapter IX 63

Why I "Love" the Navy 63

Chapter X.. 68

Revolution in Honduras... 68

Chapter XI 76

From Soldiering to Mining 76

Chapter XII 83

Revolution in Nicaragua and Riots in Panama 83

Chapter XIII 91

The Adventures of General Walk............................... 91

Chapter XIV.. 99

Fighting in the Tropics 99

Chapter XV... 110

I Become a Spy in Mexico 110

Chapter XVI.. 118

Fighting Revels and Bandits in Haiti 118

Chapter XVII 128

The Storming of Black Mountain and the Capture of Fort
Riviere 128

Chapter XVIII 134

High Jinks in Haiti..134

Chapter XIX 147

On Tour with the President of Haiti..147

Chapter XX 157

Fighting the Mud at Brest 157

Chapter XXI 169

A Devil Dog in the City of Brotherly Love 169

Chapter XXII...177

A Tempest in a Cocktail Glass...177

Chapter XXIII..183

Treading Softly in China 183

Chapter XXIV 191

My Damned Follies at Quantico 191

Chapter XXV 195

The Mussolini Incident 195

Foreword

An Opening Salute

There is an old notion that heroes, doers of great deeds, are modest, reticent, silent men. I've known quite a few heroes and doers of great deeds, some of whom were modest, reticent and silent. But some were not. Some hid their light under half a dozen bushels, while others brandished their lights aloft, casting the brilliant beams as far as they could possibly reach. So, I am afraid we must chuck into the waste basket that bit of ethics which holds that a performer of valorous exploits is necessarily a shrinking violet.

For the quantity of silence, I should rate the English as preeminent. The average Englishman simply doesn't talk about the things he has done. Anything remotely savoring of boastfulness is downright vulgar. Yet with this very reticence there may be a certain fortunate quantity of ballyhoo. That prodigious young man named T. E. Lawrence, who roused Arabia against the Turk, withal his shyness, has surely not been lost in any dim and nameless obscurity.

As for the gift of words, there's the jovial Count Luckner,* the delightful conversational Sea Devil, who at any appointed or unappointed hour of day or night will gleefully fall into his natural role of a yarn-spinning sailor and will give to the breezes of land or sea loud, roaring and laughing accounts of adventures before the mast, or tales of raiding the sea during the World War.

So much for the silent British man of scholarship and peril, so much for the rollicking German jack-tar. Let's go on to an American paladin of adventure.

If you wanted to pick a physically ideal type for the United States Marine Corps, the man I have in mind would be a natural selection. For he has all of that dash, pepper, virility and swagger associated with Uncle Sam's soldiers of the sea. And if you wanted to give a swift summary of his career, you might say there has been no time in his life when he has been entirely out of trouble.

And that should make a story. Moreover, he happens to be one of the most vivid, provocative characters of our time. To his fellow Marines he has long been known as Old Gimlet Eye.

From this point on the narrative will lapse into the first person in the hope that it may reflect the spirit of a fighting man whose career has been one of the most dazzlingly adventurous of our day. Incidentally, this is the story of one of the few men in American history twice to be awarded the Medal of Honor, by special act of Congress.

*German naval hero Felix von Luckner (1881–1966), captain of SMS Seeadler (Sea Eagle) 1916–17. 'The Sea Devil' earned admiration for winning battles without any casualties on either side.

CHAPTER I

Sixteen and with the Marines

SOMETIMES I CAN CLOSE MY EYES and see a long line of my grey-cloaked forbears pointing reproachful, ghostly fingers at me for throwing in my lot with the fire-eating Marines. But I was in good company. My grandfather Butler was put out of Orthodox meeting for marching off to the Civil War.

Father died four years ago, but I shall always remember him as a man of powerful individuality and vigorous vocabulary. He spoke the plain language of the Quakers in public life just as he did in the bosom of his family, but he garnished the plain language with choice epithets when the occasion demanded high explosives. Father had just made a speech on the floor of Congress advocating a good size navy. Leaving the House, in the corridor of the Capitol he met a pacifist, who said to him: "Thee is a fine Friend." Father replied by saying: "Thee is a damn fool."

My mother put me to bed in the middle of a golden summer afternoon for sputtering out a couple of innocent damns. I was five years old and felt outraged and insulted. I didn't understand why I should be punished for talking like my father. When Father came home, through the half-open door I heard Mother telling him all about my black crime.

"If we don't take care, he will grow up like a New York newsboy."

"Thee mustn't take these little things so to heart," Father laughed. "I don't want a son who doesn't know how to use an honest damn now and then."

Farming, law and politics have from way back been the principal occupations of my family on both sides. A Butler has sat on the bench in Chester County, Pennsylvania, almost without a break for the past seventy-five years. My father, Thomas S. Butler, was a judge for a time, but he spent most of his later life as a member of Congress, where he represented the same district for thirty-two years. As chairman of the Naval Affairs Committee of the House he occupied a key position of influence.

I was born on July 30, 1881, in West Chester, Pennsylvania, around which so much of my family history has been woven. I had a strenuous, but not particularly eventful childhood. Brought up as a Hicksite Quaker, I am still one in good standing, so far as I know. I was vigorously brushed and combed and soaped to acquire the cleanliness next to godliness before going to the Friends' Meeting twice a week. Dozing off on a hard bench to the drone of words that meant nothing to me and being "The fighting Quaker" is what my friends and enemies call me, and I'm proud of both titles—fighter and Quaker. But I'm ashamed to confess that in my first recorded fight I took unfair advantage. I was a small boy packed off to spend a vacation with my grandfather. He was sixty years older than I and not much fun as a playmate, so I searched the neighborhood for a friend my own age. I found him standing on the edge of a muddy little pond. He had yellow curls, a lace collar and a black velvet suit.

"Hello," I sang out, "What's your name?"

"I'm not allowed to speak to strange boys," he answered.

That was more than I could bear. I gave Lord Fauntleroy a hearty shove into the shallow, reed-choked water. Red-faced, mud-streaked and dripping, he ran home, howling at the top of his voice. I felt that my grandfather secretly approved of my action. Nevertheless, I was sent home in semi-disgrace a week before the proposed end of my visit.

My first school was the Friends' Graded High School in West Chester. Later I was sent to the Haverford School near Philadelphia, which was then, as it is now, an outstanding school and accepted like the Ten Commandments as a matter of course by the old Quaker families of the city for the education of their sons. Studying was not my specialty. I have always preferred action to books. I'm probably the only general officer in the United States who has never attended a war or naval college.

Our elocution teacher taught me the pump-handle gestures and dramatic flourishes of the nineties, and then said to me: "My boy, I'm going to make a first-class orator out of you." Whereupon he made me learn an oration by William Cullen Bryant* and entered me in the yearly competition. But I secretly memorized Mark Twain's "Storm on the Erie Canal." I've always liked a good storm.

*Victorian man of letters, William Cullen Bryant (1794-1878).

The annual oratory contest was a gala night at the school. Squirmingly self-conscious in my first long trousers, I mounted the platform before all the boys and their parents. The teacher was in the front row and nodded at me approvingly. Beforehand, he had taken me aside to assure me that I would win the cup. I thought I would, too, but I didn't tell him about the surprise I had for him. I drew myself up and tried to feel like Patrick Henry and Daniel Webster rolled into one. As I launched out into the Erie storm, the dignified old gentleman leaned forward, his jaw dropped and his eyes almost popped out of his head in horror. The boys clapped and pounded on the floor, but the judges didn't give me even honorable mention.

That was my first experience at speaking out of turn in public. But not my last, I'm told.

When the Maine was blown up in Havana Harbor, in February 1898, I was just sixteen. The excitement was intense. Headlines blazed across the papers. Crowds pushed and shoved around the bulletin boards. School seemed stupid and unnecessary.

War was declared two months later and we boys thought our government exceedingly slow in avenging the death of our gallant American sailors. But here was the war at last, and we built bonfires and stamped around shouting "Remember the Maine, to Hell with Spain" and singing "We'll Hang General Weyler to a Sour Apple Tree."

Enviously I watched volunteer companies marching gaily off to war to the tunes of "There'll Be a Hot Time in the Old Town Tonight" and "The Girl I Left Behind Me." I clenched my fists when I thought of those poor Cuban devils being starved and murdered by the beastly Spanish tyrants.* I was determined to shoulder a rifle and help free little Cuba. It made no difference to me that Cuba had been a vague dot on the map until the Maine was blown up. Cuba now seemed more important than all the Latin and history in the world.

*Rumors pumped out by the sensationalist press at the time greatly exaggerated the Spanish treatment of Cubans. Some of it was government propaganda to help frame the US intervention as a humanitarian crusade.

The 6th Pennsylvania Volunteers was recruiting a company in West Chester. I tried to join up but was good-naturedly told to run along home. I couldn't even break into the navy as an apprentice boy. Father refused to give his consent.

One night as I was getting into bed, I heard him say to Mother in the next room: "Today Congress increased the Marine Corps by twenty-four second lieutenants and two thousand men for the period of the war. The Marine Corps is a finely trained body of men. Too bad Smedley is so young. He seems determined to go."

The Marine Corps was little more than a name to me then, except that once I had seen a Marine officer flashing down the street in sky-blue trousers with scarlet stripes. I had been much impressed with the handsome uniform. I knew I'd like to wear it. I tossed all night. In half-waking dreams I was charging up a hill at the head of my company, with sword drawn, bullets dropping around me.

Father's seal of approval on the Marine Corps settled it. The next morning, I took Mother aside and told her I was going to be a Marine. "If thee doesn't come with me and give me thy permission, I'll hire a man to say he is my father. And I'll run away and enlist in some far-away regiment where I'm not known."

Mother sighed. "Let me think it over quietly today." That evening she agreed to go with me on the first train leaving Philadelphia for Washington next day. Father knew nothing of our conspiracy. We started out at five o'clock. In the train Mother reached over and took my hand. I drew away. I was a man now and didn't want to be fondled in public. I've always hoped that my mother in her wisdom understood my lack of affection that morning.

In Washington, we went to the headquarters of the Marine Corps. Mother waited outside when I went into the office to introduce myself to Colonel Commandant Heywood. That fine old soldier looked at me quizzically. "When I met your father the other day, he told me you were only sixteen."

"No, sir," I lied promptly, "that's my brother."

"How old are you, then?"

"I'm eighteen, sir."

His keen eyes twinkled. "Well, you're big enough, anyway. We'll take you."

The Colonel directed me across the parade ground to Sergeant Hector McDonald, a tall, sway-backed, weather-beaten old timer, who was in charge of recruits.

While I was answering his questions, I looked out of the window, and to my horror saw my father. His coat-tails were flying out behind him as he rushed wildly across the parade ground to the Commandant's office. Goodbye, war, now I'm in for a scene.

An orderly appeared at the door and said the Commandant wished to see me. I was quaking in my boots as I went to the office.

"Did thy mother give thee her permission?" he demanded.

"Yes, sir."

"But thee is under age."

"Oh, there isn't any age limit now. Congress has never fixed one," I explained to my Congressional father. "Anyway, I've attended to that."

"How old did thee say thee was?"

"I told Colonel Heywood that I was eighteen, born on April 20, 1880."

Father smiled. "All right. If thee is determined to go, thee shall go, but don't add another year to thy age, my son. Thy mother and I weren't married until 1879." The Adjutant and Inspector of our Corps at that time was Major George C. Reid, one of the gentlest and finest characters I've ever known. Not the least of his virtues was a military stride that I would have given a fortune to acquire. He had a keen sense of humor and took a great interest in me because of the way I had broken into the Marines. Major Reid's nephew, George, entered the Corps when I did. He is now a retired colonel, living in Cleveland.

The Major took George and me, one under each arm, and strolled over to Heiberger's uniform shop. With as much dignity as if he were outfitting Napoleon's grand marshals, he had us measured for two second lieutenant's uniforms.

Since we couldn't perform our full duties until we were properly garbed, George and I hung around Marine Corps headquarters, like two generals temporarily out of a job.

Our uniforms came at last. My heart thumped as I hurriedly pulled on the sky-blue trousers with the gay red stripes down the seams and buttoned myself snugly into the dark blue coat. The uniform was tight and covered with black braid. I looked thin and wasp-like, more as if I belonged to a boys' band than to a husky fighting corps. I was very much pleased with myself. I couldn't go home and parade down the streets of West Chester, so I did the next best thing. I had my picture taken.

Now that George Reid and I could dress like second lieutenants—no matter that we were so new we almost creaked—we were ordered to the Washington barracks for instruction. The school for officers was conducted by a wonderful old soldier, Sergeant Major Hayes. He had been in a Scottish regiment and had fought with Kitchener in the Sudan. After his discharge from the British army he came to America and joined up with the Marines.

Until the Spanish-American War, two thousand men and officers constituted the total enrollment of the Marine Corps. Hayes, stationed at the Washington headquarters, enjoyed the distinction of being the one and only sergeant major for the whole Corps. His principal duty was to bring up young officers in the way they should go. He was getting on in years, but he was still a magnificent two hundred fifty-pound specimen, built on heroic lines. He carried his six feet three inches as erect as a ramrod.

When we rose to recite our lessons, the Sergeant Major always stood up too. Even though he was in charge of us, he never forgot for a moment the difference in our ranks, or that enlisted men never sit in the presence of officers. One rebuke from him cut to the quick. We all admired him so much that we didn't have the heart to disappoint him. He was one of the most perfect public servants I have ever met.

Those first six weeks of intensive training planted the seed of soldiering in me. And from that time on I never felt entirely happy away from Marines.

CHAPTER II

Remembering the Maine

ONE AFTERNOON AN ORDERLY TOLD ME I was to report at once to the Commandant's office. Colonel Heywood came crisply to the point. "Butler, should you like to go to Cuba?"

Why else in hell had I joined, I thought to myself.

The Marines were the first American troops in Cuba after war was declared.* A battalion of six hundred Marines under Colonel Robert W. Huntington** had landed on the beach at Guantanamo on June 10. The Spanish guerrillas peppered them with shot from the hills and the thick brush back of the beach, but the Marines calmly planted the Stars and Stripes on Cuban soil and quickly entrenched themselves. They drove three thousand Spaniards into the jungle, captured the enemy's water supply and triumphantly held their ground at Guantanamo.

*American public opinion backed Cuba's struggle for independence and supported a US intervention against colonial Spain. But it wasn't until the destruction of the USS Maine in Havana Harbor, on the evening of 15 February 1898, in a terrific explosion that killed 258 of the crew, that President William McKinley officially brought America into the conflict. After his offer of truce was rejected, a US naval blockade formed around Cuba and Congress officially recognized this as a declaration of war in April 1898. The Cuban War for Independence that had started in 1895 was now the Spanish-American War.

** Colonel Robert Watkinson Huntington (1840-1917).

The papers were filled with their exploit. We boys in the barracks back home devoured the tale of their adventure and were green with envy that we weren't with them in the thick of the mess. The high spot was when a sergeant of Marines volunteered to stand on the beach, a prize target for the Spanish fire, and signal the American cruiser in the bay to shell the woods where the guerrillas were hiding. Good old Huntington climbed over the trench and stood beside the sergeant while he swung the signal lantern. I was beside myself with excitement. To have the luck to join Huntington's gallant Marines seemed too good to be true.

"The American steamer *St. Paul* has been chartered by the government to take the President's own regiment, the 8th Ohio, to Cuba," the Commandant explained. "You will sail with it from New York tomorrow morning at ten o'clock."

Three of us young second lieutenants received orders to go. We had only a few hours to scramble our war outfits together. I paid five dollars for a little tin trunk, tossed into it six suits of underwear, a sewing bag, an extra pair of shoes, a few toilet articles and a Bible my old nurse had given me, and I was all set to meet the Spaniards. Today, a military career is complicated by five times as much baggage.

The biggest moment in my life was when I telegraphed Father and Mother in West Chester that I was off for the war. My parents met us in Jersey City.

As I leaned over the rail looking down at my mother, my martial ardor cooled off considerably. I hoped George and Pete couldn't see me trying to swallow the lump that kept pushing up into my throat. For months afterward, I could close my eyes and see my mother on the dock in her sweet blue and white silk dress with great balloon sleeves.

We anchored off Santiago July 10, just one week after the stinging defeat of the Spanish squadron under Admiral Cervera. We could see some of the Spanish cruisers, lying like wounded creatures on the beach. One was still burning.

Almirante (Admiral) Pascual Cervera y Topete (1839-1909).

Reid, Wynne and I were transferred to the cruiser Vesuvius for transportation to Guantanamo. The long knifelike ship rocked viciously. We were just three godforsaken, seasick little Marines, and we didn't give a tinker's damn if we ever joined Huntington's battalion. The Vesuvius had one virtue.* She was speedy and, in a few hours, brought us into the beautiful hill-circled waters of Guantanamo Bay.

The 'dynamite cruiser' Vesuvius was a sophisticated vessel; and had another virtue: three 15-inch guns.

Pete Wynne, George Reid and I, still shaky, set out for Admiral Sampson's flagship, the New York, to report for duty. None of us had ever been aboard a man-of-war. Our blue uniforms, glittering with black braid and brass buttons, were set off by flashing swords and white kid gloves. We were rigged out as showily as if we were escorting debutantes to an embassy ball.

On the New York everybody was in slouchy working clothes, stripped to the regulation minimum, for it was a scorching day. One by one the members of the crew sauntered carelessly by to look us over. We must have been as good as a vaudeville act. We paid no attention to their ribald and uncouth comments but haughtily continued to face front.

On the other side of the quarter deck a tall thin naval officer in a simple white uniform was pacing back and forth. He was stoop-shouldered and his beard and mustache were turning white. He was Admiral William T. Sampson, commander of the American fleet, which the week before, in the battle of Santiago Bay, sealed the doom of the Spanish navy in West Indian waters.

Every now and then the Admiral interrupted his promenade to glance at us with quiet amusement. But he made no effort to get acquainted. It took all our self-control to maintain our dress parade manners with the sun beating down like a sheet of fire.

Finally, when it looked as if no one would come to our rescue, an orderly brought us instructions from the Admiral to go ashore and report to battalion headquarters. A small boat landed us at a rickety little dock. We stepped out gingerly so as not to wet our fine clothes.

We asked some Marines camped near the dock where we could find Colonel Huntington. We put on a brave front for we wanted to make an impression at our first meeting with these tried and true veterans. Seventy-five per cent of the Marines in Cuba had been with the Corps from five to thirty years. While the old men were outwardly polite, they so obviously regarded us as candidates for the zoo that our self-esteem fell below zero. Shifting a chunk of tobacco from one cheek to the other, one wiry, iron-jawed corporal pointed out Colonel Huntington's headquarters perched on the topmost crest of a hill close by.

On the hot, dusty climb we soon lost the spick and span, tailored appearance we had so carefully brought ashore. Our stiff collars were long since wilted, the patent leather shoes smarted. We longed to take off our coats but clinging desperately to the visible proof of our rank, we kept them snugly buttoned.

At the top of the hill near an old blockhouse which had been pounded to fragments by shell-fire, we found four or five hundred men encamped inside a line of trenches. By this time, we were so dirt- streaked and untidy that we were ashamed to present ourselves at headquarters, but an inner angel prompted us not to ask the sinewy, bronzed men lounging around the tents for soap and a basin of water.

We pushed doggedly on to the center of the camp where we stumbled upon a half-dozen unkempt-looking tramps, with white beards and white hair.

"Can you tell me where I'll find Colonel Huntington?" I asked one very bow-legged white beard, sitting in a rudely made canvas camp-chair. He was short and stockily built, with big knotty hands and a prominent nose. He cocked his head on one side and looked at me impertinently.

"What do you want with the Colonel?"

"We are under orders to report to him."

"Going to help him win the war, are you?"

"This is no time for joking," I rebuked him stiffly. "We have our orders, and you will do well to point out where Colonel Huntington is."

One of the old boys burst into a great convulsive roar and fell backwards off his cracker-box.

Pete Wynne, always belligerent, could contain himself no longer. "Cut that out," he bellowed. "Don't you know enough to stand in the presence of officers?"

This brought shrieks of joy from the whole crowd. We were by turns white with rage and purple with humiliation.

"I shall report you to the Colonel..." Wynne began.

Just then a private came up, snapped to salute and addressed the bow-legged old man in the camp-chair as Colonel. I had reprimanded Huntington himself, the head of the whole Guantanamo Marine battalion, but it had never occurred to me that a colonel could be half-washed and careless about his personal appearance. The man who had laughed himself off the box was my future company commander, Captain Mancil C. Goodrell.

Many of these old war-birds with the rank of captain or higher had served with the Corps through the stormiest battles of the Civil War. Some had been with the Marines called out to reinforce Sumter. They fought at Bull Run, Antietam, Chickamauga and were stanch sharpshooters with Farragut at the capture of New Orleans. They are all dead now.

Goodrell, when I first met him in Cuba, was sixty-one years old, tall and straight and bearded. It was the style in those days not only for colonels but for captains and lieutenants to display a flourishing crop of whiskers.

Goodrell marched me off with a paternal friendliness that won my heart at once. He ushered me to a tent outside the trenches.

"Guess you'll have to take off your party clothes and save them until you parade for the girls at home," he explained, bringing me a plain field suit of brown linen and a broad-brimmed campaign hat. "Our company is going on outpost duty tonight. You must get ready at once. Our second lieutenant is sick, and you will have to take charge of the picket known as the Salt March." With a cheerful wave of the hand he disappeared.

Before sundown I started out with thirty men. If I live to be five hundred, I could never again endure the panic and bewilderment of that night. Here I was, sixteen years old, with no training or knowledge of soldiering, marching out in the bush, in the unhealthy neighborhood of the enemy. I was frightened. My head spun. And I gave a poor imitation of sprightliness as I stepped out at the head of the column. I stumbled over rocks and trembled when I brushed against cactus. In every thicket I saw murderous eyes and a raised rifle.

After an eternity, we reached our picket. My thirty men took their positions and calmly made ready for the night without any directions from me. I wouldn't have known what to tell them, anyway.

Slater, sergeant of the detachment, had been in the Marine Corps for twenty years. He was tall, gaunt and as hard-boiled as they come, but he was a soldier first, last and all the time. He made it his job to see that the Marines carried out their orders with flying colors, no matter what the President of the United States sent along in the way of officers. He was determined that even with the handicap of my presence the Spaniards would not get through our line that night.

I stood in the background and admired the cool deliberation with which the men made themselves at home. They were no more concerned than if they were turning in at the Washington barracks. I felt awkward and embarrassed, like an uninvited guest at a party. How should I ever have the nerve to give orders to these flint-muscled men who joked about the enemy?

When the sentinels were posted and the others were beginning to snore, Slater came to me and saluted: "If the Lieutenant would like, I'll make his bed."

I didn't like. A bed was useless. I knew I wouldn't sleep. But Slater's polite suggestion was a command. Obviously, I was going to bed. He neatly arranged my little bedding roll and mosquito net in the shelter of a thicket and announced, "The Lieutenant may get in when he is ready."

It was impossible to explain to Slater that I preferred to spend the night on my feet because I didn't shake as much standing up as lying down.

About midnight, Captain Goodrell came crackling through the brush on a tour of inspection. He put his arm around me reassuringly. "You'll be all right, my lad. There's no chance of an attack tonight. But if you need me, you'll find me half a mile from here." And he turned to Slater, "Take good care of the Lieutenant."

"Can't I come with you, Captain? Night inspection would be good experience for me," I urged, but my desperate excuse fell on deaf ears. He laughed and plunged through the darkness to visit the next picket.

It was stifling hot. My tongue clung to the dry roof of my mouth. Mosquitoes, more ferocious than any I had met in Pennsylvania, buzzed and stung with tormenting insistence. Every now and then one of our guards fired, insisting that Spaniards were lurking in the bushes. I burrowed deeper into my blanket. I didn't want to see a Spaniard.

At six o'clock Slater came to me with the formal announcement: "If the Lieutenant would like to get up, it is time to go to breakfast."

I never before jumped out of any bed with such willingness. The men grumbled that it had been a very dull night. Maybe it was, but my first night in the open near an unseen enemy was a nightmare of an experience. We climbed back through the underbrush to the main camp on the hilltop. The sight of the tents, the welcome smell of coffee and bacon and the secure feeling of being among six hundred brawny Marines, revived my spirits.

Captain Goodrell realized that I was only in the way, but he always tried to make me feel that I was a necessary unit in the company. He would come quietly into our midst, grab me by the shoulder and say, "Come on, Lieutenant, you and I are going to see what the Spaniards are up to."

That old Civil War veteran was a damned good soldier. Experience and danger had made him nimble-witted for every emergency. Fear wasn't in his vocabulary. One night, after we had just taken up our position, he invited me to walk with him in front of the lines.

"We'll be back in an hour, Sergeant," and he pushed right off, with me following at his heels like a timid but faithful dog.

We walked along the trail for about a mile. The Captain was in no hurry. He stopped every few minutes to point out to me the best places for ambushes, quite unconcerned that keen-eyed guerrillas might be lurking in those very thickets. As he was giving me a good lesson in bush soldiering, a bullet— the first bullet ever shot at me— whizzed past my head with a sickening ping. I sprawled flat on the ground, panting with fright.

"What in hell is the matter?" Goodrell looked down at me.

"That was a—bullet."

"Well, what if it was?"

He made me feel so ashamed of noticing a mere bullet that I scrambled at once to my feet. All the same, I now felt Spanish bogeys creeping up on me from all sides. I pointed out what I thought were Spaniards on the crest of a hill just ahead of us. He agreed that the moving figures might be Spaniards, but he wasn't disturbed at all. He sauntered along, relating hair-breadth escapes he had had during the Civil War.

On one of these night excursions the tropical moon flooded the whole bush with silver. Every stone, every cactus plant, quivered intensely and seemed nearer and more real than by daylight. If a war hadn't been going on, the country would have seemed enchantingly beautiful. In any case, Goodrell broke the spell. He wasn't romantic.

"This is a perfect night for an attack. Nothing to worry about, my boy. A little excitement is needed now and then to keep a soldier from going stale."

He must have observed that I looked alarmed, because he went on with ghoulish cheerfulness: "You know, Butler, you came to the wrong place if you didn't want trouble. Every man except me in the 10th Iowa Regiment was killed during the Civil War. I'm an unlucky man to associate with. My friends always get shot."

He got me all worked up for nothing. The attack didn't come off.

The first time Goodrell ordered me to drill the company was also the last time. I stumbled out in front, all hands and feet, which I didn't know what to do with. The men kept their eyes centered on me. I was petrified. I turned my mind inside out to salvage a remnant of the memory course on regulations in which I had been letter perfect in Washington. Finally, I sputtered out some commands. They were so conflicting that the men were falling around on top of one another. I was at the end of my rope. The next move was beyond me. I turned to Captain Goodrell who was watching the unexpected football scrimmage from the sidelines.

"I'm afraid, sir, I don't know what orders to give to straighten them out."

He snorted. "Get the hell out of here, Butler. There are no military orders on hell or earth to untangle that mess. Company dismissed!"

The Captain was a glorious scout for a sixteen-year-old boy to run up against in his first war. Whatever luck or skill I've had in the soldiering business I attribute to the teaching and example of that splendid officer, who, according to modern standards, had no military education.

All the officers were friendly. That group on the Guantanamo hilltop was about the most genial, loyal little band of comrades I've ever known.

The spirit of the Corps! They were all filled with it. Association with these men meant more to me, just out of school, than four years in a naval academy would have meant.

We were encamped on the hill above Guantanamo, marking time for several weeks. Then our whole battalion was ordered on board the transport Resolute and we sailed away in the wake of the flagship Newark to bombard Manzanillo. The Resolute drew too much water to approach the town, so we stayed out in the open sea and blazed away with our six pounders. The other ships steamed into the harbor and when the town refused to surrender, opened fire.

In the late afternoon, Colonel Huntington, our commander, was rowed over to the Newark. When he came back he announced: "Men, we Marines are to land tomorrow morning and capture the town. And remember I said, 'capture it.' You've been hell-bent for action. You're going to get it now."

"A damn piece of foolishness. Six hundred Marines against six thousand Spaniards. We'll all be killed before we reach the shore," Captain Goodrell muttered in a tone loud enough for us all to hear.

To add to the tension, one young officer talked me deaf, giving me elaborate and precise instructions for the disposal of his priceless keepsakes. He seemed to forget that I was one of the landing party, too.

About four in the morning a small boat flying a white flag chugged up to the Newark. A dispatch was brought aboard which passed like wildfire through our squadron. The dispatch read: "Protocol of peace signed by the President; armistice proclaimed."

Never since in my life have I enjoyed such a complete sensation of relief as the fluttering of those white flags inspired. I remember the day. It was August 13. In one way or another thirteen has always been my lucky number. The war was over.

CHAPTER III

A Full-Fledged Marine

THE SPANISH-AMERICAN WAR WAS OVER. In my wildest daydreams I couldn't pretend that I helped win the war. I had not taken part in a single engagement. But boy-like, I felt most enthusiastically that I had had my share in the chapter of history that was written in Cuba in the summer of 1898. I was a veteran. More than that I was a full-fledged Marine, a seventeen-year-old leatherneck.

On the afternoon of September 1, 1898, we arrived off Portsmouth Navy Yard and dropped anchor. You might think we had been in exile for ten years. We were as delirious as Columbus's crew at the sight of land—good American land. Our one ambition was to get ashore. But I was out of luck. As junior officer of the company, I had to stay on board with our men.

My handsome uniform, tailored in the best military style by Heiberger, went ashore, even if I didn't. "Buck" Neville's uniform was in the last stages of a rapid decline. He wanted to make a good impression on shore, so he came to me and I was delighted to trade him for the day. I stalked up and down the deck in his first lieutenant's coat, but unable to understand why Neville was willing to reduce himself in rank, even for a few hours' shore leave.

Nobody could be downhearted when Neville was one of the company. He was always cheerful, always ready with a side-splitting comment. In life's darkest moments, Neville found something amusing to say.

In my later years with the Marines, Neville, John A. Lejeune and I formed an inseparable trio. Neville gradually lost his slim figure which enabled him to get into my uniform. Lejeune, known to all his friends as "Gabe," was thick, broad and stocky. The three of us fought one another's battles all through our careers. From time to time we would be reunited in remote corners of the globe inhabited chiefly by Marines. At Vera Cruz in 1914 Lejeune was colonel, Neville was lieutenant-colonel and I was senior major and it was there we served together for the last time. When we became generals, we were widely separated. A general suffers the disadvantage of remoteness. He has no one to play around with.

General Lejeune cut a brilliant figure during the World War. His driving force was behind the Marine record made on the battlefields of France. He knew how to get the best efforts out of his staff. His men worshipped him. During a lull in the battle of Meuse-Argonne, Lejeune drove up to the line.

The men rose to salute. "Sit down, men," Lejeune said. "It's more important for tired men to rest than for the Division Commander to be saluted."

Lejeune was the most successful Commandant the Marine Corps ever had. When he retired after thirty-nine years' service in the Corps, he became Superintendent of the Virginia Military Institute. Neville succeeded him as Commandant of the Corps. Everybody loved General Neville. His death, in 1930, was a real blow. I always felt as much allegiance to these two men personally as I did to the Corps.

Toward the end of September, I was ordered to the flagship New York as the Junior Marine officer, but I was first granted a week's furlough to visit my home. I had my dress uniform pressed and I polished my sword. I tried to stand very straight and look as soldierly as old Major Reed. I was blissfully happy when the men of my company lined up to cheer me as I went away.

The week at home was wonderful. It was comforting to get back again to the "thee" and "thy" of the Plain Language. To make the week more perfect for a boy proudly conscious of his uniform, the neighbors received me with all the honors of a war hero.

I presented my orders on board the flagship New York, which was lying in the Brooklyn Navy Yard. Life aboard ship was Greek to me, but a crowd of high-spirited youngsters in the steerage mess soon taught me what it was all about.

During my younger days I spared no time or effort to attain popularity, which seemed the most desirable thing in the world. I was painfully sensitive and I suffered torments when unkind comments were made about me. In later years I've acquired a thicker skin. Now I don't even turn around to see who's doing the kicking.

Twenty-four wild Indians kept things moving in the Steerage Mess of the New York. At times they made my life quite a burden. They locked me in my room until I could repeat through the door the boxing of the compass. They made me learn all sorts of nonsense, and at their bidding I acted the clown when guests from other ships came for meals.

One stormy day those young devils ordered me to walk up and down the quarter deck, carrying an umbrella, so that Admiral Sampson could see what a fool I was.

The Admiral, who was pacing up and down in his raincoat, called me over.

"Who told you to carry that umbrella?"

"No one did, sir," I replied promptly, struggling to achieve a proper salute under my canopy. "It's raining and I don't want to get wet."

He laughed. "That's the right answer, but I know those damned youngsters in the steerage put you up to this."

Admiral Sampson was no blustering, popular sea hero. Always quiet, unassuming and serious, from his Annapolis days, he had concentrated on improving the efficiency of the Navy. He was a great executive commander, and a just one.

On the flagship New York, the Captain of the Marine guard was Erastus R. Robinson. When he was living in the old Congressional Hotel in Washington he was foolishly persuaded to ride a bicycle down Capitol Hill. He collided with an ice-wagon and smashed his knee so badly that he was lame for life. Even if he had not been lame, he was now so fat that he could hardly waddle along the deck. Sampson and Robinson had been boyhood friends. Although one was now a rear admiral and the other a captain they were always "Rastus" and "William" to each other, even in public. Almost every day they went through the same program. Robinson, wearing a very dirty uniform and his cap on the back of his head, would ease down his three hundred pound bulk on a bitt-head* [mooring post] and read the newspaper to Sampson. Their violent discussions ended in their tearing up the newspaper. Sampson was often stern and formal with the rest of us, but when Sampson and Robinson got together, discipline was forgotten.

In October, I was sent to Philadelphia to join a regiment of Marines that was being assembled to participate in the Peace Jubilee Parade.

From far off and singing through the brasses I suddenly heard the spirited measures of "The Halls of Montezuma," the Marine hymn. The Marine Band was swinging down the street and our waiting ranks were to fall in behind. Towering above everybody, his six feet three inches as straight as a flag-pole, marched my old teacher, Sergeant Major Hayes, who had come with the band from Washington to act as Regimental Sergeant Major.

As the band marched toward us, my heart beat fast. Now I would have my reward. Old Hayes would unbend for once, slap me approvingly on the back and say, "You're a credit to the Corps, my boy. As your teacher I'm proud of your conduct in Cuba."

The captain of my company gave me permission to speak to Hayes. I rushed across the street. Old Hayes drew himself up as if he had never seen me before and saluted in a painfully military manner. I actually had to reach up to take his hand.

"Sergeant Major, don't you know me?" I blurted out.

"O, yes," he assured me, "I know the Lieutenant."

"Aren't you glad to see me?" I implored.

"Yes, sir, I'm very glad to see the Lieutenant," and he stepped back into position with a wooden soldier formality that put us miles apart.

Not a word of praise for my gallant service in the war. Our meeting was a dismal failure. The whole parade was ruined for me. Soon after that I received orders to leave that same night for New York to join a battalion of Marines sailing for the Orient to take part in the Philippine Insurrection.

CHAPTER IV

Marking Time in the Philippines

ONCE BEFORE WHEN THE NUMBER THIRTEEN turned up I was saved from going on a landing party at Manzanillo, which would have meant a tossup with death. Now, April 13, 1899, I started by special train across the continent with a battalion of three hundred men, bound for the Philippines. For all I knew, the natives in the dark jungle lands for which I was bound might fricassee me for Sunday dinner. A brand new first lieutenant would be a particularly toothsome morsel.

We sailed out of the Golden Gate on the Newport, an asthmatic, broken-down transport. She had but one screw and one boiler. Nearly twelve hundred of us were jammed into the old transport. The bunks were the width of an ironing-board and as soothing to lie on as bricks.

The ship was on her last legs. Between San Francisco and Honolulu, we broke down twice. Each time we had to lie for thirty-six hours in the trough of a heavy sea, while new tubes were being installed in the boiler. The steamer had not been designed to make long trips. Down below, where the men were quartered, it was necessary to stow a large supply of coal. Since the men were all seasick, the berthing space soon resembled a pigsty. But these old soldiers refused to complain. They accepted whatever hardships came their way with the philosophy of stoics.

It was a full month before we anchored in the harbor of Manila. The decaying hulks of the Spanish warships still showed above the water, where Admiral Dewey had left them after the Battle of Manila Bay, on May 1, 1898. I could picture him standing on the bridge of the Olympia, giving the famous order, "You may fire when ready, Gridley." Dewey was the hero of American youth. The quiet way he stole into Manila Harbor with his six fighting ships, right under the noses of the Spanish guns, and destroyed the whole Spanish fleet thrilled the home-folk from one end of the country to the other. Well, here we were to defend the flag Dewey had raised in the Islands.

Before us stretched the walled city of Manila. Crumbling churches and convents rose above the old ramparts. From the deck of our transport the city looked more faded and ancient and Spanish than Havana. We were ordered into barges and towed across the bay to the naval station at Cavite.

We officers were quartered in the former Spanish Commandant's palace, which was so historical that it creaked in unexpected places as if ghosts were stepping out. Each of us had our China boy, whose chief occupation was to see that the supply of whiskey, ice and mineral water didn't run low.

I was a first lieutenant of Company A, commanded by Captain H. C. Haines, later a brigadier general. He stood six feet one and was rugged, gentle and strikingly handsome. I used to go to his room and wake him up with a "Good morning, Captain, sir."

He turned on me one morning. "Damn it all, Butler. Don't call me both captain and sir again. It makes me nervous."

Slowly the gnawing desire for home wore off, but ever since I have had great sympathy for homesick boys and realize that they have to be weaned like other animals.

There was fighting still on around Manila, but we were gradually pushing back the Filipinos. The old monitor Monterey lying off Cavite, provided our only excitement, when now and then she let drive with her twelve-inch guns at the opposite shore. We Marines harbored a special grudge against the 10th Pennsylvania Volunteers, who were encamped just outside the town of Cavite, between us and the Filipinos. If there was a skirmish they hogged the show and we were kept in the navy yard.

One day we set forth in high spirits to take the town of Orani on the north shore of Manila Bay. Elaborate and theatrical preparations had been made for the attack. We procured a casco, a native flat-bottomed boat, about ten feet wide and fifty feet long, with high square bow and stern. The casco was converted into a floating fort. An old three-inch landing gun was mounted at each end and tied fast with ropes. The inside of the boat was lined with boilerplates to keep bullets from striking the company of Marines hidden at the bottom.

This monstrosity was christened the Pope, after our eccentric old colonel, Percival C. Pope. Pope was bald— not a hair on his head—but he thought none of us knew it. His most safely guarded treasures were two wigs, one longhaired and the other, closely clipped. On the first of each month he stirred up a great commotion about sending for the barber. That evening he appeared at dinner in his short wig and explained most elaborately that he had just had a haircut. About the middle of the month he changed to the long-haired wig and began to talk about needing the barber again.

Our armored scow Pope was towed to Orani by two steam launches. When we approached close enough to open fire on the town, the forward gun broke loose from its ropes and took a flying leap into the water, carrying part of the barge with it. The other gun, fired at the same time, stayed with us, but it swung the scow around like a spinning top, almost upsetting the launches.

The fifty Marines, who until now had been stowed quietly in the bottom of the boat, were suddenly galvanized into action. They thought they were going to drown. They jumped to their feet with brimstone curses and split the air with their yells for help.

Certainly, our neat bit of Trojan Horse strategy was ruined now. It had been our plan for the scow to reduce the opposition with its guns and run swiftly toward shore. The fifty invisible Marines were then to leap forth and capture the town by surprise.

Pope was commanded by Hal Dunlap, one of the finest Marines the Corps ever produced. His recent heroic death in France, while attempting to save a French peasant woman from a landslide, deprived the Corps of its only hope for a real Commandant for some years to come. He was a General at the time of his death.

But there was no opposition. Even our shouting did not inspire a single shot from shore. The only casualties were two pigs that foolishly strayed in the line of bombardment. When we landed we found that Orani had already been evacuated. The town was ours without even the asking. Some of the men ran across a rum-shop and took immediate possession. They staggered out and began shooting in all directions like bad men in Wild West days. Fortunately, no living targets were within range. We sailed back across the bay to Cavite, well-satisfied with the day's picnic. The expedition was pronounced a howling success.

In September, the infantry regiment of volunteers went away and the Marines took over the town of Cavite. In October, we had our first real fight.

The United States army, in the shape of a giant hook, was advancing south from Manila. We were directed to join the army at Nocaleta. This town, held by the insurgents, was a tough nut to crack. The Spaniards had several times attempted to capture Nocaleta. Once they lost a whole regiment, but they never were able to take the place. The town's defenses could be reached only by crossing a narrow causeway, commanded by the enemy's guns.

The Marines were assigned the job of clearing out all the rebels along the neck of the peninsula and of driving them in front of the army.

We marched out of Cavite early in the morning, a regiment of six companies, commanded by Lieutenant Colonel George F. Elliott, who had been with us in Cuba. Captain Haines of our company led my battalion. I was put in charge of the company. I was quivering with eighteen-year-old excitement. This was the first time I had ever commanded a company in action.

My company took the lead, although it should have been fourth in the column. In about an hour, we were marching down a sandy, narrow road. The ground on either side was marshy and intersected by tidewater streams.

We turned a sharp corner and almost ran into a Philippine trench, which was just in front of us. Under the mistaken impression that our other battalion was ahead, protecting us, we were nearly ambushed.

A heavy burst of rifle fire greeted us. We all fell flat on the ground. My first sergeant, McKinnon, a wild, impulsive Irishman, jumped to his feet. As I was grabbing him by the wrist to pull him down, a bullet went through his arm, crippling him for life.

I remember how my heart pounded and how my stomach seemed to shrink into a small hard ball. I longed to be anywhere on the face of the earth, anywhere except lying flat on that Philippine trail. My panic couldn't have lasted more than a few seconds, but it seemed hours. I looked around and saw my men calmly lying on the trail waiting for some orders from me. Damn it all! I had to do better than this. In a crowd, the natural desire to hide one's weakness, combined with the certainty that the others are equally frightened, gives courage to the group and spurs on some men to heroic deeds.

I got weakly to my feet and waved to the company to commence firing. They obeyed with a will. Driving the insurgents ahead of us, we plunged through rice paddies, often waist deep in mud and water. The Filipinos were pushed back across a shallow river. For a time, they kept up a weak, half-hearted firing from the nipa huts on the far bank. Our persistence wore them out and they soon fled, abandoning their rifle pits and intrenchments. At noon we effected a junction with the army. The fighting was over. Now that I had come unscathed through my first pitched battle, I pretended to myself that I liked it and that the barrack life to which we were returning would seem very dull.

About the middle of December another battalion of Marines arrived in Cavite to supplement our force and give us the opportunity to take over more territory. The day they descended upon us, a friend and I were walking from the fort to our quarters. On the street we met Captain Haines and another officer, two big men, and between them was a little fellow with a fiery mustache and a distinguished bearing. No matter about his size. He dominated the others.

"Who is the little fellow?"

"Major Waller," explained my friend, "the commanding officer of the new battalion."

At mess I had heard the older officers talking about "Tony" Waller. I recrossed the street to get a better view of the newcomer. He had short thick legs, but he was very straight and military. Somehow, I realized then that I was looking at a real soldier.

Waller was in charge of a landing party of American Marines, in Egypt, at Alexandria, in 1884 when the British under Admiral Sir Charles Beresford were putting down the Egyptian outbreak started by Arabi Pasha. He was on the Battleship Indiana during the Spanish-American War.

I served under him from time to time for almost thirty years. I can say without reservation that Littleton Tazewell Waller was the greatest soldier I have ever known. In China, he led us Marines against the Boxers. Our paths were to cross in every odd corner of the world until our last campaign together in Haiti in 1917. He left Haiti that year and was in line for Commandant of the Corps. But he didn't have a fighting chance with the pedants in Washington, because he had not gone to Annapolis. In 1926, he had a stroke of paralysis and died, a broken man.

The picture of him that stays with me is the Waller of those days of his dashing prime in the Philippines and China. His men adored him. He had a magnificent face and carriage. On a horse he was impressive. He always took off his hat with a flourish. I can see him, straight as a ruler, his head thrown back, his enormous nose outlined against the sky, as he saluted the flag. Waller may have liked to talk about himself, but he had plenty to talk about.

Colonel Elliott, in command of our regiment, was one of the kindest men in the world, but when anything upset him, he flew into a hurricane of violence.

One Sunday morning we were lounging lazily in the mess room after breakfast. A message was brought that our outpost three or four miles from Cavite was having a hot little fight with the insurgents.

"I'll send reinforcements," the Colonel decided. "Butler beat it out there with your company."

The company fell in. Keyed up to meet the emergency, we swung off smartly in double time. As we rounded a corner, we ran into Colonel Elliott.

"What the hell do you mean, Butler, by tiring out the men?"

I immediately reduced the speed to a slow walk.

"I'd like to damn you from hell to breakfast," Elliott bawled me out. "Those men out there are in trouble. Get a move on you."

Again, I started off in double time. Again, the Colonel interfered.

"Didn't I tell you before not to go so fast?" he shouted, picking up a stone and aiming it at my head.

I ducked like a deep-sea diver, and the stone hit a music boy. As time went on I realized that the fine old fellow was ashamed of his childish display of temper. From then on, I had only to mumble "stone throwing" half under my breath to make him wiggle the end of his nose in a funny, rabbit-like way and let me have almost anything I wanted. But I did not hold the little fracas against him. We all loved the old man so much that we never nursed resentment because of his outbursts. Elliott was Commandant of the Corps from 1903 to 1910—the first to be retired as a Major General.

Elliott was eventually relieved by Colonel Robert L. Meade. He was tall and slender, with a beaklike nose and high rasping voice. A fine old soldier with unlimited courage, but as full of cayenne pepper as Elliott. Colonel Meade was a nephew of General George Gordon Meade who commanded the Union Army at Gettysburg. Little more than a boy during the Civil War, he had been captured by the Confederates and held for a year in Andersonville Prison.

Apparently, he hadn't looked at the drill regulations since the Civil War. At a regimental drill, he gave orders that sounded like an echo from Caesar and tried to get us into formations that had been in the discard for thirty years. Of course, none of us knew what he was driving at. We were severely reprimanded for our ignorance.

Meade would lash out at anyone, if the mood seized him. His famous quarrel with Theodore Roosevelt when Roosevelt was Assistant Secretary of the Navy is a favorite in Marine annals. He wrote to the Secretary of the Navy:

"A man signing himself Theodore Roosevelt has written me a very impertinent letter. I request that practice to cease."

In the Philippines, Colonel Meade treated me to a sample of his discipline.

Late one night, three or four young officers burst into the room which Pete Wynne and I shared. Bottles were opened, stories were told, and there may have been a little singing. At any rate, we were enjoying ourselves without realizing what a racket we were making. Colonel Meade's room was at the other end of the building. Evidently, we kept him awake.

The next morning, he sent for me.

"Lieutenant, your boisterous conduct last night was unfitting in an officer and a gentleman. I shall have to relieve you from your command."

I turned a little sick inside, but I couldn't summon up the nerve to protest that we were only having a little innocent fun.

"Do you want to leave the company or should you prefer to stay, as second in command?" he inquired stiffly.

"Oh, sir, I'd much rather stay with my own crowd."

Humiliating as it was to step down in my own outfit, I had no alternative but to accept Meade's ultimatum. Fortunately, I won my position back a few months later.

Life in Manila was gay in those days and jazzed up with plenty of drinking. We usually gravitated to the patio of the Hotel Oriente, where Army and Navy officers were always gathered around the small tables. At five o'clock, everybody who was anybody in the city sallied forth on the Luneta, to enjoy the evening breeze from the sea. Officers in dazzling white uniforms drove by at a leisurely pace. Beautiful olive-skinned women promenaded in their carriages. The band played opera overtures. The Filipino drivers clanged the silver-toned gongs on their tiny *calisas*. And the sunsets! There are no more beautiful sunsets anywhere in the world than those over Manila Bay.

Cock-fighting was our main diversion at Cavite. The master of ceremonies was Nam Sing, the Chinese tailor who had his shop in the navy yard and made all our uniforms. Admiral Dewey had brought him from Hongkong. Nam Sing, good-natured and monosyllabic, was a fixture at Cavite. His cock fights were an institution. The birds, with razor-like gaffs fastened to their heels, fought to the death. On Saturday night the silver Mexican dollars clinked into the ring. Nam Sing was happy only when he was risking a stiff wager against us.

A Japanese tattoo artist turned up in the navy yard one day. He was all smiles, very ingratiating. He convinced us all, officers and men, that life wouldn't be complete without an example of his craftsmanship. Even Colonel Meade was tattooed. And if I remember correctly, Colonel Elliott had his arm decorated with a flight of geese. One sentimental cuss had a portrait of his wife needled into his shoulder. When he returned to the States, he learned that she had run off with another man.

I selected an enormous Marine Corps emblem to be tattooed across my breast. The Japanese required several sittings and hurt me like the devil. I even came down with a fever as a result, but the finished product seemed at the time to be worth the pain. I blazed forth triumphantly, a Marine from throat to waist. The emblem is still with me. Nothing on earth but skinning will remove it.

Toward the end of my stay at Cavite, when there was little to do in the station, I bought a native pony and tried to ride. Frazer, a sergeant in my company who had served nine years in the U.S. Cavalry, did not admire my horsemanship. Highly entertained, he watched me climb clumsily into the saddle and hunch over the pony's neck at the first break into a gallop.

"Lieutenant, I'll teach you how to ride like a ranger, if you'll start at the beginning," he drawled.

I was only too willing to accept his offer. For weeks I was required to ride round and round in a circle without saddle or bridle. Frazer stood in the middle with a whip and made the pony perform. In spite of Frazer's patience, and my perspiring efforts, I never learned to ride properly.

Major Waller was ordered to Guam in June 1900. He was permitted to choose five officers to go with him. I was one of the five who volunteered to join his command. We never even started for that godforsaken island. Just as we were about to sail for Guam, we were ordered to China instead.

CHAPTER V

Off to China to Fight the Boxers

A YOUNG OFFICER MARCHING IN A COLUMN WITH his company knows nothing of the diplomatic and political background inspiring an expedition nor can he grasp the complete picture of a campaign. He trudges along in a little world of his own and deals only with the men around him. I started off to China as innocent of Boxers as a new-born babe.

On June 19, we dropped anchor in the Yellow Sea off Taku Bar fifteen miles from shore. The sea—it really was yellow—was dotted with Allied warships, Chinese junks with square, patched sails and busy little tugs and launches. We all piled on a German freighter which came alongside and agreed to take us over the bar and up the Pei Ho to Tangku. Late at night we sailed up the river, flowing sluggishly between low marsh lands. Here and there a Chinese mud house with tiled roof. Everything silent, dark, not even the pop of a gun.

The Allies seemed to have frightened the Boxers from this thin slice of coast country. Not, however, the same Allies who fought together in the World War. In 1900, Germans, Austrians, Russians, Italians, British, French, Japanese and Americans made common cause against the Boxers.

It was two in the morning before we tied up at a little wooden dock. Major Waller, who had been paying an interminable duty call on our Admiral, climbed on deck with the latest news.

"The foreign concessions in Tientsin, twenty-five miles inland, are in desperate straits. Seventeen hundred Allied soldiers, aided by several hundred civilians, are manning the defenses. They are surrounded by fifty thousand Chinese. Boys, they can't hold out much longer. We must go to their rescue at once. We'll get together a train and start up the railroad toward Tientsin."

We first carried most of our stores a half mile up the river to the Monocacy, a side-wheeler gunboat, especially designed for river use. She could run both ways and looked no more like a man-of-war than a Staten Island ferry.

At the railroad station in Tangku, we seized an antediluvian engine and filled all the flat-bottomed freight cars we could haul with rails and ties for repair work. "Pokey" Powell, who knew something about engines, and a private, who had been a locomotive fireman, climbed into the cab. After much fumbling with the levers, they persuaded the bulky iron mule to move.

It was noon when we shoved off from Tangku on one of the most desperate trips I've ever made. We had no maps, not the ghost of an idea where the railroad would take us. At every switch we guessed and followed our instinct. But Major Waller was a war horse if there ever was one. He was right in his element, with the old locomotive plugging on, sneezing and puffing steam out of rusty pipes.

In the afternoon we overtook a column of Russians— four hundred of them from the garrison at Port Arthur— marching to Tientsin. We stopped the train and invited them to ride with us. The soldiers had been carrying their fat, puffing colonel part of the way because his feet had become so sore that he could no longer limp along in his big boots.

The Russians were husky giants, and useful, too. From now on we had to repair large sections of track which had been torn up. Two of the Russians, with no effort, could pick up a rail with which four of our men had to struggle.

Creeping along inch by inch at snail speed, we came that night to a complete stop. The bridge ahead of us had been blown to fragments. The train, with most of our supplies, was sent back to the coast for more troops. That was the last we saw of the train. We were planted in what was to us the middle of China with only the meager equipment and food we could carry.

After a supper of canned salmon, canned peaches and hardtack, we wrapped ourselves in our ponchos and sat down, dismal and panicky. Twelve miles ahead of us, we saw a glare in the sky. We heard the dull booming of cannon and the crash of rifle-fire. Rumors flew around among us of women and children massacred and hand to hand fighting in the streets of Tientsin.

"Christ," grumbled one lieutenant, "we have no baggage, we have no food supplies and we'll be eaten alive in five minutes when we meet up with the Boxers. Why can't we go back to the good old Monocacy?"

We all agreed with him. From where we were sitting the ancient paddle-wheeler seemed like home, sweet home.

Just then Major Waller breezed into our low-spirited circle.

"I've just been talking to the Russian Colonel. He wants to wait for reinforcements. He swears on all his icons that our combined column of five hundred will be wiped out if we advance a step farther. Now, it may not be good military tactics to go on. But our women and children up there are in danger. I'm going to leave it to you men. What do you vote to do? The junior officer will vote first."

I thanked my lucky stars I didn't have to speak first. The junior lieutenant's dying calf expression was pitiful. He looked at us imploringly, gulped a couple of times and said, "I vote to go on, sir."

Of course, the rest of us followed suit. A load was off my chest. It was easier to move, even if it was forward, than to sit still and feel sorry for oneself.

The Russian Colonel was a good sport. Although he had a low opinion of Waller's foolhardy plan, he lined up his men without another word of protest. In their white blouses and black boots and trousers, they led the advance, in column of four's. It was two in the morning. Waller, figuring on a four hours' march, predicted that we would be in Tientsin by daylight. But he guessed wrong.

The heavy artillery with which we were equipped to rout the Boxers consisted of one Colt automatic machine-gun and a three-inch field gun. The machine-gun, with Pokey Powell in charge, was carried on our backs. We dragged and pulled the wretched cannon across the first creek, but it was such a damned nuisance that we dumped it into the next creek. It was useless to try to advance with this encumbrance.

At daylight we discovered a gray mud village off to our left. No one was stirring. It looked harmless enough. Beyond the village we could see the roofs of Tientsin.

Without any warning the Chinese opened fire from a concealed trench directly in front of the Russian column. At the same time, we were greeted with a burst of fire from the village. Boxer Village it has been called ever since.

At the first crash of bullets, we dropped down on the flat plain and burrowed our heads as far into the ground as we could. I was next to old Waller. Leaning on his elbows, he was sweeping the plain with field-glasses.

Cool as a cucumber, he remarked in an off-hand way: "I'm waiting to hear some poor fellow shot through the head. A bullet that hits the skull sounds like a stone splashing into a pond. I haven't heard that sound for many years."

I had never heard it and never wanted to hear it. Frantically, I began building a barricade of earth and stones around my head. We were getting it hard from both sides. I thought we were finished.

The Russians, who had borne the brunt of the fire, now had enough. They were filtering through us, running back as fast as their boots would carry them.

For all practical purposes we were alone in China. Even daredevil Waller decided that a handful of Marines could not lick the whole Chinese nation. Already three of our men had been killed and nine were wounded.

Waller turned to me. "I hate to give the order. But if we don't retire at once, we'll be cut off."

"I vote to run," I urged.

"Marines never run, my boy."

"All right, then, we'll walk, but let's get out of here."

As we began the retreat, I asked the first sergeant of my company to check up on the men. He stepped up to me. "Private Carter is missing, sir."

"Has anybody seen Carter?" I shouted.

"The last time I saw him," one man called out, "he was lying in a ditch a quarter of a mile back in that hornets' nest."

Lieutenant Harding, one of the most gallant men I ever knew, and I, with four enlisted men, turned back to look for Carter. We found him, groaning and writhing, in a mud puddle near the railroad track. When we tried to move him, he was in such agony that he begged us to leave him there to die. He had a compound fracture of the left leg. The bone stuck out like another joint.

All this time the Chinese weren't exactly drinking tea. They followed us out of their trenches and kept up a running, nagging fire.

We lifted Carter out of the ditch and tied his legs together with bandages torn from our shirts. Harding and I made a chair of our hands, two of the enlisted men took his feet and the other two fired into the Chinese mob, which milled around us. They were so close we could almost count the scraggly hairs in their mustaches. If any of them ventured unpleasantly near, our two sharpshooters picked them off like pheasants.

Down the railroad track we trudged, ducking with the whine of the bullets. It was slow traveling. We couldn't make more than a mile and a half an hour. To add to the excitement, a contingent of Chinese cavalry dashed out of the village. Good old Waller was on the job. He marched his men abreast of the Chinese, holding them back with a steady fire to prevent them from circling us.

Four grilling hours. Six or seven miles. Just as I thought we couldn't hold out much longer, Lieutenant Leonard and twenty-five men arrived on the scene; they had been serving as a rear-guard and had found out we were behind the column. With our reinforcements we felt like a whole army. Four men now carried Carter on a stretcher improvised out of a poncho and two rifles with bayonets fixed.

In the early afternoon we crossed a deep stream on the tottering remnants of a bridge which had been burned. We caught up with Major Waller and our column at last. We had carried Carter seventeen miles.

An old corporal who marched with us was shot on the inside of the leg. He limped along for fifteen miles without complaining or mentioning his wound. The old Marine gave the rest of us an invaluable object lesson. Another old Marine, a sergeant, was walking beside me. Crack! A stream of blood trickled down his face. The sergeant pulled his hat down over the wound and walked right on. The amazing courage of men like these did more than anything else to swing us into our stride and make us a fighting company.

In order to make a military and warlike appearance, we officers, still pretty new at the game, had worn our swords. After I had caught mine between my legs a few times, I tore it off and flung it away. Later when I was leaving China I found it among the baggage at Taku. One of our Marines must have picked it up. I have always kept that little sword, but I never wore it again.

For the rescue of Carter all the enlisted men received Medals of Honor. Until 1914 such medals were not given to officers. Harding and I were advanced two numbers, however, and brevetted for gallantry in action.

I never understood why the Chinese didn't close in on us and wipe us out. They outnumbered us one thousand to one. On my visit to China in 1928 I learned why. Because of the terrific beating administered by the British and French in 1858, the prestige of the foreigner was so great in China that the superstitious soldiers following hot at our heels regarded us as superhuman and were actually afraid to kill us. Lucky for us that they believed in magic.

That night I devoured huge quantities of half-cooked bacon, which one of our men with a nose for food had found on the train which had just come up with Allied reinforcements. I filled up the cracks with canned peaches.

I fell asleep on a board and was having a horrible dream. Someone shook me awake. It was Major Waller, cheerful as usual. It was two thirty in the morning. I was in a state of collapse. No one else wanted to budge, either. But "Tony" Waller shot some pep into us with one of his typical orations on the honor and glory of the Corps, the finest fighting force in the world. The grumbling, footsore Marines fell into line.

At the railroad station we met a column of Allied forces under Commander Christopher Cradock. British, Russians, Italians, Americans, we now marched along the railroad tracks toward the besieged city of Tientsin. The Chinese contested every inch of the way and shot a few of our men, but now that we were a column three thousand strong we advanced with some confidence.

Half-blinded by a terrific North China dust storm, we plugged on. I had a howling toothache. I also had barber's itch, aggravated by the sand particles which lashed across my face like scorpions. I felt like hell. I sat down on the railroad track so damned tired that I didn't care how many Boxers shot me full of holes. A good-natured Russian soldier insisted on pulling off my shoes and greasing my feet with bacon fat. The heels were rubbed raw. We didn't know how to take care of our feet in those days.

The British officers carried on as usual. They were traveling with elaborate mess outfits. That evening they put on a lot of dog and sat down to an elaborate banquet from soup to nuts. How my homesick heart stirred with envy at the sight of their white tablecloth and napkins and food —especially the food! Would you believe it? They even had a table. They were seated in state about one hundred yards from the spot where some of us were crouching with a chicken which had walked entirely too far in its fife. I chewed on the leg of that chicken all evening. We youngsters thought chiefly about food. We were hungry all the time. Our one ambition was to sneak into that town of Tientsin without further scrapping and get something to eat.

We spent the night in a cluster of mud huts near the railroad. Lousy, crawling, filthy holes. The men were worn out and discouraged. They wanted to return to the Monocacy and get a good bath and rest before pushing on to Tientsin. I ought to have cursed them out as bums and cowards, but I was inexperienced. I referred the matter to Major Waller. I can see him yet, straightening up and getting hot under the collar. Then and there I had a lesson in Marine Corps determination that I never forgot.

He glared at me and snapped: "You ought to be ashamed of yourself to make such a proposition to me. As long as you serve in this Corps, never express an idea like that again, let alone think it."

I braced up like a shot and bawled the men out for making a fool of me.

Swinging a lantern, Waller came into our hut, and waked us again at two thirty in the morning. That was the hour permanently adopted by the Allies as the proper time to get out of bed. I almost hated Waller's smiling, cheerful face. Two thirty every morning for two months!

In the gray misty dawn, we crept along cautiously. The Chinese were sniping from every direction. We seemed to be getting into the heart of the Boxer country. By this time, I had heard many gruesome stories of Boxer treatment of prisoners. I was none too happy.

About noon—it was June 23—we came to a bend in the river, jammed with logs. Sure enough! On the opposite bank was the town we had been aiming to reach for four days. We crossed over on the logs—a makeshift pontoon bridge—to the foreign concession of Tientsin. All the houses were surrounded with high walls, the streets and river front were barricaded with household furniture and bales of wool and camel's hair. A continuous, if somewhat flimsy wall still held between the foreign residents and the Boxers.

The first person to greet us when we jumped ashore at Tientsin was Mr. Charles Denby, brother of Edwin Denby, who later became Secretary of our Navy. Mr. Denby knew how to welcome throat-parched Marines. He handed each of us a bottle of beer. We broke the tops off with our bayonets. The taste of that beer after eating sand for two days! That's something to remember.

After we had mopped some of the dirt off our faces, we unfurled our American flags and marched up Victoria Road, the principal street of the foreign concession. Women and children rushed out to hug us. I've marched in many parades since then. I've heard crowds cheer in a way to set Marine blood a-tingling. But the whole-hearted enthusiasm of our Tientsin reception has never been equaled.

The Marines were assigned to a godown filled with cotton and rice, belonging to the China Merchants and Steam Navigation Company. I didn't wait to see my company settled. I made a bee-line for Watson's store and bought all the jam I could carry away. Then I filled myself to the brim with jam and hardtack.

When we had enough to eat, we turned in for a good sleep, thinking the war was over. Perhaps a few days in Tientsin—then back to the Philippines. None of us had any idea that we were going to spend the next three months in China.

CHAPTER VI

A Hot Time in Tientsin

THE MARINES WERE SO DOGGONE TIRED that they could have slept for a week, but they didn't have much chance to rest. A couple of days after we arrived in Tientsin, we set out to find Admiral Seymour and his lost column. Major Waller, who never seemed to get tired, was the leader of the expedition.

In the early part of June, Sir Edward Seymour, the British Vice-Admiral, with some marines and sailors, and Captain B. H. McCalla of the U.S.S. Newark, with an American landing force, were in Tientsin. There were also Russian, Italian and other Allied forces. The railroad was cut, and they could not push on to Peking. A Chinese runner from the British Minister in Peking dashed through the Boxer lines with a message for Seymour.

"If you are coming, come at once. We are in desperate straits."

The Allied commanders in conference tossed back the pros and cons of the Peking venture. Perilous, foolhardy. Captain McCalla got up impatiently and pounded out: "I don't care what the rest of you do. I have one hundred and thirty men here from my ships and I'm going tomorrow morning to the rescue of my flesh and blood in Peking. I'll be damned if I'll sit down here, ninety miles away, and just wait."

Admiral Seymour said he would go also. The other nations fell into line. Four or five hundred men were left to defend the foreign concession of Tientsin. A force of two thousand under Admiral Seymour marched away in the direction of Peking. That was two weeks before we arrived. No word of Admiral Seymour and his column had come through since.

When Major Waller heard the story, he paced up and down in a high state of excitement. Waller was as courageous and impetuous as the missing Captain McCalla.

He also had an eloquent gift of persuasion and soon had our Allies consumed with the desire to find Seymour's column.

We were off again. Our march began at night. Through the burning outskirts of the foreign settlement we pushed off, trying to feel as plucky as Waller.

At noon time the next day we reached the Shiku Arsenal, fifteen miles north of Tientsin. We didn't have to search farther. Right there we found Seymour and his troops. They had been besieged in the arsenal for two weeks.

What had happened was this. Seymour's column advanced about forty-five miles from Tientsin—half the way to Peking—when the Chinese blew up a bridge behind them. Supplies and communications were cut off. Seymour had to beat a retreat. The wounded men were floated on junks down the river. The rest marched along the bank, firing continuously to keep the Chinese at bay. In their retreat they approached the Shiku Arsenal. Seymour decided the arsenal would make an excellent base. He stormed it successfully, captured it, and there he had been obliged to stay with his men until we came on the scene.

The arsenal was well-stocked with ammunition and field guns, if not with food. The men had amused themselves shooting nineteen-pound Krupp ammunition at pigs, when no Chinese offered themselves as targets.

I was received cordially by Captain McCalla, afterward an admiral in our navy. Right after his greeting, the Captain remarked: "I have a sore back. Wonder what's the matter with it."

When we pulled up his coat and shirt, we discovered that he had been peppered with buckshot. Several pieces of lead were still sticking into him. The gallant old sea-dog had not stopped to think of himself so long as he had had his men to consider.

We got up the next morning at the usual hour of two thirty and said goodbye to the Boxers by setting fire to the arsenal. When the magazines exploded, an ungodly racket split the air, and the sky for miles around was filled with smoke.

When Seymour's three hundred sick and wounded were loaded on improvised stretchers, we marched back to Tientsin, loaded down with souvenirs—Chinese uniforms, rifles and so on.

Among those conspicuously present in the rescue of Seymour's column was a young British Commander named Beatty—Admiral Beatty of World War fame. Beatty was a strikingly attractive man. I admired the dashing way he wore his cap on the side of his head and his talent for courting danger. He had been wounded and carried his arm in a sling.

On the morning when we were marching to the assistance of Admiral Seymour, the column halted under an embankment to dodge the Chinese shells, which were flying too close for comfort. Commander Beatty, with his arm in a sling, pranced on a white horse on top of the embankment right above my company.

"It takes a lot of nerve to sit up there on that horse with all those shells bursting around him," I remarked to the man next to me.

"He's a damn fool; he's not doing any good by it," the old Marine retorted.

But I was so impressed by his performance that later in Tientsin I borrowed a pony and rode outside the foreign concession toward the native city. I stopped the pony in an open space and looked around, as if daring the

Chinese to take a shot at me. I didn't have to wait long. Two or three bullets sang past my ears. That was enough for me. I galloped for cover.

Those were hectic days in Tientsin. The Chinese, with their heavy artillery mounted on the walls of the native city, a mile and a half away, shelled the foreign settlement day after day. The firing never let up from the time we brought Seymour back until we captured the native city the middle of July.

Shells or no shells, I still had a raging toothache. My head was being bombarded without artillery. I went in search of the European dentist recommended to me. To put it mildly, he was not a bold, brave man. I found him in a cellar. He didn't relish the idea of going to his office, which was on the second story of his house.

"Oh, come on," I urged him, "it's a quiet day. The Chinese must be asleep. If you fix my tooth, I'll get you a ride down the river to safety."

"All right," he agreed a bit reluctantly.

He placed a rubber dam over my mouth and was selecting his tools of torture when a shell burst through the front of his house. He dropped everything and ran out.

I was so harnessed up that I got to the window only in time to see him disappear around the corner. I never met him again. But the pain in my tooth died a natural death, so I harbor no grudge against him.

I spent much of my time with my company at the barricade built around the railroad station across the river from the foreign settlement. Nearly every night we were on the lines. The minute we relaxed our watch, the Chinese made a desperate attack, and we had to rush out to drive them away.

After a quiet afternoon I'd say, "I wish those damned Chinamen would jump us tonight." But when awakened at two in the morning by the rattle of musketry nearby, I would bitterly repent.

A small sofa in a joss house where some of us were quartered, served as my bunk. When I heard firing, I looked sleepily at the placid Buddhas that surrounded me and shoved my head under the pillow to drown out the noise of the guns. But I was an officer. I had to get up.

Our company was a glorious outfit. Half of it was made up of old soldiers, the other half, boys like me. The old fellows took care of us youngsters and taught us the tricks of the trade. The men got drunk every pay day and caused me endless trouble. But when I was dead tired, they carried my pack, and they shared with me the food they managed to steal. I've always had a deep affection for the veterans who brought me up.

On the Fourth of July Major Waller ordered two boys to climb with the flag to the roof of the go down which we were using as barracks. Almost at once a shell landed on the spot, and the roof crashed in. We had to take the flag down and do our celebrating under cover.

In the afternoon the Major went out to return a call on one of the foreign officers. I was left in charge of the barracks.

A sentry burst in, panting. "Lieutenant, the Japanese General and his whole staff are on their way to the barracks. They want to present us with a cannon they've captured."

Captain Bailey of the British Navy was with us at the time, helping us to enjoy the Fourth. Captain Bailey was a perfect John Bull in appearance. He was a great friend of Captain Forsythe of our navy, who could have been made a model for Uncle Sam. The two inseparables were always known as John Bull and Uncle Sam.

I was completely flustered. I had never been in the presence of a Japanese general or any other general and had no idea how to receive the Oriental dignitary. I wanted to cut and run.

"Brace up, old top," Captain Bailey advised. "Invite the old chap in, send for some champagne and drink a toast to Nippon."

I went to the door to greet General Fukushima. He and his staff were in full dress uniform, glittering with medals and decorations. We looked like tramps. In fact, we had scarcely enough clothes to cover our nakedness.

The ivory-hued general bowed and bowed. He was very friendly. He politely sucked in his breath with a hiss a few times and then, through an interpreter, presented the gun as a token of Japanese friendship on our national holiday. The cannon was an old Krupp gun of the vintage of 1890. It is now at Marine headquarters in Washington.

I was awkwardly silent for a moment. I couldn't figure out the next polite move.

Captain Bailey pushed me forward, whispering, "Get on, old man. You have to make a speech."

I mumbled out a tangle of words about the wonderful gift, the marvelous Japanese army, the great Japanese nation. The Marines gathered around and gave three rousing cheers for the General. He departed, much pleased with our expressions of goodwill.

The Chinese were making the foreign concession hotter than hell. It was high time to creep up on the native city and silence the pestiferous Boxer batteries. More troops, English, Russian, Japanese, arrived. The Ninth U. S. Infantry, commanded by Colonel E. H. Liscum, came up the river to reinforce us.

On the afternoon of July 12, I was returning to my joss house quarters after a thirty-hour tour of duty in the trench around the railroad station. Colonel Meade, our commanding officer, called me over and introduced me to Colonel Liscum, who invited me to sit down beside him. Colonel Liscum was a gentle, kindly soul. I'll never forget the fatherly way he patted me on the shoulder, telling me that he had been a boy during the Civil War and could appreciate what a hard experience I was having for a young man. The next day, in the battle for the native city, he was killed, holding his regimental flag after the color bearers had fallen. Meade had been suffering a severe attack of inflammatory rheumatism and went into the battle with his hands and feet bandaged like those of a mummy. At the moment Liscum was shot he was waist deep in mud in the field before the native city. A monument dedicated to Colonel Liscum now occupies the exact spot where he fell. Encircled by handsome modern buildings, it stands in the center of the Japanese Concession.

As I have said before, many exciting things have happened to me on the thirteenth. It was on July 13, 1900, that the Allied forces, seven thousand strong, attacked the native walled city of Tientsin, defended by fifty thousand Chinese.

Two walls stood between us and the native city of Tientsin. The outer mud wall, about twenty feet high, surrounded the scattered villages on the plain, with their rice paddies and grave mounds like mole hills. A space of fifteen hundred yards separated the mud wall from the high stone wall of the native city.

At three in the morning we left the foreign settlement and marched around the mud wall to a point opposite the south gate of the native city.

Chinese bombs were exploding about us, and Chinese snipers on both sides of the river were pouring a steady stream of bullets in our direction. The sky flashed with fiery zigzags.

Our artillery was also keeping up a heavy bombardment. The British were hammering at the stone wall with the guns they had used to defend Ladysmith in South Africa during the Boer War. It took many men to drag around these clumsy guns mounted on boiler plate wheels. But they did real damage with their big shells. We cheered every time one of their projectiles crashed in the native city.

We charged over the mud wall at seven in the morning and began our advance. The whole country was flooded. The Chinese had diverted the water from the canals into the open space between the two walls. We struggled through this filthy swamp, with bullets splashing and whining around us. The low mud walls of the rice paddies provided some slight protection. We crouched behind them, firing furiously, slipping, sliding and stumbling from one to another.

Almost to the stone wall. A horde of Chinese were swarming out of the gate, threatening to swing around behind us and cut us off. I ran up to our Colonel for permission to drive them back.

Only half my company with Lieutenant Powell was with me. The others under Lieutenant Wynne were on the mud wall protecting our left flank. Our slender line slopped on through the mud of the rice paddies toward the gate.

As we were climbing over one of the rice dikes, Partridge, our tallest private, was shot and fell backward. I stooped over him. He had an ugly gash in his left shoulder, but he was bleeding so little that I didn't think his wound was serious.

We pushed on for fifty yards, shooting every inch of the way. The Chinese who had been threatening us filtered back through the gate. But now we were close to the stone wall. A terrific fire was poured down on us. Thousands of Chinese bristled on the wall. There were only thirty-five of us. We had to retreat, but not until the Chinese flanking party had retired.

On the way back, we picked up Partridge. He was unconscious and heavy as lead. I put his legs around my waist. Two other men supported his shoulders. It was five or six hundred yards to our rice paddy trenches. Bullets were kicking up the mud all around us.

Suddenly, I felt a burning sensation in my right thigh. At first, I thought Partridge in his agony had kicked me. Then I realized that I had been shot. I could still walk; so, we kept right on to the trenches, where we laid Partridge under cover. I applied my first aid package and moved to the next rice paddy where the crowd was not so great.

Our doctor came along and offered to dress my wound. I wanted him to go across the open space to attend to Partridge and leave me until later. We rowed over this and when he finally went to Partridge, the poor fellow was dead.

With the assistance of a bugler who carried my pack and revolver, I limped across the open space to another rice paddy near a desultory graveyard and sat down in the mud. By this time, I had lost my enthusiasm for charging Light Brigade fashion, into the native city. My friend, Lieutenant Leonard, with a sergeant trailing at his heels, bent over me.

"The Colonel is afraid we'll be outflanked. He has ordered all wounded moved to the rear."

"I don't want to go. I'll stay right here," I argued.

"Come on. Get up. We'll help you." Leonard was firm.

With Leonard, the sergeant and the bugler half hoisting me along, I crept from grave mound to grave mound. Lucky for us so many Chinese had gone to their ancestors, for the live ones were finding us an attractive target. Eventually, we reached the safer side of the mud wall, where Japanese, Russian and English wounded were lined up on stretchers.

Here I found Lieutenant "Bill" Lemly, who is now a retired Colonel, living in Washington. He had been shot in the left leg early in the morning before we crossed the mud wall.

We two lame ducks linked arms and, using our two lame legs as one good one, hobbled along in the shelter of the mud wall to the foreign concession. On the way we stopped to watch the British sailors hammer their high-explosive shells at the walled city. While we were applauding their accurate firing, a Chinese shell tore off the head of one of the British gunners. We moved on!

So many seriously wounded men were being carried into the hospital that my leg had no attention until evening. Since we had only one or two doctors, Lemly and I helped dress the wounded. In the late afternoon, Harry Leonard was brought in. He had been shot in the arm. The wound became infected. Leonard, who had risked his life looking out for everybody else, and by taking me to the rear, now had to have his arm amputated at the shoulder. He stayed on the active list, however, for another ten years. Before he had entered the Marine Corps, he had studied law. He is a brilliant lawyer now in Washington. I engaged him as my counsel when I was slated for court-martial in the Mussolini affair in 1931. Leonard outwitted the crowd that wanted my scalp.

I heard the story of the rest of the Battle of Tientsin from my friends who visited me in the hospital. It was a terrific scrap—the fight for the native city. The gallant Ninth Infantry lost, in addition to Colonel Liscum, its commander, several other officers and thirty percent of its men. We Marines had equally heavy losses. It wasn't sport, floundering on empty bellies for twenty-four hours in muck up to the waist, with the Chinese guns thundering an unceasing death tattoo.

Little progress was made on the 13th. But early on the morning of July 14, a company of Japanese soldiers crept forward in the dark and blew up the south gate of the city. We were all much moved by the courageous self-sacrifice of the Japanese who were killed in bombing the gate. The Chinese garrison was completely demoralized. The defenders fled in all directions. Without resistance the Allies marched in and captured the city.

While I was in bed with the wound in my thigh, I was examined for promotion to the grade of captain. The medical board hemmed and hawed and decided I was physically unfit to perform the duties of captain, because of weakness through loss of blood. Colonel Meade and Major Waller both pronounced the decision absurd. Upon their recommendation, Admiral Remey, Commander in Chief of our naval forces in the Orient, overrode the doctors and gave me my promotion. I was a full-fledged Captain and very proud of my new rank, which I received before my nineteenth birthday.

It was tiresome to be laid up, especially when the boys were coming in with the exciting news of the proposed march to Peking. The Allies had poured additional troops into North China. A column of 18,000 men was being formed to start for the relief of the besieged Legations in Peking.

Bill Lemly and I were stirred to action. We weren't going to be cripples, left behind. We pronounced ourselves well and joined our command.

CHAPTER VII

On to Peking

WE LINED UP ON AUGUST 4 TO LEAVE Tientsin for the march to Peking. The warlike bustle, the confusion, the picturesque mingling of many nationalities, were enough to kindle any young man with military eagerness.

French Zouaves in red and blue, blond Germans in pointed helmets, Italian Bersaglieri with tossing plumes, Bengal cavalry on Arabian stallions, turbaned Sikhs, Japanese, Russians, English. The Royal Welsh Fusiliers wore three folds of ribbon down the back of their necks. One of these decorations commemorated the distinguished service of the Fusiliers at the Battle of Bunker Hill. We became much attached to the Royal Welsh on the march. When we left China, they presented us with a handsome loving cup as a memento of our friendly association.

Our force of Marines had by this time been increased to a regiment of six hundred men. Counting the Marines, the Ninth and Fourteenth U. S. Infantry, Battery F of the Fifth Field Artillery and one troop of the Sixth Cavalry, America contributed about three thousand men to the Allied column.

Up and down the American line rode General Adna R. Chaffee, who had just come to Tientsin to take command of all the American troops in China. He was magnificent. Just my idea of the way a general should look. He sat very straight on his powerfully built American horse. With everyone else in khaki, his blue coat made him look even more impressive. Later, on the weary march, his very appearance put fresh life into us.

Since Chinese carts were the only means of transportation, we were traveling light. Our stores were being carried up the Pei Ho on Chinese junks. Wirt McCreary, a Marine Lieutenant, was in command of the junk fleet plying up and down the river. Coolies walking on the river bank towed the junks by ropes harnessed across their chests. When two military junks met, the senior officer had the right of way and the junior was obliged to tie up. McCreary, being a Second Lieutenant, had to tie up so frequently that he was perpetually behind in his schedule. But he was a man of resourcefulness. The rank of passengers on the junks was indicated by the number of stars on the flags flying from the bamboo masts. McCreary made himself a flag out of an old blue flannel shirt. He pinned four white stars on his flag to indicate he was an admiral. Then he put on a pair of green glasses so he would not be recognized and sat like a potentate in an armchair in the stern of his junk. He had the right of way for a month.

His deception was not discovered until he collided with a junk carrying a genuine Japanese Admiral.

The ninety-mile march to Peking stretched out into an infernal ten days. The Boxers stubbornly opposed our progress. But the Russians and Japanese who were ahead of us in the column drove off the Chinese without calling on us, unless the resistance was determined.

The blasted discomfort bothered us more than the fighting. The temperature rose as high as 140 degrees in the sun. There was no shade, not a drop of rain, nor a breath of air.

The cavalry and artillery kicked up clouds of dust, which beat back in our faces. The blistering heat burned our lungs. Nearly fifty per cent of our men fell behind during the day, overcome by the sun. In the cool of the night they would catch up with us and start on again the next morning. I was overcome myself one day, but I clung to the horse of a mounted officer and managed to worry through.

Our throats were parched, our tongues thick. We were cautioned not to drink the water along the road, but no orders could keep us from anything that was in liquid form. On one occasion we found a big earthen bowl of water in a hut that we stormed. We drank lustily and immediately became ill. The bowl had been covered with scum.

Now and then we passed villages surrounded by mud walls. The houses were smoldering, the walls riddled with bullets, the dead Chinese piled in the courtyards. Most of the time we pushed through fields of grain ten feet high. It was like walking through a blast furnace. For days we struggled through these jungles of grain. We even bivouacked in them at night, eaten alive by mosquitoes.

One day we passed near a watermelon patch, but to my sorrow it was not the time for our hourly halt. I couldn't get those melons out of my mind. That evening with my friend Fritz Wise and some volunteers I returned to that patch, four miles in our rear. I hurriedly ate the hearts out of thirteen melons. The others were equally greedy. Then we loaded ourselves down with as many melons as we could carry for our whole crowd. As we passed a little village, I suddenly felt quite sick. I was about to sit down to rest, when to my horror I saw two Japanese soldiers with their eyes and tongues cut out, nailed to a door. Undoubtedly the poor devils had left their company to forage like us. I forgot my stomach ache. We beat it back to our column in double quick time.

My wound had not yet healed and my leg was giving me constant pain. Over and over I asked myself why in thunder I had been so eager to take part in this rotten Peking show when I might have stayed in the hospital. I swore to all within hearing that I would stop soldiering as soon as I returned home. The rest of the Marines expressed similar feelings. They splintered the air with their oaths, sparing no one from General Chaffee to the Chinese "bastards."

This attitude, I observe, is common to all soldiers. They curse the service when they are in it, and they yearn for it when they are out. I have also learned that as long as a command growls it is in a healthy state of mind. It's when your men are quiet and sullen that you have to watch your next step.

My old company commander in Cuba, Captain Goodrell, advised me: "When your men are hard pressed and heavily burdened on the march, if you will insist on carrying but the canteen of a single man, your company will move. Then when you are older, the men will not expect this of you, for you have earned a reputation for giving them your strength in your youth."

An easy and friendly relationship prevailed between officers and enlisted men on the march. We were sharing the same hardships. I remember affectionately a private in my company named Pete. He was a Greek who had served in the Marine Corps nearly thirty years. He was a little fellow, weighing not more than one hundred pounds, and wore brass earrings, which gave him a wild pirate look. But he was all muscle, bone and Marine loyalty. After the second day's march I was sitting on the ground with a hopelessly empty stomach. Pete sat down beside me and offered me dry bread and cheese. Moldy and stale as they were they went to the right spot. Pete had his knapsack filled with bread and cheese, and every evening he divided these questionable delicacies with me.

On August 13, we rested all day in the walled city of Tungchow, about twelve miles from Peking. It must have been a rich town before it was struck by war. Now, corpses, with skulls smashed in, lay sprawled across the streets. Brocades and fragments of porcelain spilled out of the broken fronts of shops. The gilded archways were shattered. Carved teakwood furniture was being split up by the Allied soldiers for firewood. But the Boxers had done most of the damage before we arrived.

Several of us ventured through the open door of a house. It seemed deserted. We explored adjoining rooms until we came to an elaborately furnished bedroom—all gilt and gewgaws. On the Chinese bed, which was covered with brocades that a museum would have envied, lay an old mandarin. He was flat on his back with a ferociously ugly sword pinning him to the bed.

As we walked along the street toward a narrow canal, a whole family leaped into the water. Father, mother and three children. They wanted to drown themselves. We jumped in, dragged them out and kept a strangle hold on them until they calmed down. Our Chinese interpreter followed the drama with detached calm. When it was all over, he declared:

"Now that you have saved their lives, you are responsible for these people. You are their guardians and must take care of them from now on."

"Not on your life," we yelled in chorus. Off we ambled again.

We stopped at a Chinese cook-shop, with an open front. A wrinkled Chinese chef officiated. We were hungry as usual. Pancakes, surely, spreading and steaming on the hot irons over the charcoal fire. We ate some. They were soggy and vile-tasting and landed like lead in our insides. I have never liked pancakes since.

Altogether, Tungchow was not a pleasant place. I was glad to start for Peking at dark that night. We pushed on through a heavy rainstorm and reached the outskirts of the Chinese capital by daylight.

As we came closer, I could not help being impressed with the dignity of the walls surrounding the ancient city. There were miles of massive battlements, with huge gate houses. But I had no time to admire the architecture and atmosphere of Peking. I wasn't a tourist.

The walls, however, were part of my job. First came the great stone wall of the rectangular Chinese City; then the wall, forty feet high of the square Tartar City; within the Tartar City, the Imperial City, also surrounded by its red wall; and finally, enclosed by a very special wall the Forbidden City containing the yellow-roofed palaces of the Empress Dowager of China. Peking was all walls, and every wall held possible danger for us.

We advanced along the east and north walls of the Chinese City, keeping close to the wall in the shelter of the houses. The Chinese held the Tartar City and Chinese were stationed on the Tartar wall near the northeast gate. We halted near this gate beside a pond where ducks were peacefully swimming. But it wasn't peaceful. The Chinese on the wall were firing hot and fast.

With Major Waller I climbed up on to the ramp of the outer northeast gate. We could see the Boxers shooting at our men from the embrasures of the Tartar wall.

"Send out and get your company. We'll get through the gate and drive those pests off the wall," Waller said.

Instead of sending for the company, I ran down myself to the road and hustled the company along. As I turned to follow the last man through the gate, a bullet whizzed toward me at an angle. I spun around in a circle and passed out of the picture.

When I came to, I was lying in a small guardhouse adjoining the gate. Captain "Mike" Bannon was bending over me. "Give him air," he ordered.

Someone commented, "He's shot through the heart." I struggled to get the men to understand that I had not been shot through the heart. Every bit of wind was knocked out of me. Finally, I forced enough breath to murmur, "No, not the heart."

Captain Bannon and the bugler William Carr, who had helped me when I was wounded in Tientsin, tore open my blouse. The bullet had struck the second button of my blouse. The ring on the flattened-out button dug a hole in my chest and carried off part of "South America" from the Marine Corps emblem tattooed on my breast. I carried that flattened-out button in my pocket for years. Medical aid in battle was not elaborate thirty years ago. A little pad of dressing was bandaged on the wound. That was all. For weeks my chest was black as ink, and every time I coughed I spit blood.

When my friends were reassured that I was very much alive, they caught up with our company and helped drive away the Boxers who were annoying us on the Tartar wall.

I lay in the guardhouse for some time before I could make the effort to get up. I was very weak and leaned against the gate. Lieutenant Summerall, subsequently Chief of Staff of our army, was riding by with his artillery. When he saw me staggering and reeling along, he lifted me on his horse and escorted me in style to my company.

Although my chest was painful, I did not intend to miss any of the fun. In the evening, with some of the other officers I crawled through the Water Gate, a kind of open sewer leading under the wall from the Chinese City into the Legation Quarter.

That night we bivouacked under the Chien Gate, just beyond the Legation Quarter, on the south side of the dividing wall between the Chinese and the Tartar cities. We rolled up in our blankets and slept on the ground right under the Tartar wall. The rain swept down in torrents, and it was cold. A devilish night. I kept still about my chest, which was aching abominably. I wanted to get into the scrap next day.

Early in the morning we shook ourselves awake. "Buck" Neville, then a captain, pulled us out of our grouch. Cheerful and lovable always, he kept the column moving by his gift for laughing off disagreeable experiences.

The artillery boys, glad to get into action, lustily bombarded the gates of the Imperial City and of the Forbidden City, still held by the Chinese. My company, stationed in the tower of the gate on the floor above the guns, picked off the Chinese at the other end of the wall as soon as they showed their heads. We fired so rapidly that many of the rifles got hot and jammed.

When my company was relieved, I went below to the level of the guns. I had been there only a moment when a bullet struck Captain Reilly in the mouth and killed him. That fine old officer fell back into the arms of his lifelong comrade, Major Waller. Much depressed, we carried him inside the Gate House. He was a great soldier. No one in the army had so many friends. But there was no time to lament.

Reilly's Battery knew their business. They kept up a steady and accurate hammering with their shells and succeeded in making a wide breach in the gate of the Imperial City. Under the protection of the artillery bombardment and our rifle fire the infantry moved forward, pushing back the Boxers, who fought like demons.

By noon—it was August 15—the Chinese had evacuated the Forbidden City. Peking was now in the hands of the Allies. The Legations were saved. For the next week or so, Chinese snipers caused us a little trouble, but the real danger was over.

Sections of Peking were assigned for protection to the different national groups composing the Allied column. For nearly two weeks my company remained on the stretch of wall between the Chinese and Tartar cities. Then things quieted down, and the tension relaxed. It seemed to me now like unbelievable luxury to move into the Palace of the Eighth Prince, after I had grown accustomed to sleeping on a board in the open. The palace, which was our barracks until we shoved off for home in October, consisted of a series of courtyards leading one into the other, with tiled roofed one-story buildings built in the form of a quadrangle around each courtyard. The vast rooms were decorated with intricate carvings, beautiful silk hangings, cloisonné and porcelain vases six feet high, bronze gods and handsome but deucedly uncomfortable teakwood furniture. I didn't think much of my bed, a long brick couch covered with cushions filled with a rocklike substance. Underneath was a small oven, not a bad idea with the weather turning cold. But Chinese pillows are as hard and unrelenting as marble.

After the Boxers were routed from the Forbidden City, we had nothing to occupy us except guard duty. In our spare time we rode around the city on Chinese ponies, gathering up souvenirs that were not securely nailed down.

Now, I know a big rumpus was kicked up over the looting in Peking. The people at home threw up their hands in holy horror when they learned their soldiers took things they had not bought and paid for. But some allowance should be made for the fact that during the excitement of a campaign you do things that you yourself would be the first to criticize in the tranquil security of home.

Moreover, the Empress Dowager, with her whole court and the rich people of Peking, leaving the palaces unguarded, had fled to the north just before our arrival. The Peking rabble was free to loot. Nearly everything worth taking had already been carted off by the Chinese themselves, who were far better judges of value than we were. We found the contents of whole shops spilled out in the streets. It took stronger wills than we possessed not to be tempted by brocades and furs lying in the gutters.

One evening three of us were scouting through an empty palace and stumbled on a hidden recess. In the light of our lantern, a pile of candlesticks, boxes and trays gleamed invitingly.

"Gold!" we whispered in high glee.

Staggering under the weight of the loot, we hurried to the barracks and buried our find in the back courtyard. A few days later we secretly dug up our treasure. To our disgust, our fortune turned out to be brass.

Although we had received no pay for three months, we weren't bothering our heads about it. One of my friends found a storeroom filled to the ceiling with Chinese cash— those round brass coins with a square hole in the middle. We piled up four or five tons of the money in our courtyard and paid our bills with a shovel. Each week our Chinese servants took as much as they could carry for their wages. But our whole pile didn't amount to much. Since it took ten strings of cash to make a cent, one needed a wheelbarrow full to buy a package of cigarettes.

Peking was settling back to normal. But to show the Chinese that their power was entirely broken, the Allies decided, about September 1, to march through the Forbidden City with a column composed of officers and men selected from all the Allied forces. "Buck" Neville and I had the good fortune to be chosen from our regiment. I was looking forward to a special view of all those gorgeous palaces and throne rooms about which I had heard so many tales.

The palace eunuchs left behind in the flight of the Empress Dowager were ordered to open the big gates. From south to north we marched straight through the Forbidden City. We were the first foreigners, I was told, to desecrate this holy territory. But what a disappointment! Dust and neglect everywhere. The one-story and two-story palaces with their heavy yellow-tiled roofs were filled with uncomfortable-looking furniture. There were no gold, silver and precious jewels, only some gold pillars. The men investigated these gold pillars with the tips of their bayonets, only to find them covered with thin gold leaf. As we swung out the north gate, we were filled with contempt for those Chinese rulers who were satisfied to live in musty, old palaces.

Before we started for Peking, Colonel Meade, commanding our regiment, was invalided home with inflammatory rheumatism. A new colonel arrived on the scene, Henry Clay Cochrane. He had a square-cut, gray beard that waggled when anything went wrong. And for him nothing was ever right. His god was efficiency. Although the war was over and we were merely doing garrison duty until we were ordered home, he set about to enforce strict discipline and apply war tactics.

Almost at once he had an inspection of the regiment. I know my company looked like tramps. No new clothes had been given out since we had left the Philippines the first of June. Not a man was completely clad in an American uniform. As they lined up for inspection, some of them wore blue or rose Chinese trousers, others, mandarin coats, and almost all of them were shod in Chinese silk boots.

Cochrane looked us over, snorting with disgust.

"Captain, your men don't even look like soldiers. You'd better send them to the Forbidden City to keep the palace attendants company."

"No, sir. They may not look like soldiers, but I assure you, sir, they are soldiers of the first water."

We all had our rifles and ammunition, our good nature and health, which are, after all, the prime requisites for soldiering. I was furious at Cochrane, but since he was my commander, I had to control my feelings.

On October 10, our regiment left Peking and started for Tangku and the coast. My company had been longest in China and had suffered the greatest casualties. Twenty-six of our men had been killed or wounded. As a reward for our service, Admiral Remey invited us on board his flagship, the Brooklyn, for a trip around Japan. It was no pleasure trip for me. Two days after going on board I came down with typhoid fever. I was very sick. Weighing ninety pounds, I was carried off the boat at Manila by old Corporal Simonson and my music boy, Carr, who seemed to be around whenever I had to be helped. I was moved to the naval hospital at Cavite. The hospital, being located over the boiler-shop, did not hasten my recovery. The doctors packed me home.

I reached San Francisco December 31, 1900, in time for a New Year's Eve celebration. It was a most successful celebration. My mother and father, who had been notified that I was at the point of death, came across the continent to meet me. I had now gained thirty pounds and ate like a lumberjack; so, they felt reassured about me.

My neighbors in West Chester gave me a fine welcome home. The local Grand Army post held a public reception and presented me with a handsome watch and chain, which I have worn ever since in whatever part of the world my service has taken me. A few days later, the town of West Chester held a reception. The Secretary of the Navy, the Commandant of the Marine Corps and other distinguished guests came over from Washington with the Marine Band. On this occasion I was given a beautiful sword, still one of my most prized possessions.

Next image: Major powers plan to cut up China for themselves; America, Germany, Italy, UK, France, Russia, Austria. Punch Aug 23, 1899, by J. S. Pughe.

CHAPTER VIII

"Those Damn Knapsacks"

THE WALLS AND TILED ROOFS OF PEKING were slipping rapidly into a blurred background. In my two restful months at home I recovered completely from the effects of fever and the Boxer expedition. Even Marines don't fight all the time. I went back to duty at the Marine Barracks in the Philadelphia Navy Yard under a great old character, Colonel James Forney.

Those eccentric, exasperating and often delightful old Trojans of twenty-five and thirty years ago! They have all disappeared from the service. It would take a Dickens to immortalize their amusing twists and idiosyncrasies. Perhaps we old-timers now look as ridiculous to young officers as our commanders did to us. After all, it's only a question of where you are sitting when you view the show.

Colonel Forney rarely straightened out to his full length of six feet seven. During the Civil War he had been a Captain in the Marine Corps, and he had long ago lost his active interest in soldiering.

While burying an Admiral in the late Sixties, Forney, then a Captain, had command of a Battalion of Marines, acting as a firing squad. They were armed with old muzzle loading rifles and Forney forgot to give the order to withdraw the ramrods from the bores of the pieces. He gave the order to fire and 300 ramrods sailed across the cemetery and broke 1,000 panes of glass in a greenhouse. All of which helped to break up the funeral.

The details of routine service life bored Colonel Forney. It irritated him beyond measure that he was required to hold school for his subordinate officers. Three times a week, at five minutes to twelve, his orderly notified us that the Colonel was ready for school. Six or eight of us promptly tramped to his office and seated ourselves according to our rank. As the senior I sat at the right of the row, the junior lieutenant at the left. The Colonel, who had not studied a treatise on his profession for twenty-five years, picked up a book, any book, from his desk and carelessly opened it. Then he called upon the junior Lieutenant to recite the text of the page to which he had accidentally turned. The unfortunate Lieutenant, not even knowing the title of the book, floundered helplessly for a minute and then admitted his ignorance of the subject. By this time the noon mess call would sound.

Closing his book, the Colonel would say: "Lieutenant, you get zero for this lesson. It's dinner time. School is adjourned."

I attended the Colonel's war college for six months and was never asked a question. The poor second lieutenant was always the goat.

One day, to tease the old man, we placed on his desk a copy of the new firing regulations which had just come in the mail. We watched through a window as he sat down at his desk. He took one look at the pamphlet and then, much annoyed, shoved it out of sight under a pile of papers.

Later in the morning, Colonel Forney appeared on the parade ground to take command at formation. As usual he had not bothered to collect a complete uniform. He was wearing a frock coat with uniform trousers and carried his sword without a scabbard. Standing before us, he addressed the whole command solemnly.

"Some damned fool has brought out new regulations. In my forty years in the service I've been expected to learn at least a dozen sets of regulations, none of them any better than General Scott's tactics, which I absorbed in 1860. Now this new-fangled set has come just to worry me in my old age.

"However, I'm studying it. I don't want any of you to look at the book. It's my job as commanding officer to do all the instructing. I'll feed it to you little by little in drill practice. This morning we'll try one of the simple new movements described in the book."

He gave the command, "Right step," a movement probably dating far back of Caesar's day. The three hundred men went right step for fifty yards.

The Colonel called, "Halt!"

"Now that you have successfully performed this new movement, we'll try another. Left step."

We returned to our original position.

The Colonel complimented us enthusiastically. "You have done so well that I'll reward you by abandoning the rest of the hour's drill. Thank you for your close attention." We were dismissed.

Once a week Forney drilled us for five minutes, good-naturedly praised our efforts and let us go.

Several of the younger officers wanted to show their best girls how attractive they could be, stepping smartly through fancy maneuvers in full military regalia. We wheedled old Forney into holding a dress parade. Anxious for our commanding officer to make a spectacular impression on the visitors, we even persuaded him to do the reviewing on horseback.

The hour came for the parade. Harnan, the dear old sergeant, who was Forney's orderly, was reeling drunk. He laced the Colonel's leggings on the inside instead of the outside. Inside or outside, it was all the same to the Colonel. As he started across the parade ground, he tripped on the laces and sprawled out his full length to the hilarious amusement of the men and our guests. Assisted to his feet, the Colonel held up the parade while he launched into a violent and prolonged discussion with his orderly on the proper method of putting on leggings.

The problem now was to swing the parade into action, since the old man, much upset by the accident, refused to get on his horse. After soothing words and repeated pleading on our part, he at last magnanimously agreed not to spoil our big day. The horse was brought to the barracks steps, where with the assistance of a chair, our commander was safely deposited in the saddle.

The band struck up "The Halls of Montezuma," the Marine hymn. The horse began to prance, and the Colonel fell off. He was so rip-roaring mad that he decided to ride that horse if it killed him. Once more we went through the elaborate performance of mounting him. This time the horse was led through parade by two strong privates. Forney never tried a horse again.

In the spring of 1902, Colonel Forney was succeeded in command by Cochrane, the Colonel who hauled my company over the coals for wearing Chinese silk boots during the last days of our service in China.

When I was convalescing from typhoid in the Philippines, I had the privilege of witnessing the sham battle Cochrane pulled off at Cavite. It was one of the historic events of the Marine Corps. Cochrane, who did not reach China until the fighting was over, decided to stage his own little war in Cavite.

The sham battle was so well advertised that nearly every American in Manila brought his family to the show. The bay was dotted with small boats. A grandstand was erected at one end of the field to accommodate the guests.

Cochrane divided the Marines into two forces, one to attack the old Spanish fort, San Felipe, and the other to defend it. Between the fort and the town was a flat open stretch about one hundred yards wide. To make the attack seem more realistic, it had to be assumed that the hundred yards was three thousand yards. The attacking force had to cross the parade ground thirty times before "reaching" the fort.

The first twenty times across, the defenders could shoot at the assailants only with artillery. This consisted of some muzzle-loading Spanish cannon, mounted on little wooden wheels. The defenders rammed the powder into the antique pieces of ordnance with any old rags they could find. On each discharge the air was filled with shirts, underclothes and socks.

After an interminable period of crossing and re-crossing, the assaulting column was considered to be under rifle fire. The casualties were heavy. The ground was so covered with wounded and dying that the troops could scarcely move without stepping over their unfortunate comrades.

Finally, the commander of the assaulting column stepped up to Colonel Cochrane and complained that his men were suffering unnecessary losses. Under normal conditions there would be bushes and trees behind which they could take cover.

Cochrane hoisted the white flag to indicate a temporary armistice and blared through a megaphone to one of the attacking companies, "Captain, march your company double time to the corral, put wisps of straws in the necks of their blouses and act as bushes."

The captain was dumbfounded but obeyed the order. Soon he reappeared with his company, stumbling along in a column of fours. Each man had stuffed the collar of his coat with straw which bristled around his head and stood several feet above his hat. We could hardly see the men's faces but we could hear them sneezing from one end of the column to the other. Once the burning underwear vomited all over the "battlefield" by the old Spanish artillery set fire to these human bushes.

The animated bushes were distributed, on their knees, three yards apart the length of the field and moved forward with the attacking force. The shrubbery added great zest to the battle.

Toward the end of the afternoon the assailants placed the bamboo scaling ladders, which they had been carrying patiently all day, against the wall of the fort. But when the invaders tried to climb up, the defenders poured down on their heads buckets of hot water and garbage. There was no sham about the fist fights which followed. No decision was ever rendered as to who won this particular war.

And now here was Cochrane, again, the fussy old martinet, bringing his war college ideas to the Philadelphia barracks.

With a detachment of sixty Marines, I was at that time stationed on the receiving ship Lancaster, an old wooden frigate dismantled of warlike gear and used as a barracks for sailors. Every Thursday morning, we joined the Marines of the Navy Yard barracks in battalion exercises.

On the first Thursday after the arrival of Cochrane, I marched my men to the barracks and reported to the new commander for the weekly maneuvers.

Three companies of barracks Marines were assembling on the parade ground. Mine made the fourth in the battalion. We were all in parade clothes, and none of us carried packs.

When Colonel Cochrane threw back his head to address the battalion, his square grey beard stood out stiff and straight. His voice came through his whiskers with a whistling sound. He kept us standing at attention in the hot sun for twenty minutes while he made a tiresome speech on the art of war and the conduct of soldiers during battle.

Then he announced: "We'll now have a review followed by inspection. Since no high-ranking visitor is with us today, I'll set up a stick to represent the reviewing officer."

Our eyes bulged as we watched him pound a stout peg into the ground between two flags which indicated the reviewing stand. He then put the battalion in motion. We all solemnly saluted the stick as we marched by. The Colonel turned out of column after he had saluted and took up his position at the right of the stick. We could see him telling his inanimate reviewing officer the names of the companies as they passed.

We were then formed for inspection in column of companies, one company behind the other with my company leading. On that particular day my company had only thirty-five men, while each of the other three companies had seventy. In order to make them all appear the same size to our distinguished visitor, I was directed to form my outfit in single rank.

Saluting, the Colonel invited the stick to inspect the battalion. Apparently, the invitation was accepted, for Cochrane pulled his stick out of the ground and carried it along with him.

We had been told to "open ranks," that is to have the rear rank step back three paces in order that the inspecting officer might pass between the ranks. Since I had no rear rank, I didn't give the command.

Cochrane stormed up at me. "Why haven't you opened ranks?"

"It's not possible, sir. I have only one rank."

"You've missed the point," he fumed. "It's necessary for the military education of your men that you conduct yourself as if you had two ranks. Have the rear rank step back."

A little dazed with this play acting, I complied and reported my company ready for inspection.

Walking down the front rank and firmly grasping the stick in an upright position, old Cochrane apologized: "These men are not part of my command, General. They join me once a week for instruction. I'm not responsible for any defects you may observe in their conduct or equipment."

As he started down the imaginary rear rank, continuing his idiotic, one-sided conversation, we could hardly contain our merriment.

"You see, General," he explained, pointing to an imaginary Marine, "the shoes worn by this man are of inferior quality, but it's not his fault. They are issued by the government. We have great difficulty in securing first-class articles."

When this nonsense was finished, he told me to unsling my knapsacks and prepare them for inspection.

"I'm sorry, sir, my men have not brought their knapsacks with them."

His whiskers pointed significantly forward and the whistling sound was ominous as he said: "Captain, must I tell you again that we are preparing our men for war? You will unsling those knapsacks, or I'll relieve you from command."

"I'd be glad to obey the order, Colonel, but I don't know how."

"Your responsibility is at an end when you give the command," he barked in a high-pitched voice. "Then it's up to the men in the ranks properly to execute the order."

By this time, I was ready to roll on the ground with joy. Almost in hysterics I called out, "Unsling knapsacks."

The men, entering into the spirit of the thing, waved their arms about, bumped into one another and stirred up a commotion worthy of heavily packed knapsacks.

"Several knapsacks in the front rank are out of line," the Colonel pointed out. "Straighten them."

After some confusion and argument about which ones were out of line, the front rank was finally accepted. In the rear rank he had me call on certain numbered men in the squads to move their knapsacks forward or back. Since there were neither men nor knapsacks, it was difficult to know when the movement was complete. The Colonel, by some occult reasoning of his own, finally decided that the knapsacks were straight.

"But, Captain, haven't you forgotten something?"

Stifling my desire to shriek with laughter, I admitted: "Perhaps I have forgotten something, but I can't think what it is. Won't you be good enough to tell me, sir?" Throwing out his whiskers at a fierce right angle, the Colonel turned to the stick. "I wish to apologize, General, for the Captain's conduct. Young officers of the present generation are careless and don't take their profession seriously."

He then faced me solemnly. "You have failed to open your knapsacks for the inspection of the visiting General." I promptly acknowledged my fault. "Open knapsacks," I shouted.

The Colonel with his stick proceeded along the front rank. He halted beside an old Marine and poured out his wrath.

"For a man who has been in the service as long as you have, your knapsack is very poorly packed."

"Why, Colonel," I protested, "these men all know how to pack their knapsacks. They do it frequently aboard ship. I don't think it's fair of you to jump on this man when he hasn't a knapsack with him."

Ignoring me, the Colonel addressed his friend the stick. "You see, General, this young officer entirely misses the object of the inspection. I'm merely preparing this man's mind. If he ever receives a reprimand for the condition of his knapsack, he will know how to act."

The Colonel continued along the imaginary rear rank, commenting, "The rear rank is better than the front rank. Apparently, these men have been properly instructed." With that, he told me to sling knapsacks, and dismissed the company.

Telling the First Sergeant to march the company back to the ship, I bolted for the barracks to talk the drill over with the captain of one of the other three companies of the battalion, my friend Captain A. E. Harding, who had been with me in the Philippines and China.

While we were talking, a bell rang three times. Harding jumped up.

"That's my number. The old man wants me. Come along, Smedley; you'll see some fun."

We found Cochrane at his office window, mournfully gazing out over the parade ground.

"Captain Harding, come here. Don't you see them out there?"

Harding stared and stared without being able to discover anything unusual.

"No, Colonel, I don't see anything but grass."

"Don't you see them out there in rows?" Cochrane persisted.

"No, sir, I don't."

"Look well, Captain. Don't you see two long straight rows of government property?"

Harding was irritated. "No, Colonel, I don't see anything. Now, what is it?"

"Don't lose your temper," Cochrane advised. "This is part of your military education. I've sent for you to remind you that you left your knapsacks on the parade ground when you marched your company into the barracks."

Harding, thinking that the quickest way out of the difficulty was to agree, said "Oh, yes, sir, yes, sir, that's right. I did."

"What do you intend to do about it?" pursued Cochrane.

"Tomorrow morning, Colonel, when I go out to drill, I'll bring in the knapsacks."

Cochrane straightened out like a ramrod and whistled through his whiskers: "Captain, do you mean to tell me that you will leave those knapsacks out all night? The navy yard workmen might steal them."

"I don't think the workmen in the navy yard are dishonest," Harding said hopefully.

"I like to hear you speak so well of our laboring classes but," Cochrane explained, "it might rain."

"But I don't think it will rain." Harding was hopeful again.

"You can't be positive that it won't rain," the Colonel argued.

"No, sir, I can't," poor Harding had to admit. "Therefore," the old man went on relentlessly, "since you are not positive of the security of government property, you must take steps to protect it. What do you propose to do?"

"I'll just go out, Colonel, and gather them up."

"You can't carry seventy knapsacks," replied the adamant commander.

Harding was beginning to wilt under this steady bombardment. "I'll make two or three trips."

"That isn't satisfactory. Now, what will you do?" Harding heaved a deep sigh and surrendered at last. "All right, Colonel, I'll take the company out and let them get their own knapsacks."

"Really, Captain Harding, I think there is some hope for you," said Cochrane, thawing out with a stiff little smile.

Harding flung out of the Commandant's office and pounded angrily up the stairs of the barracks. From below I could hear his men banging their rifles and stamping over the floor as they struggled into their parade clothes again.

A glum, sullen-faced company marched out of the barracks with a more glum and sullen captain at their head. Harding formed his men in line at the place where he guessed the imaginary knapsacks were located. But one usually guessed wrong with Cochrane. The old man, ready to pounce down like a predatory bird, was watching the scene with gimlet eyes from the barracks.

"Captain, you're wrong," he shouted, "the knapsacks are over there," and he pointed vaguely to the other end of the parade ground.

Harding moved his company "over there," but Cochrane wasn't satisfied.

"No, no," he fumed impatiently. "Don't you see where I mean? Over there!"

Three or four hundred men were leaning out of the windows of the barracks, cheering gleefully and howling down ribald and uncomplimentary remarks at the scapegoat captain and his unlucky company. Harding reached the limit of his endurance. Beside himself with rage, he threw his sword on the ground and shouted at the Colonel, "I can't find those damn knapsacks."

Cochrane turned to me and said in a tone that dripped with icicles: "It's distressing to see a young officer fail. However, in the course of time, I think that Captain may become a useful public servant."

In a voice that rang out across the parade ground the Colonel announced that he would find the knapsacks himself. He went out on the parade ground and drove four stakes into the grass, one on the right and one on the left of each imaginary row of knapsacks.

"Now, Captain, here are your knapsacks."

In order to make no mistake this time, Harding ordered four of his men to station themselves with the four stakes between their feet. Then he lined up his two ranks between the men serving as guide posts.

All was serene until the Colonel let out a shriek. "Captain, the whole thing is a failure! Don't you see that your knapsacks are ruined?"

"No, Colonel, I don't," Harding spit out sourly.

"Well, then, you should. Your men are standing on the knapsacks instead of slightly in the rear. You might as well march your company into the barracks. Your mind is not receptive to ideas this morning. We'll try this another day."

That was Cochrane, fantastic, serious, pompous, mean as the deuce. The war college idea must have sprung full grown from his disciplinary brain. He could think up a dozen ways of making the lives of his subordinates miserable. Generally, our fury kept us from laughing right in Cochrane's face when he was engineering his absurd maneuvers and sham battles. We were so damned mad at being dragged through all his monkey business in the heat that we usually forgot how funny he was.

Chapter IX

Why I "Love" the Navy

To most people Culebra means the cut through the Panama Canal. Few persons have ever heard of the island of Culebra twenty miles east of Puerto Rico. On this picturesque but desolate little island not more than five miles at its widest and longest, the United States government at one time maintained a naval station. Our warships rode comfortably at anchor at the south end of the island in Great Harbor, which afforded an ideal natural protection.

It was September 1902. Trouble was brewing among the explosive population of Panama. One battalion of Marines had already been sent to that turbulent neck of the woods.

Two additional battalions were now landing at Culebra, to be within easy hailing distance in case they were needed on the Isthmus. I was with them. As I stepped off the transport, my outlook on life was particularly cheerful because my Major was Harry Haines, to whom I had been devoted in the Philippines. As an excuse for our presence in southern waters, the Navy was to engage in fleet maneuvers off Culebra, and the Marines were to fortify the island, according to plans worked out by the Naval War College.

My battalion was stationed at Camp Dewey at the northern end of the island. Even if the Navy had not been continually nagging at us, tenting on Culebra would have been unpleasant. The island was infested with scorpions, tarantulas and other poisonous members of the crawling tribe. One day a centipede six inches long started up my bare back. A husky Marine yelled for me to stand still. With a heavy flat board, he crushed the centipede and incidentally almost broke my back.

There were no wells. We had to send barges to a neighboring island for drinking water. As I look back, the only recommendation I could hand Culebra was the beautiful crescent-shaped coral beaches beckoning an invitation to the fine surf bathing. But we Marines had little time to sport in the surf or indulge in any idle resort recreation. Our middle name was work.

We sweated and heaved to mount four and five-inch guns for the defense of the island from almost the moment we arrived. Each gun weighed several tons. It was no joke to drag those guns up hills four hundred feet high. We also had docks to build and other jobs to occupy us, so that by the first of December we had not made much headway toward mounting the guns and digging emplacements for powder magazines. The Admiral of our squadron, Joe Coghlan, was furious at the delay. He got it into his head that we were slackers.

*Rear Admiral Joseph Bulloch Coghlan (1844-1908), a veteran of the Civil War.

"I'll show those lazy, good for nothing Marines how to mount guns," he announced.

He collected one hundred and twenty-five experts in gunnery from his squadron to set up a gun in record time. He'd let the world know how inferior the Marines were to a good battleship crew. My company, which was chosen to represent the Marines, had only sixty men available for the contest.

The competition started at four o'clock in the morning. Each outfit was given its gun—a naval gun without wheels —at the water's edge. The guns were to be mounted on huge wooden platforms, which had to be buried in the ground. Each detachment had to drag fifteen tons of material up the rival hills.

All the equipment was carried to the top of our hill by afternoon. We had even dug the pits for the foundations. We caught fleeting glimpses of the bluejackets working on their hill around an arm of the bay. Our spies, no doubt to spur us on, ran up to us with the report that the Navy was gaining on us. We were not surprised. Our opponents had double our number. But we bent to with a will. Every man took Coghlan's slur on the Marines as a personal insult.

Nearly every man of war that the United States owned seemed to be anchored off the island. Admiral Dewey had just come to Culebra to command all the assembled squadrons.

The famous Admiral took a personal interest in our contest. He issued orders that a shot should be fired from the first gun mounted, so that he could know on his flagship which group was victorious. Because of the danger of hitting his ship, no shot, however, was to be fired at night.

About four in the afternoon, when we were ready to mount our gun, we discovered that two of the heavy oak platforms, weighing six thousand pounds apiece, could not be made to join together. Through a blunder, we had one platform belonging to another gun. This was a terrible disappointment. We had planned to fire our gun just before sundown. The platform mix-up set us back several hours.

We held our breath and pricked up our ears at sundown. The jackies* didn't fire. We had as good a chance as they to send off a shot in the morning.

*Meaning the 'blue-jackets.' This slang term for American sailors is based on the US Navy's original (ceremonial) deep-blue uniforms, which had been phased out by this time.

I sent out a call for volunteers to work all night. Every man in my company, cooks, bakers, clerks, came up the hill after supper. We worked like Trojans and finished at midnight. Our scouts brought us word that the sailors had not yet pulled their gun to the top of their hill.

At sunrise we fired the winner's shot. The shell sailed gaily out over the Mayflower, Admiral Dewey's flagship, and struck the water a mile beyond. For some reason this angered the hero of Manila Bay. He sent me a reprimand for firing. The only kind word we received from the Navy was a message signaled by a Lieutenant-Commander Buchanan from his gunboat in the bay. And that poor man was given a stiff calling down by the Admiral for congratulating the Marines.

Weary and half-dazed but elated with our victory, we hobbled down the hill to celebrate a well-earned holiday.

Holiday, indeed! We had hardly stretched our aching bones on our cots when a signal came from the flagship. The successful company of Marines was awarded the privilege of mounting the sailors' gun. The privilege was a command. It made me boil to gather together my tired men to finish the mounting of that damned navy gun. With plenty of healthy cussing we got the gun in place and fired off a shot. Our victory was complete, but the Navy was embittered toward us.

Admiral Coghlan was so enraged that the Navy had been licked after all his bragging that he punished the speed artists whom he had sent ashore to mount his gun.

Some fertile-minded naval official who had nothing to do but pace up and down his deck in a starched white uniform and invent work for the other fellow, now conceived a brilliant idea. A canal was to be constructed through the narrow peninsula from the inside harbor to the outer bay, so that the admirals and other naval potentates could come through in their steam launches by a short cut.

Admiral Coghlan sent ashore one hundred and fifty sailors to dig the canal. One day after the sailors had been working a little more than a week, a junior naval officer burst into our camp, half a mile from the embryo canal.

"The sailors refuse to work any longer. They're throwing mud at the officers."

I was on duty as officer of the day. I collected some Marines and ran to the excitement. The sailors were raising Cain, but we subdued the incipient mutiny. Sixty-five irrepressibles were sent to Admiral Coghlan's flagship for punishment.

The Admiral now detailed me to dig that damned canal with Marines. In his order he had stated that Americans could not work under such unhealthful conditions, but he neglected to explain how Marines failed to be Americans.

The next day I marched out two hundred and fifty men from our battalion and took charge of the canal digging. No wonder the sailors had mutinied. Sometimes we were blasting and digging through solid rock, sharpening our picks every hour. Again, we were shoveling through stagnant marsh land, alive with mosquitoes.

To add to our misery, the Navy required us to work in uniform with leggings on. We were fifteen to eighteen feet down in the ground, with a blistering sun beating down on us. Our friends in the Navy could not have devised a more fiendish torment. Finally, we succeeded in getting an order permitting us to take off our shirts and leggings.

At the beginning of the Christmas holidays, two-thirds of the canal was completed. The Admiral issued an order for the fleet to scatter through the various Caribbean ports for the holidays. My canal diggers, however, were excluded from this sight-seeing excursion.

The Navy had towed over an old clam shell dredge from San Juan, Porto Rico, to dig the salt water approaches. Since the sailors who ran the clam shell dredge were off on their holiday, it was up to us to keep the dredge running. Thinking anything but charitable, Christian thoughts toward our absent naval tyrants, I operated the controls of the dredge Christmas morning.

We worked continuously during the two weeks the fleet was away enjoying liberty. I must say the Marines were magnificent. Although they disliked the loathsome routine of digging from daylight to dark and resented the injustices that had been piled upon them, they were loyal and devoted to one another and their officers.

Not long after the first of the year Chagres fever broke out among my Marines who had been transformed into tropical day laborers. I had a severe attack myself. One night when I was burning up and delirious, it was believed that my end was near. Haines, my Major, asked the flagship for ice. He was refused, although there was an ice machine on board. The Major, a rugged, powerful man whose strength was tempered with great gentleness, walked five miles around the bay to a little canteen where he bought twenty-five pounds. By the time he returned the ice had melted.

In desperation, the Major insisted that I should be moved across the bay to the hospital, a temporary wooden shack. I was hardly conscious. Waves of ether seemed to float around me. My men carried me out on my cot and gently lifted me into a boat to be rowed over to the hospital. I was only half aware of the change. I thought I was still down in the canal with the sun burning a hole in my back.

A Marine officer on one of the ships wrote to my father in Washington, telling him what had been happening in Culebra. My father raised hell with the Navy Department. By the time I recovered, the Admiral had a message from the Secretary of the Navy, who directed that no more Americans should be worked on that canal.

But as soon as I came off the sick list, I was detailed to finish the canal with sixty-five natives hired to do the job. After working top speed for two weeks and almost finishing the canal, I had a relapse of the fever.

While I was still tossing on my bed, the Navy had the grand opening of the canal, with much ceremony, full dress uniforms and all the gala trimmings. Flowery speeches were gracefully tossed off, but no mention was made of the men who built the canal. There was not one word of praise for the Marines. I have never forgotten that. My lack of affection for the Navy dates from my Culebra experience.

CHAPTER X

Revolution in Honduras

A TYPICAL CENTRAL AMERICAN REVOLUTION HAD broken out in Honduras. Admiral Joe Coghlan, ordered to protect American interests, steamed away in February 1903, with an ill-assorted relief squadron, consisting of his flagship, the Olympia, the little gunboat Marietta and the transport Panther, an old banana freighter.

Our battalion was put on board the Panther. We wanted to give three cheers for Honduras. A revolution was a welcome escape from the wretched islet of Culebra, where we Marines had been prodded beyond endurance.

But our high spirits sank to zero when we became better acquainted with our banana transport. It was a small ship and the three hundred and fifty of us were jammed to suffocation. We could have accepted the discomfort with Marine philosophy, if the Captain of the Panther had not been a very disagreeable naval commander named Wilson. His quarters were in the forward end of the deck house next to the forecastle, outside of which the enlisted men congregated to get a breath of air.

One afternoon the Captain summoned the whole ship's company to the quarter deck. He separated the sheep from the goats. The Marines were lined up on the port side, the sailors on the starboard. He struck a Napoleonic pose between the two crowds and addressed us pompously.

"Somebody has been using profane language near my cabin. I want you all to understand that I will not tolerate profanity. I know the guilty party cannot be one of these fine men," he said, waving his left hand toward the sailors; "therefore it must have been one of these—these men enlisted from the slums of our big cities." And he aimed his right hand at the Marines.

I was standing ten feet from him, with my sword drawn and resting on the deck. My hand itched on the hilt. I was overwhelmed with a desire to run him through. Then and there I made up my mind that I would always protect Marines from the hounding to which they were subjected by some of the naval officers.

After Wilson told the Marines what he thought of them, he issued an order dividing the deck for the use of officers and men. He confiscated for himself most of the starboard side of the ship, gave the naval officers one-fourth of the port side, and cramped the Marine officers, fourteen of us, into space twenty feet long and twelve feet wide. We were forbidden to take our exercise on any other part of the deck.

Wilson imagined himself something of a John Paul Jones and liked to kid himself with the idea that he was commanding a real man of war instead of a stuffy little banana boat. He kept us out of mischief with drills in vogue during the time of the ark.

Apparently, he was convinced that eighteenth century pirates still infested the Spanish Main. One day he mounted the bridge and bellowed orders at us through a huge brass megaphone. He informed us that we were about to be boarded by the crew of a hostile ship lashed to our side with grappling irons. We were directed to repel boarders coming over the starboard side. But our skipper got his antique commands so mixed up that the whole main deck was soon a seething scrambling mass of sailors and Marines, piled four deep, shouting and struggling to get untangled.

In more than thirty years I've served with all sorts of men, but for downright cussedness I never met the equal of the Captain of the Panther.

And we certainly had a good dose for him as we sailed the length of the Caribbean. Our little gunboat could make only eight knots an hour, hence the squadron traveled at a snail's pace. It was ten blistering days without a puff of wind to ripple the water before we reached Puerto Cortez, the principal port on the north coast of Honduras.

We drifted slowly into the beautiful harbor, with its palm-fringed shore line and a range of translucent blue mountains in the distance. The water was crystal clear. We could see the bottom one hundred feet below us. For climate, though, we had jumped out of the frying pan into the fire. It was so hot that steam was actually rising from the shore.

As we entered port, we noticed that the blue and white government flag was still flying over the custom house. We fired the regulation national salute of twenty-one guns. A friendly power is expected to return the salute, gun for gun.

We waited and waited. Not a sound. Several hours slipped by. Finally, a tremendous explosion spit forth from a hoary, muzzle-loading cannon ornamenting the mud fort at the edge of town. Silence again. In an hour another boom groaned out. This was repeated at intervals of an hour until dark.

Just before sundown a launch chugged up to the flagship. A swarthy little officer in bright red pants and green coat stepped on deck to see the Admiral. He was all apologies. He spoke English very slowly and precisely, with an ingratiating shadow of an accent.

"We are very sorry," he explained. "We could send off only twelve guns today. We shall finish the salute in the morning. To get the powder for the cannon we have had to empty all our rifle shells."

As he departed, the officer volunteered the information that a revolutionary attack was expected any moment.

It wasn't exactly clear to me what all the fighting was about. As far as I could learn, General Terencio Sierra was President and wanted to stay

President. The head of the revolutionary faction, General Manuel Bonilla, insisted that he had been elected President by a large majority, and he wanted to be President. Bonilla was supported by a General Davila. In fact, there were hosts of generals in both parties. Every twentieth person one met was a general, but I'm hazy on their names.

It all seemed like a Gilbert and Sullivan war. The supporters of the government wore blue and white hatbands, and the revolutionists wore red and white hatbands. Since the hatbands meant revolutionist on one side and government on the other, they offered a flexible as well as a convenient method of identification. At a critical moment a man could quickly shift his allegiance by turning his hat-band inside out.

Puerto Cortez was not hard to defend. The town was built on a sandy island. Its only connection with the mainland was a small bridge over which rattled the rickety trains of the narrow-gauge banana railroad to the terminus thirty-five miles up in the bush country.

The night of our arrival an outpost of one officer and a few men was stationed on the bridge. The soldiers knew the enemy was miles away. It was a hot night and the men were sleepy. The whole group, including the officer, lay down on the tracks, using the rail for a pillow.

Toward morning a banana train wobbled along the bridge and ran over some of the sleeping sentinels. The tragedy was bad enough, but the slur on the vigilance of a government outpost was too much. The pride and honor of the Honduran army was at stake. The engineer and conductor of the train, who were Americans, were seized and sentenced to be shot at daylight.

The American Consul, hearing of their plight, immediately notified the Admiral. A few of us Marines hurried ashore. There wasn't much time before daylight. By a considerable display of diplomacy, graphically emphasized by our pointing ominously in the direction of our squadron, we succeeded in rescuing the unfortunate train crew.

For the most part we led a rather dreary existence while we waited for something to happen. Puerto Cortez was the most uninviting place I have ever seen. It was dirty, hot and hummed with flies and bugs.

It was hard to understand why fifteen hundred people wanted to live here. The houses were little more than mud huts with corrugated iron roofs generously patched with sides of Standard Oil cans. Down the middle of the one and only street the railroad ran from the custom house and dock at the eastern end of town.

Near the custom house was the Louisiana lottery, which found a welcome asylum in Honduras when it was outlawed from the States. We all bought tickets regularly and just as regularly failed to win.

Bananas were everywhere. I almost hated bananas. A little fleet of banana boats, unconcerned about the revolution, was continually coming and going. Among them, I recognized some of the transports used during the Spanish-American War.

We amused ourselves sailing boats around the bay, took rides up the toy railroad into the banana country and did what Intelligence work we could without offending the Hondurans.

We had been living on board our ships anchored in the harbor for about a month before the revolutionary movement came to a head in Puerto Cortez.

The commander of the local government forces was not a Honduran, but a native of one of the islands in the West Indies. He had gray hair, a gray mustache and a great deal of black blood in his veins. The little fellow strutted around importantly in the impressive plumage of a French field-marshal.

One fine morning the three hundred soldiers quartered in the barracks near the railroad bridge turned their hat-bands inside out and became revolutionists. They sallied forth to attack the small garrison at army headquarters in the custom house.

The battle took place in front of the American Consulate and opposite our ship, so we had box seats to the performance.

The loyal troops formed a line and advanced down the street toward the rebels. The dusky Commander-in-Chief, rigged out in his best French uniform, advanced with them, but very much in the rear. He was being dragged slowly and cautiously along on a hand car, which he was using for field headquarters. His son, more gallant, was in front of the troops and fearlessly urging on a band of some thirty followers.

The hand car with its precious load of military brains kept at a safe distance from stray bullets. It retired early in the action. The comic opera Generalissimo disappeared into the custom house. He never even glanced in the direction of his son, who was in the thick of the fighting. The boy was shot before the battle was over.

The handful of government troops was soon overcome. After suffering a few casualties, the loyal army melted into thin air by the prudent method of turning hatbands.

The whole mob, now comrades in arms, surged toward the custom house, where the government funds were stored.

The wily old General had been too quick for them. He had carried the six thousand dollars cash on hand on board the Honduran navy, which consisted of a small Delaware River one-cylinder tug boat, rechristened the Blanco.

The crowd ran at top speed to the shore end of the dock just as the dirty old tub was shoving off into the bay. Their howling and yelling were futile. The treasury was beyond their reach.

As the Blanco started to steam out of the harbor, the General changed his mind. His wheezy little tug swung about and headed toward the mud fort at the edge of town. Impudently, he poked the stern toward the beach and drove at the fort with an old cannon.

At first the fort did not answer this insult. But in a few minutes, there was a terrific explosion, and the Blanco was engulfed in smoke. When the clouds cleared away, we saw that the blast had knocked a big hole in the stern of the boat. Later we learned that the fort defenders had stuffed their one piece of artillery with powder and a diabolical mixture of railroad spikes, bolts and other hardware.

The Blanco was in a sinking condition as she put-putted her way toward our flagship, where some first-aid repairs were rendered.

Eventually the old bandit disappeared out of the harbor with his loot. Not many days before, when I had called on him, he had eloquently sobbed out his love for Honduras and declared with tears in his eyes that he intended to die with the Honduran flag wrapped around him.

The rising tide of popular indignation against the government in power was extending to other little towns scattered along the coast. Our consular representatives were calling on us for help. We Marines cruised around on the Panther to keep an eye on the revolution.

Ceiba was our next port of call. All I knew about it at the time was that one William Walker, notorious American filibuster,* who looted Nicaragua for some years, sought refuge around 1860, on a Man of War at Ceiba. The captain of the ship promptly turned him over to the local authorities, who ended the filibuster's career by shooting him. Today Ceiba chiefly lodges in my memory as the place where ice, brought on little schooners from Nicaragua, cost one dollar a pound.

The original meaning of filibustering and one still used internationally, is the intentional military intervention in a country to support forces fighting against that country, with the hidden intention of ultimately casting rebels aside and taking over. The notorious William Walker (1824-1860) inserted himself and his militia forces many times into trouble hotspots in South America, hoping to found a state with him as sole ruler, and operate it based on a slave economy. Walker succeeded briefly in Nicaragua but was soon after apprehended by authorities in Honduras and executed for his crimes.

Following image: Walker as President of Nicaragua.

The town was as unattractive and dirty as Puerto Cortez. An impenetrable tropical jungle filled with wild animals was pushing in on the town and, without the vigilance of the inhabitants, would have swallowed it up. Even fence posts burst into full bloom when it rained. The native population was enlivened by a sprinkling of foreigners who had left their own countries without bothering to say goodbye.

Since there was no harbor, we anchored in the open sea, a few hundred yards off the beach. When we went ashore we discovered that the local army had not yet turned their hat-bands. The government party was still in control.

The generals—as usual, there were several of them—received us cordially. They explained that ammunition was too precious to waste on a salute. Would we honor them with our presence at a review?

The review took place late that afternoon in the open space in front of the fort, which was nothing more than a long wall with loop holes.

The commanding general was coal black, heavy set and solemn, but he tried to make himself agreeable as master of ceremonies. He wore a high silk hat and a frock coat of mellow vintage. The only evidence of his profession was the huge, old-fashioned saber which dangled at his left side.

We stood around, sweating and blistering under the broiling sun. Finally, the bugles sounded, and the army, which had been lying in the grass waiting for orders, yawned, stretched and shuffled lazily out on the parade ground. The officers stamped up and down, brandishing their swords and scolding in noisy Spanish. After much shifting and assorting, the three hundred half-clad lads were in line.

Then the band appeared. An enormous drum was pushed forward on a wheelbarrow. The other instruments were of bamboo and emitted weird sounds. But the native soldiers seemed to appreciate the band and stepped smartly to the rhythm of the crazy music.

At sundown three men climbed up on the wall of the fort where the national colors were triumphantly fluttering. A little cannon was pushed out, also on a wheelbarrow. There was a quick jerk, a tiny puff of smoke, and the sunset gun went off. The three men, instead of pulling down the flag, picked up the flagpole and lowered it to the ground, where it was laid to rest for the night. The troops scattered in the direction of supper. The ceremony was over.

Two or three days later the soldiers calmly turned their hatbands and shot their general—the one who wore the plug hat. Ceiba went over to the revolutionary party, without any fighting.

Since no American interests were threatened in Ceiba, we moved eastward along the coast to Trujillo.

Apparently, we had arrived none too soon. As we dropped anchor, we could hear the sharp cracking of rifles. A message was brought to the squadron that our consular agent, a Honduran, was in great danger. A boat load of Marines was at once sent ashore to rescue him.

When we breezed up the street, we discovered that the government forces were in the town hall on one side of the plaza and the revolutionists were in the church on the other side. Between them, right in the line of fire, stood the American Consulate.

Upon our approach, the shooting stopped. It was a sort of armistice. Both sides came out to look at us. But we didn't linger to pass the time of day. We marched right on to the consulate, over which the American flag was grandly waving.

The place seemed to be deserted, but soon we heard stifled cries for help underneath the house, which was raised from the ground on heavy timber props.

We crawled under and found our agent tucked away between the beams in the middle of the building, where he could place the greatest amount of wood between him and the contending armies. We assisted the trembling, quaking Consul from his hiding place and stood him up, blinking, in the sun. He was dressed in a sort of Mother Hubbard, concocted out of an American flag.

As soon as he recovered sufficiently from his fright to recognize that we were American soldiers and not Hondurans, he struck a pose of great dignity, which contrasted idiotically with his masquerade costume. Shore held no attraction for him. He demanded to be taken at once to the commander of our ship.

Delighted to show off our circus exhibit, we rowed him out to the Panther, where he was received with the honors due his rank, but not, however, until the Captain made him take off his patriotic chemise and change into civilized clothes. He refused to go ashore until the fighting was over.

The government leader at Trujillo was a real soldier. He was determined to stick it out, no matter what happened.

Several of us went to see him at his headquarters in a dingy little house near the plaza. The room itself was enough to take the heart out of anybody. The plaster was falling off the walls, the ceiling was sagging down. Wounded men, with rags tied around their heads and arms, were lying, groaning, on the dirty mud floor.

The commander was sitting at a bare table, his face lighted dimly by two smoky lanterns. He was a native Honduran, a clean-cut fellow, with flashing teeth.

"I have staked all I have on this struggle," he told us through an interpreter. "I'll stick it out, no matter what happens. The insurgents will shoot me anyway. I can't even depend on my own troops not to mutiny. I can't count on any help from the central government at Tegucigalpa."

Generally, when a military leader is in a tight place, he has some hope of rescue. This man knew only too well that he didn't have a chance in a thousand. The other towns along the coast had fallen. His, too, would pass into the hands of the *insurrectos*. I had the greatest admiration for this obscure commander who stoutly refused to change his hatband. The scrap at Trujillo lasted several days. The bullets kept striking so close to us that we had to move a little distance out in the bay. The outcome was the same here as in the other towns. The local forces went revolutionary. I was genuinely sorry to learn of the death of the determined and gallant leader of the little government army. As soon as the rebel flag went up, he was shot. It was just another human tragedy on the outskirts of the world.

Not only the coast, but the mountain region in the interior had now gone over to Bonilla's revolutionary party with very little bloodshed. So long as Americans and their interests were not jeopardized, the job of the Marines in Honduras was finished.

Chapter XI

From Soldiering to Mining

PHILADELPHIA HAD A NEW CHARM FOR ME. I was viewing the old Quaker City through rainbow colors. I had the good fortune to meet my wife here. She was Ethel Conway Peters, a Philadelphia girl. Her family had been prominent in the affairs of the city since Colonial times.

We were married in June 1905. How can I write of the blissful, tranquil happiness of a long-married life? I'm a soldier and my words are blunt. The years have been golden. I haven't the poetry to describe them. Whatever storms have broken around my head, my wife has stood at my side. I can't think of much that I do to please her; except perhaps to wear grey suits and blue ties, because blue and grey are her favorite colors.

Right after our marriage, I was ordered to the Philippines as captain of Company E, Second Regiment. We made a leisurely journey to Manila by way of Europe, India and Singapore. That was our wedding trip.

I didn't return to Cavite, where I had been initiated into some of the duties of a soldier's life five years before. This time I was stationed at the Olongapo Navy Yard on Subig Bay, about sixty miles north of Manila.

Major Joe Pendleton was in command of the thousand Marines at the Olangapo post. He was genial, and hospitable, his wife kind and motherly, but almost stone deaf. He adored her and loved to tease her.

The Major talked a blue streak and he always managed to swing the conversation around to the fact that he had been on duty in Sitka, Alaska, for six or seven years, and had learned that his family tree entitled him to a totem pole with two frogs on it. All we had to do was to press the button. Out would come the totem pole and the frogs.

The garrison never tired of the latest Pendleton story. I remember, for instance, the night that Captain Skenk was to dine with the Pendletons. They were giving a dance in his honor.

"Captain, I hope you will enjoy the dance tonight," said Mrs. Pendleton.

"I'm sorry, Mrs. Pendleton, but I shan't be able to come. I've just had a cable that my mother has died," Skenk explained.

"Oh, how nice," beamed dear, deaf Mrs. Pendleton. "Bring her along."

We had good times at Olangapo. The old crowd kept drifting in and out. Fritz Wise, who had been on the trek to Peking, was there. We both let out a few whoops when we learned that Hiram Bearss was coming. No one could be bored when "Hi" was in the offing. He kept things moving.

He had just been married, and Fritz Wise and I went to the dock at Olangapo to meet him when he arrived with his bride, one of the prettiest girls I've ever seen.

As they stepped off the tug, Fritz said, "I bet you a dollar, Hiram, you're wearing someone else's undershirt."

"I won't bet," said Hiram, "and I won't take it off."

"We'll do it for you, then."

We dragged him around a corner of the dock and jerked off his blouse. Sure enough, his undershirt was marked D. D. Porter. Hiram never seemed to have any clothes or funds of his own. He was always borrowing. But Hiram was so likable that he could get away with anything. He was fearless, wild, always playing practical jokes.

We stayed more than two years in the Philippines. My daughter Ethel was born at Olangapo on November 2, 1906. She was named Ethel Peters after her mother, but we always called her "Snooks." The crowd got drunk to celebrate the event. All night long I could hear my bachelor friends yelling, "Three cheers for the totem poles—and the frogs!"

"Snooks" started out in life as a Marine. As soon as she was born, she was christened and adopted by the regiment. The biggest member of the 2nd Regiment was a man named Snooks and as my baby was the smallest, the men called her Snooks also, a name that has clung to her ever since. The First Sergeant made a formal application for her to become a member of Company E. On Thanksgiving I gave a big dinner for the enlisted men and carried her on a pillow to the function as guest of honor. She was always a Marine, so it seemed fitting that I should give her in marriage in March 1932, to a Lieutenant of Marines, John Wehle.

Naturally, I enjoyed garrison duty, which meant that I didn't need to leave home. But about ten days a month I had to march my company over the country on long hikes.

We averaged two hundred miles a month with our packs on.

When we halted for the night on one of these cross-country expeditions, a private was given an entrenching tool and ordered to dig a garbage pit. The man, suddenly mutinous, struck his corporal with the shovel and almost killed him. He became wild and hit at everybody within reach.

On my way to Culebra in 1902 I had taken a course in knotting from Chief Bos'n Hill, an old-time tar. He taught me twenty-seven different knots, splices and hitches. I've never forgotten them. We had no guardhouse in camp; so, I now applied what I'd learned from the old bos'n. I made some rope handcuffs called a Tom Fool's Knot. Several of us then tied the mutinous private by his wrists to a tree. As soon as he calmed down I let him loose. But when I returned to Olangapo, I had him tried by general court-martial for assault and battery.

The private was put in the brig, where he became the soul mate of what is known as a "sea lawyer." In a fire and brimstone letter to a United States senator, the sea lawyer charged me with tying his friend to a tree by his thumbs so that his toes just touched the ground. I had ruined his thumbs for life. What was going to be done about it? The senator in a white fury of an outraged sense of justice took up the matter with the Navy Department. The Navy Department cabled to the Philippines for an investigation.

An inspector came to Olangapo. Without my knowledge, he questioned all the men in my company. Then he came to tell me that he had been investigating my conduct.

"Well, what did you find out?" I asked.

"They told me there was not a word of truth in these charges."

"If you had come to me in the first place," I said, "I would have given you the facts. The fellow was mutinous. I did tie him by his wrists—not by his thumbs—to a tree and left him there until he calmed down."

I found out that the hundred and sixteen men who had been on that march all swore to the same story. The whole company lied to protect me when they thought I might get into trouble. Said they didn't even know this private. There had never been a man in the company by that name. Nobody had been tied up for anything.

It has been my experience all through the service that an enlisted man will lie and even die for an officer who gives him a break.

I did, however, quite innocently, get into a mess which terminated my stay in the Philippines.

With a detachment of fifty men I was sent from Olangapo to the opposite shore of Subig Bay. We spent a couple of months in that godforsaken spot, dragging six-inch guns up the mountains to defend the bay in case of a problematical future war with Japan.

It was a miserable existence. Water poured in torrents under our tents, pitched on a steep mountain slope. All we had to eat was hardtack, coffee and canned beef. We lived on hash—baked hash one meal, fried hash the next.

Enviously, we watched the navy supply tug from Olangapo bounce over regularly to an island in the bay where a Marine battalion was stationed. That darn little tug never brought us supplies. It didn't even know we were alive. Finally, we were down to our last rations. Even the last crumb of hash was eaten. We kept frantically signaling the tug, but it blithely ignored us. Maybe I wasn't mad!

It was a march of ninety miles around the horseshoe bay to Olangapo, the supply base. It was only a few miles by boat across the mouth of the bay.

I picked out a native dugout with a tiny sail made out of flour sacks. The outriggers were bundles of bamboo poles. With Corporal Lytle and Private

Thompson, I shoved off to cross the bay. Lytle is still in the corps as a Senior Non-Commissioned Officer.

We hadn't been gone five minutes when we were caught in a real typhoon. The damned little dugout spun around and around in circles. It filled up so quickly with water that we couldn't keep it bailed out. A howling blast of wind tore off our sail. Two or three mountainous waves swept away our paddles. We tried to paddle with our hands and clung desperately to the outriggers.

It looked as if we would be swallowed up in the black rage of wind and water. Once in a while through the fog and gusts of rain, we caught a glimpse of the beacon revolving on the lighthouse at the point. It was like a forlorn beam of hope.

I don't know how we did it, but we got to Olangapo at last. We were five hours making four miles.

Drenched to the skin, teeth chattering, covered with mud, I went to the Commandant of the navy yard for permission to carry back our provisions in the supply tug.

The Commandant had swallowed considerable cheer to fortify him against the weather.

"Do anything you want. Take anything you want," he tossed off genially.

I lost no time. By daylight I had the tug loaded and started off from Olangapo in another storm. When we reached our side of the bay it was impossible to put in to shore. The little dock we had built at our camp was washed away. The waves were tossing us around like a peanut shell.

We tore off all the false work of the boat and made it into rafts. Then we lashed the beef and vegetables to the rafts and threw them overboard. When they drifted near enough to shore, the men in camp formed a chain and pulled them up on the beach. I was quite pleased. It had been hard work to bring back the rations.

For this stunt I was condemned by a board of medical survey, which decided that I had displayed evidence of nervous breakdown by taking the dugout and later the tug. And a few days later I left for Manila, under orders home.

That's life in the Marine Corps. You never know when you'll have to pick up and leave your friends. You say goodbye to one crowd, but somewhere else you greet another group with whom you've campaigned in some odd corner of the world.

That wasn't my experience with the Olangapo outfit. I served with them in many other places. Yes, and I heard old Pendleton's totem pole story again six years later in Central America. And from time to time I'd run into Hiram Bearss, always cheerful, always without a wardrobe of his own. He was base commander at Bordeaux during the World War. As for Fritz Wise—Fritz saw enough action in France to satisfy even a Marine. As a Colonel, he led a battalion of the famous Fifth Regiment at Chateau Thierry, Bois de Belleau, St. Mihiel and the Argonne. Whenever the Marines were making history in France, Fritz was there.

When I returned home, I was assigned to recruiting duty in Philadelphia. But the old Chagres fever I contracted in Culebra came back with a vengeance. I ran a temperature every day for several months.

What I really had was a bad case of malaria, but a board of doctors suspected my ailment was tuberculosis and granted me nine months' sick leave. I was told to live in a high altitude and seek light employment. That was in January 1908.

All of a sudden, in the nick of time, along came an offer. Although I'd never seen a coal mine in my life, I was asked to take over the management of a coal mine in West Virginia. And I took it because I didn't intend to be an invalid.

The mine was near Firecreek, fifty miles southeast of Charleston. My family and I found ourselves in the midst of seven hundred Hungarians and Slavs. The only law recognized down there was the gun.

On top of a peak I built a little cabin. Every morning at five thirty I took my dinner pail and went down to the mine. Mrs. Butler and the baby were alone all day. To protect them I bought two bull dogs, Clincher and Susan. Everybody and everything, including the snakes, in that end of West Virginia were afraid of the dogs. In fact, I could hardly get a message up to my house. No one had the courage to face Clincher and Susan.

The first unpleasant duty that confronted me was to fire Mike, the superintendent of the mine, because he refused to stay sober after repeated warnings. He came swaggering into my office where I was sitting behind a narrow little desk, much too narrow. He pushed a pistol within an inch of my face.

"I've killed plenty of men before. I'll kill you too."

The shining muzzle of his firearm looked as big as a field-gun.

I snatched the gun out of his fist and locked it in the safe. Then I took a running jump and kicked him out in the snow.

John Harris, the foreman, was now promoted to be superintendent. In my queer outfit with which I was gradually becoming acquainted, there was a blacksmith called "Doc."

One morning John, the new superintendent, burst into my office.

"Doc's over at the boarding house breaking up the company stove with an axe. The landlady can't get breakfast, and the miners won't go to work without their breakfast."

When I approached Doc, he meekly handed me the axe without an argument. I tied him up temporarily so that he wouldn't break out into more mischief. Then I called up the sheriff in the nearest town and told him I had a man to be locked up.

"How long will you pay for?" he asked. "It's a dollar a day."

"Thirty days."

"All right. We'll sentence him to thirty days."

A hard-faced thug came to take Doc away and I forgot all about him. At the end of thirty days the sheriff telephoned.

"Do you want to pay any more board for that man of yours?"

"No, thirty dollars is all I can pay."

Doc was released and returned in an amiable mood to his job as blacksmith.

About this time Ed Littlejohn came as superintendent. He weighed 120 lbs. and his wife 250. Ed named his grandson after me.

One noon I was at the storage bin with a Negro helper. Everyone else had gone to lunch. An empty car was under the chute, and I wanted to get it loaded. The coal seemed to stick, and so to loosen it I jumped on top of the pile. Before I could catch the beam above the chute, the coal began to slide. I went down into the chute with ten tons of coal. I was buried up to my neck. The engine crew had to dig me out. I was crushed and bloody and black with soot. My mother-in-law, who was staying with us at the time, was very nearsighted. When she saw me limping up the path, she thought I was a drunken miner invading the premises and shrieked at the top of her lungs.

Another time I started the coal car without a brake stick. Away I went down the mountainside. I couldn't stop, and I didn't want to jump. I went bang into a train of cars and was thrown twenty-five feet. My ribs were smashed. I was black and blue from head to foot. Again, I dragged myself up the hill covered with blood.

My wife told me I might as well go back to war. More blood seemed to flow here than on the battlefield.

I got to liking those darn miners. We planned a Fourth of July celebration for them. Mrs. Butler worked like a slave for a couple of days, baking cakes and making lemonade and sandwiches. I sent to town for fifty dollars' worth of fireworks. Mrs. Butler put on her best dress to receive the miners and their families. I was clean for once and all spruced up for the occasion. At dark we were to set off the fireworks.

Not a soul came to our party but two little colored boys. We made them eat all the cake. The miners were not antagonistic. They were really my friends and named their children after me. But they had an idea they were being patronized and were unwilling to come to the party.

My nine months' sick leave was slipping by. In the late summer I went to Washington for my physical examination. I got off the train early in the morning and strolled along the street, waiting until the Navy Department should open.

I saw a Marine walking toward the barracks. I just had to follow him. The band was playing and the guard was mounting.

I had been asked to stay permanently at the West Virginia mine. It was a tip top offer, and I was seriously considering it.

But that glimpse into the barracks settled it. I knew right then and there that I couldn't take the West Virginia job. The Marine Corps was in my blood.

In September 1908, back to duty I went in Philadelphia, and a month later was boosted to the rank of Major. I don't think the promotion meant so much to me as mingling again with the men I loved. I felt that I had returned from exile.

CHAPTER XII

Revolution in Nicaragua and Riots in Panama

IT'S QUITE IN THE ROUTINE OF MARINE LIFE to get orders to leave a place within four or five hours. For years I kept my trunk packed so that I could start off at a moment's notice.

In command of the Third Battalion of Marines I sailed at the end of 1909 for Panama, where I was stationed until the Panama Canal was opened in 1914.

With Marines, a station is more like a gypsy encampment than a conventional residence. From Panama we went off on three expeditions to Nicaragua when revolutions broke out in that temperamental little country.

When you reach one of those fidgety spots to which you're been ordered, you usually find everyone busily exchanging diplomatic notes. That's the inoculation period. But in the end the attack of measles comes on anyway, and the Marines go ashore.

We had hardly planted our feet on Panama soil when we were packed off on the railroad crossing the Isthmus and loaded into a transport at the Pacific side for Corinto, on the west coast of Nicaragua.

This expedition we dubbed the "First Punic War," although we Marines scarcely had a sniff of battle smoke. For three months we lay off Corinto, one thousand of us packed like sardines into our little transport.

Corinto is the hottest place this side of hell. Even with the fan going, it was 110 degrees in my cabin.

The only time I did anything more than stare at the sizzling corrugated iron roofs and tumbledown shacks of Corinto was when I made a trip of reconnaissance, travelling the length of the Nicaraguan railroad for military information.

On this trip I met two native sergeants, holding the ends of a rope to which were fastened six pitifully dejected men with slip knots around their heads. One of the sergeants told me he was bringing "volunteers" into the army. If one man had tried to make a break, the slip knots would have pulled snugly around the necks of all six. Obviously, the poor miserable peons didn't want to fight.

The trouble all started between the Liberals and Conservatives. The Liberals had been ruling with a high and tyrannical hand for sixteen years. The Conservatives were up in arms, hoping to drive the Liberals out of power. In Nicaragua the usual pattern for revolutions was reversed. The Liberals were the government party; the Conservatives, the revolutionists.

As far as we were concerned, matters were still in the diplomatic note stage; so, in the spring of 1910 we returned to Panama where my battalion took permanent station at Camp Elliott.

Mrs. Butler, with Snooks and young Smedley, who had joined us at the Philadelphia Navy Yard on July 12th, 1909, arrived at Camp Elliott on May 1 1910. Word came on May 27 that another revolution was in full swing at Bluefields, on the east coast of Nicaragua. We received orders to leave at eight thirty in the morning and by eleven thirty were on our way—two hundred and fifty officers and men. Mrs. Butler had taken the early morning train to Panama to do some shopping. When she returned at noon, I was gone, and I didn't see her again for four months.

Adolfo Diaz was running the revolution. He was secretary and treasurer of La Luz Mining Company, in which Philander C. Knox, then our Secretary of State, was reported to own stock. Juan J. Estrada, a carpenter who had become governor of the province in which Bluefields was located, was selected to be provincial president of the new government if the revolution was successful.

When we reached Bluefields, the jumping off place of the world, the American Consul informed us that the situation was desperate. The revolutionists had been driven from the lake region in the interior of Nicaragua and were now hemmed in at Bluefields with the remnants of their troops. They had only three hundred and fifty men. Right outside the town was the government army with fifteen hundred men and some little cannon. Unless something drastic was done at once, the revolution would fail.

It didn't take a ton of bricks to make me see daylight. It was plain that Washington would like the revolutionists to come out on top.

I wrote a letter to Lara and Godoy, the two government generals besieging the town, informing them that we were neutral and were on the scene merely to protect American residents. We had no objection to their taking Bluefields, if it could be managed without shooting. We requested that the government troops cache their guns outside the town and attack without firearms, because their soldiers were poor marksmen and might accidentally hit American citizens.

"In order that we may be certain that you do leave your arms," I concluded, "we will station Marines outside to check the rifles."

"How are we to take the town if we can't shoot? And won't you also disarm the revolutionists defending the town?" the government generals wrote back to me.

"There is no danger of the defenders killing American citizens, because they will be shooting outwards," I replied suavely, "but your soldiers would be firing toward us."

The generals bombarded everybody of importance with letters of appeal, without gaining support for their position. Finally, they sputtered out the Nicaraguan equivalent for "Oh, hell," and moved away.

We garrisoned the town, while Estrada with his revolutionists followed the government army in their retreat westward through the interior. Estrada's spunk was noticeably increased when he knew we were standing back of him. The government army, discouraged by the setback at Bluefields, abandoned the struggle and melted away.

The Liberal government soon collapsed, and the revolutionary Conservatives climbed into the vacant seats of power. Juan Estrada was made president, according to promise, and Adolfo Diaz, vice president.

Telling the story of that election got me into trouble with the State Department twenty years later, when I was making a speech in Pittsburgh. What I said was that we Americans wouldn't support any president who wasn't legally married to his wife. But I had proof for my point.

Well, this is what happened at Bluefields, in 1910.

As soon as the revolution proved successful, word was passed around town that an important wedding was on the social calendar. It seems that Estrada had never married the partner who shared his domestic felicity. Now that he was to dispense the hospitality of the presidential mansion, the hint was slipped to him—in what way it is not necessary to explain in detail—that the first lady of Nicaragua required the dignity of a legal status.

The American Consul requested me to go with him to the big event of the Bluefields season. The wedding was to be celebrated at the army barracks on the high bluff across the harbor. Not much of a ship could push through the narrow channel, three and a half feet deep, between the mud flats of the harbor. The wedding barge was a clumsy, flat-bottomed boat with a paddle wheel at the stern. Its regular occupation was to carry bananas up the river.

Madame Estrada, wearing a red plush gown that looked oddly like the red plush upholstery of Bluefields' furniture, came on board well-fortified by her ladies in waiting. The ladies sat in splendid isolation on the upper deck. On the lower deck, which was only six inches above the water, was a very popular bar illuminated by a smoky lantern. The men started toasts in the spirit of the occasion and were soon reeling drunk. Every now and then one of them would walk overboard and flounder up to his chest, yelling lustily for help. Then we had to turn the clumsy paddle wheeler around and drag him out of the water.

The marriage was performed with due solemnity, however, and the wedding guests were properly regaled with an elaborate banquet laid out in the filthy and unprepossessing atmosphere of the barracks. It was observed with satisfaction by all present that the feminine Four Hundred of Bluefields, who had snubbed Madame Estrada for years, were now eager to kowtow to her. Thus, was Estrada's private life rendered secure from reproach.

While we were at Bluefields, Adolfo Diaz, the efficiency manager of the revolution, came to me one day in great distress. Officers in his army had contracted with "General" Victor Gordon, a New Orleans adventurer, to bring down a foreign legion at so much per head. Gordon had gathered together forty or fifty beachcombers and had brought his collection of tramps to Bluefields some months before to bolster up the revolutionary army. The members of this motley crew were all generals and colonels, of course, but they didn't have any regiments and they never saw a battlefield. All they did was live on the fat of the land and bask like lazy lizards in the sun. They were quartered at the El Tropicale Hotel, which we dubbed the "war college" because it was the headquarters of these high-ranking bums.

"These miserable fellows are eating us poor," Diaz complained to me. "They were to get a dollar a day for fighting and grants of land for helping to win the revolution. But now the war is over, and they didn't lift a finger in the fighting. How can we get rid of them?"

"I'm with you, Diaz," I said. "I'd like to get those tramps out of here."

The American Consul and I held a conference and decided to deport them.

Diaz made an arrangement with a Jamaican, the captain of the Sunbeam, a two-masted auxiliary schooner, to dump the colonels and generals at Limon, in Costa Rica. Five hundred dollars was the captain's fee. The colonels and generals refused to budge, however, so the moving job was wished on us.

At seven thirty we descended upon the "war college" and rounded up the staff. A corporal of Marines jerked "General Vic" Gordon out of the barber shop and pulled him along the street by an unwilling ear. One half of his face was shaved and the other half covered with lather. We routed out the rest of the crew and chased them down to the beach.

The colonels and generals looked very down in the mouth at the loss of their free meal tickets when we planted them safely on the deck of the Sunbeam. But we had hardly turned our backs, cheerful that this unpleasant business was over, when the damned rascals jumped off the boat, waded through the shallow water to shore and scattered among the houses back of the water front. We played hide and seek for hours before we found them all and had them back on board again. This time we were taking no chances. We clapped them securely below and battened down the hatches.

The Costa Rican authorities refused to accept this precious human cargo, however, and Panama wanted none of them. The captain of the Sunbeam finally unloaded them on a semi-desert island where they would have starved to death if they had not been rescued by a freighter.

At Bluefields life was returning to normal, the dull apathy of a third-rate Central American port. For six weeks there had been no sign of trouble. We had little to do but lounge around our quarters, sedately located in a Sunday school building and a former missionary's house. I was glad when our orders came the first of October to return to Panama. I was particularly eager to get my men out, because several of the native soldiers were down with yellow fever and smallpox.

Just before we left Bluefields, a column of shopkeepers marched in with their chits. The Marines had not been bashful about using their "jawbone." The unsuspecting merchants of Bluefields flourished sixteen hundred dollars' worth of paper signed by George Washington, Abraham Lincoln, Yankee Doodle and other famous but deceased celebrities. I picked out the George Washingtons, Honest Abes and the rest by their handwriting and subtracted the money from their pay for the next six months in Panama, until all the bills were settled.

Thus, ended the "Second Punic War."

Camp Elliott, where we did garrison duty for the next two years, was at Bas Obispo, at the end of the Culebra Cut, sixteen miles from Panama and thirty-five miles from Colon. I was the major in command of a battalion of fifteen officers and four hundred and fifty men.

At that time the Canal Zone was in a spasm of engineering convulsions. Locks and dams were being built, steam-hammers were pounding, dredges snorting, and a ceaseless activity was going on along temporary tracks and iron superstructures. Work on the great canal was under the keen and masterly direction of General George W. Goethals, then Colonel.

Goethals might have seemed hard-boiled, since he spared neither himself nor others to push a job through, but he had a fine character. Everyone in contact with him admired and loved him. When he was tired and out of sorts, he often sent for me to cheer him up with amusing stories about the Marines. The famous engineer was fond of children and never too busy to plan surprises for his young favorites. On Snooks' sixth birthday, marking the half fare age, Goethals gave her a tiny railroad pass made out to Miss Snooks Butler, good for the Panama railway.

One morning I took the early train to meet my wife's uncle who was coming to visit us. Secretly I admired him, but he was the family tyrant, and I didn't like the idea of being bossed around. I was in a most unpleasant frame of mind. Goethals strolled down the aisle and stopped at my seat.

"You look like a thundercloud. What's wrong?"

"I had to get up at dawn to meet my wife's uncle." "What's his name?"

"S. M. Felton."

"Sam Felton? Why, he's an old friend of mine. How'd you like to make a hit with Uncle Sam? My gasoline car is down at Colon. You pretend it's yours and escort your uncle home in state. Then he'll think you are somebody." Uncle Sam was duly impressed when I led him to Goethal's magnificent big car.

"You must have a very important position on the Isthmus to own a car like this."

I decided to say nothing until we reached home. I wanted him to think for a short time at least that his niece had married well.

His visit went beautifully until the engine of my car stopped in the middle of the high bridge at Culebra. It was a suspension bridge two hundred feet above the bottom of the canal. It inspired a sinking feeling of flimsiness, especially when one was stuck on it in a heavy car.

My sergeant, a good mechanic, worked on the engine, I fussed with it, and Uncle Sam contributed advice. Finally, I had the bright idea to look in the gas tank. It was empty. I had to send the sergeant to a railroad station three miles away to get gas. Uncle Sam and I sat on the bridge, which swayed in the wind. His silence was anything but golden. Finally, he grumbled that he wasn't trained to walk tight ropes in the circus. Snorting and puffing, he pushed the car while I steered it across the bridge. Making an impression with a borrowed car was not as successful as Goethals had pictured it.

Later, I had a car of my own, the first one on the Isthmus outside of the towns. There were no roads for automobiles in those days. We couldn't even get out of our camp except by railroad. But Goethals gave me some cement and old rails, and "with the help of God and a few Marines," as we say in the Corps, I built a bridge so I could run the car out to the wagon road.

It was an old American Traveler, all red paint and brass. Every time I bounded forth in my fiery chariot, the Marines hitched up the mules in order to be ready to start when my SOS came. Once, after the automobile inconsiderately fell over a bank on top of me, seventeen stitches had to be taken in my leg. Ever since, I've been given credit in physical examinations for a gunshot wound. The old nuisance was an expensive toy, averaging a dollar and a quarter a mile. The tires cost seventy-five dollars apiece. When the original set wore out, I couldn't afford to buy others, so I filled the old tires with rope and ran the car several months longer.

President Taft was our most distinguished visitor during this period of marking time. With the Canal Commissioners I went down to Colon and paid my respects to the President, on board the U. S. S. Tennessee. Two days later Goethals telephoned me.

"The President's train will stop at your station at noon, Butler, but he has a sore foot and will have to review your men from the back platform."

"Ask him if he won't let us haul him up our hill in a wagon," I urged.

The President was game, and we took him to the parade ground in our creaking old mule wagon. He stood with me on the reviewing stand, asking for news of my father and plunging into a lively discussion of Pennsylvania politics.

Mrs. Butler, in the meantime, hurriedly collected all the women on the post with their servants and prepared a buffet luncheon fit for the gods. The President ate very sparingly for a man his size, but his brother Charles, who was in the party, took care of the family reputation. As for Goethals, he pulled up a chair to the serving table and sailed into the sandwiches with gusto.

The President held my two babies, Snooks and Smedley, on his lap—what there was of it.

"You know," he said, "you people have the most comfortable place on the Isthmus. I wish I could stay longer."

He was a simple, lovable man, with a delightful gift for putting folk at ease.

Lindley M. Garrison also came to the Isthmus, when he was Secretary of War. I invited him to inspect my camp. My Marines bent over backward to impress the war department. Their equipment was shining, every button flashed. They paraded as they had never paraded before. The band struck up "Onward, Christian Soldiers." Garrison stood next to me, deeply moved.

"It's my favorite hymn."

"Somebody told me so. That's why I had 'em play it."

"You're a bunch of bums," he said, genially.

Everything was serene in Panama until the great riots of July 1912, interrupted the routine of garrison life.

The Army, Marine Corps and civilians were holding a joint field meet in Balboa. The Marines won the greatest number of points in the sports.

The Army couldn't swallow the decision. Several hundred Marines and soldiers swung down into the saloons of the red-light district to argue the matter out. Hot, profane words sprinkled with hiccups soon led to fist fights. The struggling groups swarmed out on the plaza for elbow room. A Marine and a soldier stepped out of the seething mass like two fighting cocks and decided to settle the dispute for their respective branches of the service. The whole crowd, with their backs to the houses, formed a big circle around their two champions.

The boys were minding their own business, but the Panama police lost their heads. In company formation they bore down the street and fired into the crowd. Two men were killed and fourteen wounded.

The Army and Marine Corps forgot their differences. Their blood was up. Although the Panamanians had guns and our men were unarmed, Marines and soldiers pitched into the police in good old American style. Iron fists flew out and heads crashed right and left. Native reserves were summoned to quell the fracas.

The Colonel of the army regiment was out of town, so the responsibility of straightening out this unhealthy mess fell upon me as senior officer. I didn't even know there was a fight until I sauntered back from the water sports. An army officer dashed up to me with the news.

"Major, a thousand soldiers and Marines are breaking into the shops to get guns and kill the native soldiers. We'll have to act fast."

I ate up the distance to the trouble belt. I tried to hurl thunder at the men, but they were beyond the rational stage. They were drunken mad and vicious, so I corralled the whole mob in the railroad station and set guards outside. Then I telephoned for a special train to take the men back to their camps. The railroad official refused. I telephoned my troubles to General Goethals.

"You just wait a minute and you'll have your train," he assured me.

I learned that some of our men had been clapped into underground prisons. When I appealed to the American

Minister to have them released, he promised to write a note about it in the morning.

"But I want them out now," I insisted. "They have no business to be in those dungeons. I'll attend to their punishment."

I got in touch with Goethals again.

"I'll get President Arosemena on the telephone and he will release your men," he said, "or I'll authorize you to take five hundred Marines and restore order."

In five minutes he called me back.

"Butler, your men will be released immediately. Just go and get them."

We found one man in a cell half under water. His jailers had pinched the irons on so tight that his circulation was stopped. We had to saw him out of his misery.

Some of the Panama policemen had their jaws broken in the fighting. It cost me ten dollars a jaw to settle for the facial damages.

The incident was over except for officialdom, which tried to blame the soldiers and Marines and kicked up a hell of a row. The investigations continued for more than a month.

CHAPTER XIII

The Adventures of General Walk

REVOLUTION WAS BECOMING A NICARAGUAN HABIT. Shortly after the Panama riots, a third revolution bubbled up in Nicaragua.

General Luis Mena was behind this new outbreak. I knew him in Bluefields, where he was the chief military prop for Estrada and Diaz. He had been an ox driver, a rough giant of a man with great physical strength and vitality. President Estrada made him Minister of War. But Mena turned against Estrada and started the ball rolling by blowing up the presidential barracks. Estrada, who had been quaking, anyway, in an uneasy seat, was now thoroughly frightened and bolted.

The Vice President, Adolfo Diaz, succeeded to the presidency. Mena, as the real head of the government, remained on good terms with Diaz for several months. At last President Diaz, encouraged by the groups hostile to Mena, removed the powerful general from office.

Mena was not the man to take a slap like this sitting down. He left Managua, the capital, with a host of the government troops, personally loyal to him, and in a flash gained control of Granada, a few miles south of the capital, where the national stores of ammunition and artillery were kept.

Revolution was on again, and we Marines were off again.

On the tenth of August we left Panama—eleven officers and three hundred and fifty men. Three days later we were at Corinto. When I had sailed from that infernal hole two years before, I had hoped never to see it again. Well, here we were, but we didn't linger long. We had pressing business elsewhere.

The United States Minister telephoned me from Managua that the rebels had been bombarding the capital for three days and hundreds of people were wounded.

After we reached Managua, about ninety miles south of Corinto on beautiful Lake Managua, all railroad and telegraph communication was cut off. The town itself was quiet. For the moment the seat of trouble was centered at Leon, which had always been a revolutionary hotbed. The government forces were badly beaten at Leon by the rebels and were now retreating south toward Managua. With insufficient troops and ammunition the government army could not hold out long.

Prospects looked bleak for the regime of Adolfo Diaz, our American protege.

So long as the trains could not get through, Managua was cut off from the outside world except by a roundabout route through Honduras. The rebels were controlling all the approaches to the capital. The troops of Diaz were losing heart. Something had to be done at once, so I took unofficial command of the government of four thousand men. I had absolutely no authority for this step, but the government could not win without our support, and I knew which way the wind blew. Our state department certainly wanted the Diaz government then in power to win, even if it didn't say so in a red sealed document.

This mess was beginning to promise some real excitement, but I wasn't prepared for a comic interlude.

At Managua the senior officer of our little American force was a Commander of the Navy. He had one hundred sailors from his ship and I had the three hundred and fifty Marines.

Toward the first of September the Pacific fleet steamed into the harbor at Corinto. Our Naval Commander was delegated to make a special report of conditions to his superior officer on the Denver.

A special train with an escort of fifty sailors and twenty-five Marines was provided to shove him through the danger zone from Managua to Corinto. Not at all anxious to exchange the comparative safety of Managua for a trip through the rebel country, he waited for ice, Apollinaris water and other vital military supplies and delayed his departure until late in the day.

About nine o'clock the next day my senior officer telephoned me from a railroad station twenty-five miles along the line. His voice was very faint and even over the telephone I could feel that he was trembling with fright.

"Can—can you get permission for me to ride in on the wood train which has stopped to collect firewood here?"

"Sure," I said, thinking my permission a bit superfluous, "just hop on and come along back, if that's what you want."

"Well, I had a terrible experience in Leon—terrible."

He rang off without further explanation. I naturally assumed that several of our men had been wounded in a nasty fight.

I went to the railroad station with our medical personnel and an ambulance. When the wood train pulled in, about four in the morning, I discovered the senior officer sitting on the wood box of the locomotive. His uniform was anything but white, and his head was grotesquely swallowed up by a large brimmed native straw hat.

I jumped on the running board of the engine. "Captain, I have the ambulance here ready to take care of the wounded."

"There are no wounded," he admitted surlily.

"What happened to your train then?"

"I had to leave it at Leon."

"Didn't you have a fight?"

"No," he snapped.

"How did you get from Leon the thirty miles to that station where you telephoned me?"

"We walked."

"And you didn't even put up a fight for the train?" "Oh, you don't know that crowd. They're bloodthirsty. Even the women spit in your face. One of those female demons sharpened her bolo on the very window where I was sitting in the train."

"Then we can't do anything to help you now?"

"No, I'm bound for the Legation and I'm going to bed." The sailors and Marines in the ranks told me a different story. They felt miserably humiliated and came to me boiling over with indignation.

According to their version the train was stopped at Leon by a crowd of excited Nicaraguans. Their threats and wild gestures threw our Naval Commander into a panic. Without any argument he bolted from the train, leaving behind his cap, his check book and all his personal belongings. A horse and a large straw hat to replace his cap were secured, and the Commander bobbed up and down along the railroad track in frantic and undignified retreat. The guard of enlisted men, frothing at the mouth, followed on foot. The sailors wrote a song about this ignominious expedition, which became known as "General Walkemback's Retirement." It ran something like this:

"Walkemback, never mind the engine.
Walkemback, to Hell with the train.
Walkemback, never mind the check book.
So, he walked 'em back to Managua in the pouring down rain."

I was ready to hit the ceiling myself the next day when I was told that the rebels were distributing a handbill in Leon, describing with malicious gusto how a senior officer of the United States Navy had been bluffed out of his train by a twelve-year-old girl. The devil of it was that our rebel friends didn't even have to exaggerate the story.

Determined that the reputation of the United States military services should be upheld, I blazed down to the Legation, where I found my senior officer in a suit of blue silk pajamas sitting up in bed, with a bottle of Scotch and mineral water beside him.

"Captain, we'll have to take the train at the station and recapture the one you left in Leon, reopen the road and establish communication with the fleet."

"No, we'll do nothing of the sort," he said, pouring out some more Scotch, "it's too damn dangerous."

"Well, then, may I go without you?"

"No. It's too dangerous."

He wouldn't go, and he wouldn't let me go alone. I was disgusted and left him with his Scotch.

I dashed off a letter bristling with ultimatums and shot it right back to him by my adjutant. I pointed out that it was necessary for the reputation of our armed forces as well as for our own safety to retain our lost ground and open the railroad immediately. If he didn't join me, I would resign from the service, giving the story of the train as my reason. This brought' him around.

"All right, I'll go," he growled, "but you'll have to take a horse, so that I can ride back. I'm too old to walk these long distances."

"If you ever come back, except on the train you left at Leon, it will be feet first," I replied.

I did get him the horse, however. A freight car was rigged up with a bunk at one end for the senior officer and a private compartment at the other end for the horse. When General Walkemback climbed into his freight deluxe he looked like an elderly jockey on his way to a Derby.

The same seventy-five men who had been walked back the first time piled gleefully into the train, together with twenty-five additional men and officers. The Nicaraguans in the capital, like our senior officer, considered the trip very dangerous and strenuously opposed our making the venture, but we laughed them off.

Pulling out of Managua at midnight, we crawled a few yards at a time toward the town of our disgrace. We worked all night repairing damaged culverts and torn tracks.

I was riding on the locomotive with Lieutenant E. H. Conger, who, because of his mechanical engineering training, volunteered to run the train.

As we approached Leon about ten in the morning, we came to a long trestle bridge. Here we were stopped by a band of thirty rebels who had built a barricade of adobe stone across the track at the entrance to the bridge. They jeered and raised their rifles in a threatening manner, but we decided to try diplomacy first.

Conger knew Spanish. He leaned out of the cab and talked politely to them.

"We aren't making war on you people. We don't even want to pick a quarrel with you. We are simply opening the railroad, which we have a right to do, because it is American property."

This was more or less true. In the capital we had been given to understand that the railroad had been taken as security for a loan made to the Nicaraguan government by American banking interests.

We finally bluffed the rebel detachment out of their position. They rolled the stones off the track and retired to the far end of the bridge, where a second stone barricade bristled with a dozen red flags. At least a thousand excited little soldiers, armed with every kind of weapon from rifle to razor, seemed to pop out of nowhere and now swarmed around the barricade.

I was afraid the rebels might have been clever enough to weaken the bridge and thus invite us to a neat death plunge into the deep valley below. Before risking the train, Conger and I walked across the bridge and climbed around under it to examine the braces and framework. The rebels jumped up and down like maniacs, yelling bloodcurdling threats and Central American insults at the top of their lungs. I couldn't take them seriously.

After some argument among themselves, a delegation of ferocious little men swaggered over to us and ordered me to back my train beyond their outposts. I laughed at them.

"We're going to Corinto," I explained through Conger. "It will be a pity if you fire on us, because much unnecessary blood will be shed."

"Then you come with us to see our commanding General."

"I should say not! If your General wants to see me, he can come here. We'll be at the bridge an hour taking on wood and water."

The General trotted back with the delegation. His black eyes flashed with rage. We stood facing each other. When he scowled, I grinned.

"What's the use of wasting time?" I burst out. "I'm going on to Corinto. Now what are you going to do about it?"

Before I could wink an eye, he jerked his pistol out of his belt and shoved it into my midriff.

"If the train moves, I shoot."

One hundred red blooded Americans were clustered around the locomotive at the other end of the bridge, watching tensely to see what I would do. I couldn't retreat and lose face. If I signaled to the Marines to shoot, there would be a frightful slaughter. I had to act quickly. I made a grab for the General's gun and had the luck to tear it out of his hand. A bit theatrical I emptied the cartridges out of the barrel. His army burst out laughing. They could appreciate a joke, even when it was on them.

I made the General ride with us as a hostage and the train proceeded across the bridge.

On the other side we stopped and arranged for the rebels to return the train General Walkemback had abandoned in Leon. The Naval Commander, who had remained snugly concealed in his box car through the trip, now chose this most inauspicious moment to stroll out and exhibit himself in a passenger coach. When the rebels learned that their timid friend was on the train, they rushed back in high glee to badger him. They almost frightened him into a nervous collapse, and he sent for me.

"We'd better surrender the train at once or we'll all be killed."

"We'll do no such damned thing. We're getting your train back, and we're going straight down to the coast."

In Leon the feeling against the government party was very bitter. During the few hours we spent there before pushing on to Corinto, I heard the story of two American boys who were killed by the rebels ten days before we came.

The boys were "bilgers"—failures—from West Point, who had run off to Nicaragua and received commissions as colonels in the native government army. They served under Duron, a mercenary general from Honduras who had been hired by the Nicaraguan government to crush the revolution. Revolutions were Duron's specialty.

Duron demanded thirty-five hundred dollars in gold from the Nicaraguan government for his valuable services. After much dickering he pocketed the cash and set out from Managua with the three hundred mercenaries he had brought across the Honduran border and four hundred Nicaraguan soldiers who were passed over to him for the expedition. Among the latter were the two American boys.

When Duron marched into Leon the situation was threatening. The people were sullen and quiet—the quiet before a storm.

He quartered his army of seven hundred together with the mules and horses in the Lacayo House, an enormous structure covering a whole block, which had been built by a rich Nicaraguan, but was never quite finished. Doors and windows were still missing and there was no furniture except a few iron cots on the second floor, but the walls were covered with gaudy and atrociously executed oil paintings.

Instead of attending to his business Duron went out with the American boys and got staggering drunk. His troops, wild and uncurbed, were turned loose on the town. They looted and raped and killed some of the leading citizens. The people were incensed and struck back to avenge the outrages. Everybody in Leon was a revolutionist now.

The American boys dug holes in the street and mounted their machine guns just where the people could fire down on them from the houses. In a few minutes they were wounded and dragged themselves back to the Lacayo House.

Most of Duron's soldiers, in a panic at the unexpected and stubborn defense put up by the people, scurried like sheep into the Lacayo House for protection.

Duron decided to cut his way out. He formed his men in a column and led them out of the gate with their horses. The people lined up on the roofs of the houses and picked them off like clay ducks in a shooting gallery. Before they had advanced six squares, the seven hundred men and their horses were completely wiped out.

The two American "colonels," half-conscious from their wounds and still drunk from their debauch the night before, had remained in their room. The moment the angry mob of citizens stampeded into the house, the boys crawled under the bed. When they were discovered, the people thrust their bayonets through the bed and killed them.

Duron's men and horses were thrown into a long trench on the plaza. The Americans were buried with the others. The father of one of the boys appealed to our government and the Nicaraguan government for the return of the two bodies. Our Marines subsequently had to spend a couple of weeks digging among the six weeks' old corpses before they found the boys, who were identified by their West Point cadet buttons.

Naturally, since we were associated with the government party, we were not over popular when our train went through Leon to the coast. One woman, who had earned revolutionary laurels for splitting Duron's head in two with a butcher knife, rushed to the engine where I was sitting in the cab with Conger and announced that she was now going to split my head open too. With the crowd cheering her along she sharpened her bolo on my leather legging. I just reached down and chucked her under the chin. The fire-eating Amazon was so embarrassed that she quickly backed away.

From Leon to the coast we had to repair sixteen breaks in the track and several bridges. But we reached Corinto and our fleet without mishap, and we were proud of it, after our Naval Commander's "retreat from Moscow."

When we left Corinto for the return journey, we bundled into the train a couple of hundred sailors from the fleet to reinforce our little party. In our brief absence, the rebels had been busy messing up the line. Before we got back to Managua, we had to build three new bridges and several miles of track.

At Leon I was afraid the rebels would blow up the big steel railroad bridge, so I marched seventy men across the town, and we guarded the bridge all night.

One of the rebel colonels bustled importantly with his little staff into our midst about midnight, when we were drinking coffee around our campfire. He explained in dramatic but broken English that there was to be a battle at this bridge early in the morning between his troops and the government army. Would I please move? If not, my men would most certainly be hurt, to his great grief and the equal bereavement of his comrades in arms.

In equally dramatic style I put my hand on my heart and assured him that we would all lie down flat like door mats and let his war roll over us. I even stretched myself out on the ground to illustrate the door mat plan.

His eyes bulged and he stared at me as if he believed me demented. He turned and muttered something to his followers who were armed to the teeth like a comic opera army. Flinging up his hands in despair at having to deal with a pack of damned fools, he pompously withdrew. Needless to say, there was no battle in the morning.

Leaving the main body of sailors and Marines at Leon to keep the rail-road open, I started back to Managua late in the afternoon with fifty men. Two flat cars were placed in front of the locomotive to prevent the engine from leaving the track if the rails were torn up. Most of the Marines were packed into the box car behind the engine.

It was a hair-raising ride. The road climbs to about fifteen hundred feet and then descends rapidly to Managua. We had no brakes and no whistle and our only light was a lantern.

One of my lieutenants rode with me in the first flat car to enjoy the fine mountain air. We had plenty of air and thrills, too. We ran into a cow, through a flock sheep and around the edges of precipices with perpendicular drops of a thousand feet.

Slipping down to the low country without brakes, we shot right past the government outposts at Managua like a toboggan on ice.

The sentinels, thinking we were a rebel attacking party, blazed away at us, but they didn't hit us. Our speed was too great. We raced right into the railroad station, smashing the wooden gates placed at each end of the platform to keep animals from biting passengers, and only came to a stop when we struck an upgrade.

In Managua I went to bed. I had had exactly seventeen hours sleep during the week I had been away. It was the hardest time I had experienced since Boxer days in China.

CHAPTER XIV

Fighting in the Tropics

COLONEL JOE PENDLETON—MY FRIEND OF THE TWO FROGS and the totem pole back in Philippine days—now showed up in Managua with an additional battalion of four hundred Marines. That sturdy old soldier and genial companion was in command of all the Marines in Nicaragua. Trickling in from the fleet a handful at a time, about three thousand of us were posted at various strategic points.

In the interior the rebels still had the upper hand. With our government in Washington unofficially but definitely taking sides against the rebels, it was necessary to make a swift and concerted effort to restore law and order—also unofficially.

I was now given the job of opening the railroad southward from Managua to Granada on Lake Nicaragua, right in the heart of the rebellion.

But I was forced to take to my bed again. I came down with a mean attack of malaria and was running a temperature of 104. The expedition waited and waited while I tossed restlessly about, worried crazy with the thought that I might not be able to go into the interior with my column. Finally, I held some ice in my mouth to lower my temperature, so that the doctor would pronounce me well enough to leave.

Everything swam around me and my knees crumpled up like paper, but I managed to get to the train, where I lay on a cot in a box car. I wasn't strong enough to stand up.

We creaked along asthmatically from Managua toward Granada. Every jolt stabbed through me. Of course, I was an idiot to go, but nothing short of chains could have held me back.

As we approached Masaya, fifteen miles beyond Managua, the train had to pass between two hills, Coyotepe and Barranca. The summits were crowned with rude forts, provided with field guns. Those little hills were a tough nut to crack. They commanded the valley and effectively guarded the approach to Masaya.

When we were two miles from the hills, a rebel shell lighted in a field near the train. One of our men vigorously waved the American flag, but we had not advanced two hundred yards when a second shell crashed closer to us. A quarter of a mile farther, a third shell exploded in the ditch beside the track.

This was one shell too many. I climbed out of my box car and ordered the train back to a safer position. With Lieutenant Edward A. Ostermann, my adjutant, and Sergeant Pursell, who spoke Spanish, I walked down the track toward the hills. At a barbed wire entanglement where rebel guards were posted, we had to halt.

The soldiers looked at me curiously. They must have thought I was a ghost out for an airing. I was burning up with a high fever and stared wildly about me. My cheeks were flushed and cavernous, my eyes were sunken and bloodshot, and it was a long time since I'd had a shave.

Swaying weakly on my feet, I told the guards I wanted to see General Zeledon. He was Mena's chief subordinate and commanded the rebel forces in Masaya, just behind the hills. The guards disarmed us and dispatched a messenger to Zeledon.

For two hours we sat on the railroad track in the broiling hot sun. I was so dizzy with fatigue and fever that I almost fainted before the guards returned.

They blindfolded us and dragged us along the track. Then they conducted us over what seemed an endless series of barbed wire entanglements. My clothes were torn to pieces. I cursed those damned rebels back and forth, to the horror of my sergeant interpreter.

"Please don't say that, Major," he implored. "Some of these folks understand English."

But I kept right on cursing until the air around me was thick with undiluted Marine language. Later, when I captured this place, I discovered that those little devils had just taken us back and forth repeatedly across one fence.

At a road beyond the two hills our bandages were removed. General Zeledon galloped over to us in a lordly manner, but I refused to speak to him until he dismounted from his horse. He was a short plump man with a dark mustache and he didn't look very military in his Panama hat and civilian clothes.

"General," I said, through my interpreter, "you can't fight along the railroad. I'm giving you your chance to move away and take your revolution elsewhere. I have hundreds of men, a whole army down below, to carry out our orders to keep the railroad open."

Zeledon accepted my terms. He was about to give instructions to abandon the two hills when the fool sergeant, said to me in English, "This will please the Admiral." Unfortunately, Zeledon understood some English. Up to that moment he thought I was commander in chief.

"Oh, there's an Admiral?" he said. "I can't surrender the hills without talking to the Admiral."

Now we had to begin all over and wait for the Admiral to come up on a special train. The Admiral of our fleet at Corinto, William H. H. Southerland, was one of the finest commanders I have ever served under, but all admirals, like diplomats, love conferences.

The Admiral and Zeledon started to confer in the afternoon and conferred all night. When I realized it was going to be a long drawn out affair I returned to Managua and stayed in the hospital living on quinine and limeade until the Admiral telegraphed for me.

"Everything will be all right," the Admiral said, as he stepped on to the train I came down on. "You can go through without any trouble tomorrow morning."

When I saw the long-winded document that had been prepared for Zeledon's bedtime reading, I had my doubts.

Colonel Pendleton, our Marine commander, had come to the conference. Before he went to Managua, I persuaded him to send Zeledon an ultimatum that he was to surrender the hills by six o'clock the next morning or we would attack and capture them. Zeledon agreed, but I put no faith in his word.

At four in the morning we marched into position, ready to attack the two hills. Exactly at six o'clock the white flag went up. We were all disappointed because we knew we would have to come back sooner or later and put up a fight for those hills.

It was six in the evening before our guns and stores were reloaded on the cars, and we steamed up to advance through Masaya. Eight flat cars were in front of the first locomotive; then came eight box cars, a second locomotive and four more cars trailing behind.

Without any handicap it would have been difficult for the locomotives to push the cars up the 3½ per cent grade between the hills. But the natives had placed milkweed on the track. The wheels spun round and round without gripping, and we slid back down. Sticks were laid under the wheels, and our four hundred men used their brawn and muscle to push the train over the hills. They swore a blue streak at the natives who were concealed in the underbrush, laughing at our predicament.

We drifted down the other side of the hills toward Masaya. The town was pitch dark, and it was raining. Not a light in a window. I was sitting on the front end of the first flat car. Beside me was a sergeant watching out with a lantern for switches which might be turned to derail us. At the station, a long wooden shed, a crowd of excited people waved an enormous white flag to stop us. But I paid no attention to them. Our objective was Granada, and I was going on to Granada. We pushed slowly up the track through the middle of the town.

Suddenly, by the light of our lantern we saw a man in black galloping on a white horse down the path along the railroad track. He fired right in our faces. The bullet whizzed past my shoulder and tore through the hand of a Marine sitting behind me. I jumped off to chase the man, who cantered back, firing right and left into the cars. The train was dark and he disappeared without any more hits.

In the meantime, our train had stopped at a cross street. Around the corner swung a detachment of one hundred and fifty horsemen, all shouting and armed to the teeth. At their head, urging them on, was the man in black.

They opened fire on the train. A stream of bullets rattled against the box cars. We were in a damned nasty position.

I yelled to our men to shoot. Sixteen machine guns were mounted on the roofs of the cars. The Marines blazed away. Almost immediately an answering wall of flame poured out from both sides of the street. The track ran down the middle of the street. The darkened houses were crammed with soldiers sniping down at us.

When the fight started, Lieutenant Conger climbed out of the front locomotive to join his company and left the native engineer to run the train. The native, frightened to death, had crawled under the seat. I jumped into the cab and pulled the whistle, which was a signal for the second engine to go ahead. The native with me had now collected his wits sufficiently to start his engine. The heavy train was under way.

I climbed in the fireman's seat and leaned out of the cab window. It was a gorgeous spectacle. A sheet of fire was spitting into the darkness on both sides of the road. Four hundred Marine rifles were popping with tongues of flame, the sixteen machine guns were rattling out a staccato beat, the engines were screaming and puffing—all in one narrow little street, while the natives shot back at us from both sides of the street. The whole performance lasted only about twenty minutes.

We lumbered slowly forward and stopped a mile or so out of town to check up our losses. Five of our men were wounded, three were missing. While we were deciding what to do about the missing men, a handcar bobbed along the track toward us. Four dignified envoys stepped out and solemnly presented me with a letter of apology signed by Zeledon. He was sorry. His troops had got beyond control and acted without his orders. I knew that this alibi had been prepared before the event. Later, when the government army captured Masaya, they found Zeledon's plans for ambushing us.

"Look here," I said to the bowing and so-sorry committee, "we are short three men. Unless you produce them at once, I'll come back in the morning and capture your town."

In an hour they returned with our men. One was badly wounded in the foot and had toppled into the ditch from the train. The other two were unharmed.

It took us five or six days to travel the remaining fifteen miles to Granada. A short distance from the city at a little railroad station called San Bias we camped for a couple of days to reconstruct a long section of torn-up track.

I rushed a messenger, Lieutenant George De Neale, from our camp to Granada with a letter to General Mena, the leader of the revolutionary army. I warned him that we were advancing steadily along the railroad. If he didn't interfere with us, there would be no fighting. He answered that he was sending a delegation to treat with me.

We made elaborate preparations to impress Mena's delegates with our strength. When we put poles in the muzzles of our two little field guns and covered them with tent flies, they looked as long and as deadly as fourteen-inch guns. My four hundred men were packed around me in a closely knit semi-circle so that it was impossible to see over their heads. Thousands of Marines might have been back of them.

As for me, I was sitting like a potentate in the center on a wooden camp chair with long stilt-like legs, which the men had built for me. I was still suffering from the effects of the fever which kept my eyes bloodshot. It was at this time that the Marines started to call me "Old Gimlet Eye" —a nickname which has stuck to me through my service years.

The delegates were blindfolded as they approached us, so that they couldn't count how many soldiers we actually had. The blinders were taken off in front of my ridiculous wooden throne, and the rebel officers seemed a bit awed by our stage setting. I tried to glare fiercely down at them out of my bleary and sunken eyes.

"You must move your troops out of the railroad station so that we can come in without a conflict," I explained through my sergeant interpreter.

"We'll take your terms back to General Mena."

"We had a verbal agreement with Zeledon, and he shot us up at Masaya. Now we'll have to have a written agreement from Mena delivered by midnight."

At midnight a messenger brought me a long, involved argument on the rights of the revolutionists and a discussion of the Nicaraguan Constitution and why Diaz shouldn't be president. My proposition was evaded. I was out of patience. I sat right down and wrote an agreement for Mena to sign. He was to surrender the railroad property and the steamers on Lake Nicaragua belonging to the railroad and move his soldiers from the railroad area. If Mena refuses, I told the messenger, I will attack Granada with my big guns and all my regiments. I put emphasis on the regiments, which required a magician to conjure up.

At four in the morning there was still no word from Mena. We were three miles from town. Taking my guns off the train—and my regiments—I started to advance on the town, in order to reach it by daylight.

As we marched down the track, we noticed a lantern swinging toward us. It was the delegation from Mena carrying a white flag and my paper, which Mena had signed opposite an X, where I had written: "Sign here."

Mena's agreement read:

"I, General Luis Mena, do hereby agree to the following:

"1st. I will immediately turn over to American forces commanded by Major S. O. Butler, U. S. Marine Corps, all the property of the railroad, including all the rolling stock, telegraph lines, instruments, and all steamers. If the Victoria is at present not in Granada, I agree to order her to return to Granada at once in order that she may be turned over as above mentioned, and I do declare on my word of honor that I will not again disturb the above mentioned or any other property of American citizens, or interfere in any way with the operation of the above mentioned property.

"2nd. I do declare on my word of honor that I will not molest (or permit any of my troops to do so) any American forces which may come within the districts controlled by me, nor American citizens and their property.

Sign here (signed) Louis Mena

22nd September 1912."

At daylight we moved into the western section of the city, which was empty and deserted. We pitched our camp on the plaza in front of the railroad station. No one interfered with us, and we minded our own business, which was the railroad. Everything seemed calm.

But that night bells were ringing and whistles blowing madly at the other end of town. Cheering and shouting people poured into the streets to welcome a rebel reinforcement which increased the revolutionary army in Granada to two thousand.

With the people tense and excitable, the situation did seem a little critical. But the demonstration was centered in the other part of the city, separated from us by an arroyo—a deep gully spanned by a bridge. We mounted our guns to defend our side of the arroyo and settled down peacefully to a well-earned sleep.

Down in Managua the same evening President Diaz had invited all our senior officers to a big dinner to celebrate the recapture of the railroad. In the midst of their toasts and compliments a messenger burst in with word that we were besieged in Granada and fighting for our lives in the streets. Colonel Pendleton with two battalions set out at once to the rescue. They arrived two days later to find us tranquilly washing our clothes. It was news to us that we had actually been in a perilous situation with our backs against the wall.

Just the same, with the rebel forces on one side of town and the Marines on the other, there was danger of an explosion at any time. I wanted to avoid any friction that would lead to serious conflict. With two hundred men I marched to the three huge barracks where the revolutionary troops were quartered.

"You must take your soldiers off the streets and keep them in the barracks," I told the commanding officers.

I left a guard of Marines to see that the rebels stayed in the barracks until we could conduct negotiations to disband Mena's army.

When I returned to the little house where we had established headquarters I found Admiral Southerland and his staff. I had urged him to come down from Managua to see what was going on and decide what he wanted done.

"What's your solution?" he asked me.

"Admiral, I'm in favor of getting Mena to surrender and throw himself on your mercy and then have him sent on an American ship to Panama."

The Admiral agreed to the plan.

That night I felt impelled to go at once and talk things over with Mena. I had a hunch that it was a good time to settle the business. It was midnight. The moon was in the last quarter, and it was gruesome walking through the dark, deserted streets past ghostly white houses half hidden behind thick screens of rustling trees.

I went to the San Francisco Cathedral, where Mena and a garrison of seven hundred men were quartered. I was alone, but a company of Marines was stationed up the street within hailing distance. I knocked at a postern gate in the wing of the Cathedral and said to the guard "General Mena." That much English he understood. After a little delay the guard returned with Daniel Mena, the son of the General, to lead me to his father.

I knew Mena was ill, but, until I set eyes on him, I had no idea how ill he was. He was lying on a canvas cot behind one of the great stone pillars of the church. An American nurse was bending over him as he moaned and writhed in pain. His face was drawn and haggard from suffering. He had been flat on his back almost from the beginning of his revolutionary show and was obliged to delegate most of the responsibility to his son and to Zeledon.

With one of his officers to interpret, I sat down beside his bed. Carefully and in great detail I went over the whole situation with him. I told him that if he would surrender himself with all his army in Granada, the Admiral would provide a warship to take him to Panama.

Mena closed his eyes and pondered silently for some time. Finally, he consented.

Much relieved, I rushed back to our little house and woke up Admiral Southerland. Over a can of salmon and some apricots I explained the obligations to which I had bound him. The old Admiral promised to carry out his end of the bargain.

The next morning a cablegram from our Secretary of the Navy directed the Admiral to turn over all the rebels he might capture to the government in power.

I slumped in my chair, wilted and miserable at the thought of breaking my word to Mena. The Admiral patted me on the shoulder.

"Don't worry, Butler, I'll stick by you."

He promptly cabled to the Secretary of the Navy that his message was received too late to carry out the instructions, as he had already given me orders.

Reassured by the Admiral about Mena, I went down to the dock to accept the formal surrender of the two little lake steamers which the rebels used as gunboats. The next number on the peace program was disarming the army and sending the rebel soldiers home. The soldiers who had been recruited from the revolutionary city of Leon hated to be separated from their comfortable lodgings and three square meals, and they were afraid the folks back home wouldn't welcome them with open arms. We had to start them forcibly on their way.

Mena was still lying in the cold stone shadows of the gloomy old church. Late at night, with a Marine escort I went to the San Francisco Cathedral. Gently the men lifted Mena from his cot to a wide comfortable stretcher and carried him out through the great front doors, which had not been opened in twenty years. His powerful frame was wasted away. He had been a man of boundless energy and tremendous physical courage. It Was pitiful to see him now, emaciated and helpless. With our guards surrounding the stretcher, the little procession trudged slowly through the deserted streets. Mena's son and one servant were permitted to accompany him. He was sent by train to Corinto and shipped off to Panama. That job was wound up. Mena never returned to Nicaragua.

Emiliano Chamorro, a member of one of the most influential old families of Nicaragua, was general in chief of the government army. He had been granted dictatorial powers by the legislature to put down the revolution. I had met him in 1910, at Bluefields. He was a handsome man, with finely chiseled, aristocratic features. Because of his courage, frankness and personal charm, I was more attracted to him than to other Nicaraguans of my acquaintance. Later he became president.

I made a wager with Chamorro that I could capture Mena and take him out of the country without a shot. Chamorro offered me a fine horse if I could accomplish what he believed was impossible. I now wired him that I had succeeded. Two or three days later a magnificent black Peruvian stallion was brought to my door. He was a beauty, but unmanageable, and I never enjoyed riding him.

As soon as Mena was disposed of, I opened the dungeons under the cathedral and released citizens of Granada who had been kept as hostages in black, damp caverns for weeks. Most of them were too weak to stand up and some of them had lost their minds.

With the rebels out of the picture, there was for the moment no governor in the province of Granada. I had the job of taking over the administration temporarily until a new election could be held.

Mena had put outrageous levies on the people and his army had looted right and left. I found the cathedral filled with horses, cattle and stocks of silk, laces and general merchandise. I invited Dr. Juan J. Martinez, a graduate of Bellevue Hospital in New York, who ran a hospital of his own in Granada, to help me return all this confiscated property to its rightful owners. The influential politicians, who expected to be specially favored, were dissatisfied with the redistribution and enraged at me. They appealed to the Admiral, and I was relieved as governor. But the general population apparently appreciated my effort to deal justly with them. The citizens of Granada held a public demonstration in my honor and presented me with a gold medal for restoring peace to their city.

Granada was cleared of rebels, but the revolution still smoldered in Masaya and Leon. Zeledon had not yet surrendered. He clung defiantly to his fortifications on the two hills guarding the approach to Masaya. I knew we'd have to come back some time and take those hills.

Well, here we were on October 2, setting out from Granada for the final clean-up at Masaya.

A mile or so from the town we unloaded our stores from the train. Eight oxen hauled our three field guns around to a position from which we could shell the hills.

The more formidable hill, Coyotepe, was about five hundred feet high, with steep slopes on all sides; Barranca, the other hill, was only half as high. The summits of the two hills were a thousand yards apart. An army of two thousand rebels armed with machine guns and rifles was defending the forts.

Colonel Pendleton with six hundred Marines and sailors chose a position a little to the west of the hills. I was five hundred yards west of him with my two hundred and fifty men. Pendleton ordered me to begin shelling the Coyotepe Thursday, October 3, at eight in the morning unless Zeledon surrendered and had white flags flying from both hills by that time.

We were up at daylight. Our eyes were glued to the hills. Remembering our last experience with Zeledon, we were afraid the white flags would be displayed to cheat us out of a scrap again. But when no flags appeared at eight o'clock we started shelling. The Colonel's guns spit fire all day, but not a shot was returned, not a soldier showed himself on the summit, although we knew the rebels were massed behind the entrenchments.

Shelling from below was no good; so the combined forces were directed to make a surprise assault on Coyotepe at 5:15 Friday morning. Colonel Pendleton's six hundred men were to advance from the east and my men, on their left, from the southeast.

With two companies I spent the night in a little farmhouse on a coffee plantation. The outfit stretched out on the cement coffee-drying floors to snatch what sleep they could.

We were up again at three-thirty. Without breakfast we slipped through the darkness to our position at the base of the hill. No one smoked, no one spoke. We marched forward in two lines, holding hands to keep from losing one another. I was in the center of the first line and signaled to halt or advance by squeezing the hands of the men at my right or my left.

Exactly at the appointed hour, quarter past five, we met the Colonel with his six hundred. As we charged up the hill, the rebels opened fire and kept up a devilish hot blazing. But in exactly forty minutes, we climbed the hill, killed twenty-seven of their men in the trenches at the top, captured nine and put the rest to flight. Then we turned the Coyotepe guns on the Barranca fort opposite, and that garrison fled, too. Zeledon's rebels were all scampering down into Masaya as fast as they could run. Zeledon himself was killed by his own troops when he tried to escape and save his own skin. That's all there was to the scrap.

The government forces were supposed to attack Masaya, while we were making our charge, but they discreetly waited to find out first what was going to happen to us.

When they saw the American flag floating on the summit of Coyotepe, which had never before been captured in the whole history of Nicaragua, they let out wild whoops and pounced violently on the town.

From our position on the hill we had a panoramic view of the whole show. The storming of the cathedral, the last stronghold of the rebels, was quite spectacular. The government troops battered down the big front doors with their artillery and then swarmed across the plaza into the great stone building. The racket of exploding bullets, shouts and shrieks within the church was terrific. The rebels climbed into the tower, fighting savagely back at their invaders as they tried to escape. Many of them were pushed out of the tower to crash in the street below. Suddenly all firing ceased. The rebel flag came down, and the government colors went up.

I took my battalion down the hill. As I passed through Masaya to load the guns on our train and steam away, the four thousand government soldiers were already hard at it, looting and celebrating. Native soldiers, half naked, were parading in high silk hats and women's underclothes. Everybody was reeling in circles, drunk and hilarious. A few were playfully shooting their own comrades. Otherwise there was no violence.

When the city of Leon surrendered the next day to Colonel Long of the Marines, the Nicaraguan revolution was ever.

The Admiral now decided that Colonel Pendleton should go on a good-will mission to Matagalpa, one hundred miles across the mountains, in the interior of Nicaragua, where news was slow in percolating. The Colonel took me with him as commander of the troops. From Leon we marched overland for seven days with a column of one hundred men and fifty pack animals. We visited the gold mines and rode through the country around Matagalpa, informing the people that the revolution had been put down and that the Americans were friendly to them.

We left Nicaragua the end of November 1912. The third and last Nicaraguan revolution of my acquaintance had kept the Marines on the jump for four months.

I went home on a short leave and spent Christmas with my family but brought them all back with me to old Camp Elliott on the Isthmus in January. My second son, Tom Dick, was born there in October 1913.

While I was on the Isthmus in 1913, the Panama Canal was formally dedicated with much ceremony and many speeches, although it was not open to general traffic until the following year.

When the last dam across the Culebra Cut was blown up, removing the final obstruction, a group of important and pompous army officials boarded a tug to make the first trip. None of the Marines had been invited to join them. I walked down to the Canal to watch the festivities.

By golly! A dugout shot around the bank. It was proudly flying a little Marine flag, and two Marines were paddling like the devil. They went through first, cheered and applauded by the crowd.

CHAPTER XV

I Become a Spy in Mexico

THE MARINES WERE ORDERED TO ABANDON THE ISTHMUS in January 1914 and proceed to Mexico. Mrs. Butler packed up the house and returned with the three children to Pennsylvania. A Marine officer no sooner hangs "Home, Sweet Home" over his fireplace than it's time to take it down again.

With our battalion of four hundred I boarded the battleship Minnesota bound for Vera Cruz. A few men stayed behind to break up Camp Elliott. I felt downhearted to lose this fine post in Panama.

Whys and wherefores are not in the Marine vocabulary. I knew that President Wilson had refused to recognize

General Victoriano Huerta, the Mexican President, that Mexico was bursting its jacket with internal conflicts and that the Mexicans had no love for Americans. The intricate ramifications of the situation were not our affair. Marines are given orders, and they go.

Indigo water, sand hills, white walls and coconut palms, mountain peaks piercing the clouds, an island scarred with the grim old fortress prison of San Juan de Uloa—that was my first glimpse of Vera Cruz.

Admiral Frank Friday Fletcher was in command of the six or eight United States warships riding at anchor off Vera Cruz. He was a great old sea dog. I reported to him at once; for I had been assigned to his staff. Perhaps it was his keen sense of humor that inspired him to fling out this greeting:

"I don't know why all you men are here. Why didn't the department consult me? I've no use for Marines and less for you. I don't need you."

Much crushed, I returned to the Minnesota and wrote to the department, requesting a transfer, since the Admiral bluntly informed me that I wasn't wanted. By the time my letter reached Washington, the Admiral had dispatched me on a confidential mission to Mexico City.

After he'd enjoyed his little joke, we became good friends. In a few weeks he invited me to live on his flagship, the Florida. One had to become acquainted with Admiral Fletcher to appreciate his sterling character and his charm. He was an efficient officer, but no martinet. The human side was always uppermost.

One Sunday morning I was taking a bath in the Admiral's cabin on the Minnesota. I heard the Admiral's barge chugging up under my port. Its two engines had a distinctive, broken beat that I easily recognized. Lieutenant

George Courts, the Admiral's aide, pounded on my door. I jumped dripping out of the tub to let him in.

"Hurry up and get dressed," Courts said. "The Admiral wants you to go ashore with him."

"We're going to take a little ride and see something of the country," the Admiral explained.

At the station in Vera Cruz, we climbed into the private car of the Superintendent of the railroad. It was attached to the morning train for Mexico City. We rode for about fifty miles until we came to Jalapa. Then we switched back on the afternoon train for Vera Cruz. The Admiral and I were alone. I was puzzled. What was his purpose in dragging me out on this Sunday excursion? He talked about everything under the sun except the matter obviously on his mind until we were drawing near town.

"By the way, Butler, how should you like to take a little trip to Mexico City?"

"A fine idea, Admiral."

"For various reasons of state, our officers have been requested not to go outside Vera Cruz, but I'd like an accurate description of conditions in Mexico City. I want to know how many soldiers the Mexicans have up there. The statements have been conflicting.

"You'll have to go without orders and assume all responsibility. If you're caught, I can't help you. You must tell nobody, not even your wife, where you are going."

In plain language, I was to be a spy. I thought it over for a few minutes.

"All right, Admiral, I'll go."

When we pulled into Vera Cruz, the Admiral unfolded our plan to the railroad Superintendent, who had been an employee of Sam Felton, Mrs. Butler's uncle, at one time president of the National Railways of Mexico. He was very friendly because of his former connection with Uncle Sam and offered to take me under his wing in his private car to Mexico City.

The Admiral chugged me back to the ship. I hurried to my cabin, made a lightning change into civilian clothes and dropped my bag out of the port into the Admiral's boat. Fortunately, the crew was being entertained with moving pictures, and I could slip off without being seen. I went ashore, crept through the unlighted private car and tucked myself into bed.

As we rolled along early the next morning I looked out at the old Camino Real, built by Cortez—the road which our troops would probably use if they advanced to Mexico City. On various pretexts the Superintendent stopped the train frequently, so that I could examine the lay of the land and make rough military plans.

At Puebla the Superintendent introduced me to the leading citizens as a nephew of S. M. Felton and an expert interested in public utilities. They couldn't do enough for me. They showed me the electric power plant and the water system. They drove me around town, pointing out all the sights boring to a tourist but vitally important to an invading army.

My courteous guides explained the good features of the reservoir, built on top of a hill just outside the city, but I was much more interested in two little forts nearby which overlooked the town. Those forts commanded Puebla. Pretending to chase a butterfly, I dashed into one of the forts and made a hurried inspection before the astonished guards could shove me out.

We arrived in Mexico City the following evening, and my friend the Superintendent and I took a carriage to the American Legation. The Admiral had arranged to get in touch with me through the Legation, where I was to explain the object of my visit. Our Minister had been recalled. Nelson O'Shaughnessy was acting as Charge d'Affaires and trying to keep our relations with Mexico as friendly as possible during the period of non-recognition. Only the O'Shaughnessys and the Superintendent of the railroad were to know who I was and why I was there.

Mrs. O'Shaughnessy received us in her drawing room. She was a gloriously radiant and beautiful creature, and in her high-backed, carved chair she looked like an empress.

"I'll be shot as a spy if I'm caught," I remarked.

"Well, I'll call you Mr. Johnson," she insisted. "That ought to be a safe name."

In the book she wrote later about her Mexican experiences she mentions me as the wild-eyed Mr. Johnson.

O'Shaughnessy finally came in, saying that he had just been sitting on Huerta's bed, having a long talk with him. Although Huerta and our State Department were not on formal bowing terms, Huerta and O'Shaughnessy were warm personal friends. The weather-beaten, leathery old fighting man admired our Charge, who he knew was playing fair and square with him.

The ten days I spent in the city I lived at the Superintendent's house. I became acquainted with a foreigner in Huerta's secret service and let him believe that I was in the United States secret service, looking for a dangerous criminal who was supposed to have enlisted in the Mexican army. I always carried in my pocket a fake tintype of my imaginary desperado.

Huerta issued an order permitting the Secret Service man and myself to visit all the garrisons in my search for the criminal. I used my eyes and ears in the garrisons and gathered valuable information on the Mexican troops and their munition stores. I even made an imposing collection of military maps.

The American residents whom I interviewed either believed I was a representative of the State Department or an author jotting down data for a guide-book. I listed the names of all Americans in the city, where they lived and what food supplies they had.

Early in the morning and late at night I roamed around town to observe how much movement there was. The best plan for attacking Mexico City, it seemed to me, was to make a rush on Chapultepec and seize it before anybody was awake.

The hill of Chapultepec, crowned by the President's summer palace and surrounded by a park of beautiful trees and gardens, was the military key to the city. Everything else I had seen, but I had not yet been able to examine Chapultepec with an eye to its strategic possibilities. I kept urging O'Shaughnessy to take me.

"I can't abuse the diplomatic privileges by taking a spy in there," he insisted.

One morning I called at the Legation and found O'Shaughnessy at breakfast.

"Come on out and take a drive," I urged. "It will do your head good. It must be bursting with Mexico and America."

We drove out to Chapultepec and lingered in the restaurant at the base of the hill for two or three drinks. While I continued hopelessly to press my Chapultepec proposal on O'Shaughnessy, who should come in but Huerta himself.

"The very person," I said. "If you're so intimate with the President, you might ask him if you can show me through. If you don't, I will."

O'Shaughnessy finally went up to Huerta, who nodded his head good-naturedly.

O'Shaughnessy told the guards at the gate that my name was Johnson and I was writing a guide-book. We went all through the palace, a handsome and dignified structure. But I was not interested in the silver bed where the ill-fated Empress Carlotta had slept or in the other museum pieces.

The palace was built above an old fort. All I wanted was to examine those old fortifications. With artillery the top of the hill could be smashed to kingdom come. But here O'Shaughnessy drew the line. He refused to press the guards to take us below.

I had the list of American citizens and a roll of maps; I had seen all the troops and visited every place of military importance except the old Chapultepec fort.

The Admiral's last words to me were "Butler, my advice to you is not to dilly-dally."

I now decided that I'd better heed the Admiral's warning. I tucked my maps into the false bottom of my bag and had a farewell tea with the delightful O'Shaughnessys, who put me on the train for Vera Cruz.

I took the maps out of the bag and put them under my pillow. I was nervous and restless. I felt I should not draw an easy breath until my feet were planted on an American deck in the harbor. During the night two men got on the train at Jalapa. I heard whispers near my section, and the porter gave a little tug at my curtain. I looked through a crack and saw two Mexicans walking to the other end of the car. I was convinced that they were secret service men. Obviously, they wanted me. I had been a little too energetic in Mexico City.

At Vera Cruz the trains run out a Y and back in to the station. When we reached the Y, I fooled the secret service men. I took my bag and clothes to the washroom and hopped off the train before it switched back. I scrambled into my clothes among the freight cars and made a dash for the American Consulate, where I signaled for a boat from the flagship.

While I was waiting at the water front, a gang of Mexican hoodlums pounced on me, began searching my bag and nearly tore my clothes to pieces. But a launch was now bounding toward shore with our bluejackets, who saw that I was being manhandled.

"Major, shall we dump those lousy guys in the bay?" they shouted.

"No," I shouted back, for the crowd melted away at the approach of the launch. The last thing I wanted at that moment was to pick a quarrel with any one in Vera Cruz. But our boys were rather gloomy as they pointed the launch toward the flagship. They had been itching for a good scrap.

The two weeks on Admiral Fletcher's mission were a strain, as though I had been sitting on a barrel of dynamite.

One of the principal objects of my trip was to prepare a plan to rescue the Americans in Mexico City in case the Mexicans rose up against them.

The harbor was like a busy city street. American, British, German and French ships rode at anchor. Launches and barges were continually plying back and forth. Admirals and captains toasted their foreign guests at formal dinner parties. There was a gay exchange of international courtesy and hospitality. This was 1914, before the deluge.

Rear-Admiral Sir Christopher Craddock [sic]* was in command of the British squadron at Vera Cruz. When Craddock learned that a Marine officer named Butler was with the American fleet, he remembered that I had served with him during the Boxer uprising. He invited me to lunch with him on his flagship, the Good Hope. We reminisced about Boxer days in his comfortable and luxurious cabin, furnished with easy chairs and many books, with old silver, carvings and souvenirs of China, Malta and other countries he had visited on his long voyages.

*Rear-Admiral Sir Christopher "Kit" George Francis Maurice Cradock (1862-1914).

Craddock was handsome, entertaining and very much the English gentleman. He was something of an art connoisseur, and he wrote books on fishing and hunting. When he paid official calls he never used a steam launch. He always sailed his own gig. The old tars loved him for it. Craddock knew ships inside and out. He was a superb naval commander.

About the middle of April, I raced up the Gulf of Tampico. Things were buzzing in the oil port of Mexico.

A week or so before, the paymaster and crew of the USS Dolphin were arrested by the Mexicans while they were loading gasoline into a whaleboat at the Tampico wharf. As soon as the Mexican general at Tampico heard of the arrest, he released the Americans with an apology.

Admiral Henry Thomas Mayo, the best type of American sailor, in command of our men at Tampico, was not satisfied with the apology. He demanded that the Mexican General should raise the American flag in a prominent position on shore and give it a salute of twenty-one guns. Huerta now stepped in and insisted that the Mexican salute be returned gun for gun by the Americans. Mayo would not agree to this. The incident was approaching a crisis.

We had three hundred Marines up the Panuco River at Tampico and a thousand more at the mouth of the river on the Hancock. My good friend Lejeune, then a Colonel, was senior officer of the Marines on the Hancock.

Captain William A. Moffett, the late Admiral, commanded a scout cruiser, the Chester, at Tampico. He was a daring, skillful seaman, but unless he originated a suggestion, he seldom agreed with it. I must admit that he was a great sailor, and courageous. When my father was a member of the Naval Affairs Committee of the House, Moffett always made a great fuss over me, but after my father's death he joined the pack that tried to destroy me.

Admiral Mayo had delivered a twenty-four hour ultimatum to the Mexican general at Tampico. While he was making preparations to take the town, the excitement suddenly shifted to Vera Cruz.

The German liner Ypiranga* was on its way to Vera Cruz with a bulging cargo of machine guns and ammunition for the Mexicans. In order to prevent that explosive cargo from reaching its equally explosive destination, Admiral Fletcher, with orders from Washington, now decided to land at Vera Cruz, and take over the custom house.

*Following image: Photograph of the deck of SS Ypiranga c. 1911.

Admiral Fletcher radioed on April 19th to Tampico that he was landing at Vera Cruz. Moffett declared that he was going right down to Vera Cruz to get into the scrap. I was with Moffett on the Chester. We put oil on the fires until we were running at top speed: twenty-one knots. The old cruiser rattled like a tin pan.

Fletcher put his men ashore about noon. Every time a radio report of the fighting reached us, we tried to push the Chester along a little faster. I paced up and down the deck impatiently. Like Moffett, I was bursting to be in the thick of it.

We dashed inside the breakwater at Vera Cruz about eleven that night and dropped our anchor near the Prairie, which Fletcher was using as his flagship. The lighthouse was dark. There wasn't a light in the harbor. Every now and then we heard the sharp staccato report of firing along the water front.

Almost at once the signal came for me to land. With one company of Marines and one of sailors in small boats, I went ashore. I reported to "Buck" Neville, then a Colonel in command of five companies of Marines in the town. "Buck" ordered me to post my men on the line near the roundhouse in the northwest section of the city.

At daylight we marched right through Vera Cruz. Mexicans in the houses, on the roofs, and in the streets peppered us from all directions. Some fired at us with machine guns. Since the Mexicans were using the houses as fortresses, the Marines rushed from house to house, knocking in the doors and searching for snipers.

Just as two of my men were smashing through one door, they were mysteriously shot in the stomach from below. The house was deserted, but from the angle of the bullets, the Mexicans were obviously under the floor. We poured a volley through the floor and then ripped up the boards. There they were, two dead Mexicans dangling between the cross beams. Our fire had caught them.

The sailors who traveled openly through the streets were badly shot up, not only by Mexicans but in at least one instance by their own men, but the Marine casualties were slight. Two of my men were killed and four or five wounded.

We Marines decided on different tactics from the sailors. Stationing a machine gunner at one end of the street as a lookout, we advanced under cover, cutting our way through the adobe walls from one house to another with axes and picks. We drove everybody from the houses and then climbed up on the flat roofs to wipe out the snipers.

During the day the First Regiment of Marines, commanded by Lejeune, came ashore in small boats from the transport Hancock. I'll never forget that landing. The British jack tars lined the rails of their ships and cheered our boys for all they were worth. It was a heartening display of friendship.

All day we fought like hell through the streets, advancing in two or three long lines, driving everybody with a rifle in front of us. By night we had complete control of the city, although the sniping continued for several days. One hundred and thirty-five Americans were killed and wounded at Vera Cruz.

As a result of the Vera Cruz campaign, Congress authorized officers to receive Medals of Honor, which had formerly been awarded only to enlisted men. About twenty-five were issued. I received one, but I returned it to the Navy Department with the statement that I had done nothing which entitled me to this supreme decoration. The correspondence was referred to Admiral Fletcher, who insisted that I certainly deserved the decoration. The Navy Department sent the medal back to me with the order that I should not only keep it this time but wear it also.

While we were at Vera Cruz, news came of the assassination of the Archduke Francis Ferdinand at Sarajevo, but we didn't pay much attention to it. None of us realized that the world was heading swiftly into a war that was to make this Mexican fracas look like a dog fight.

But the British and Germans knew something was up. One day the German warships put on full steam, and before we knew it they were gone. The same day Admiral Craddock sailed out of the harbor with his cruisers. I never saw him again. Two months later Von Spee sent the gallant Craddock and his squadron to the bottom of the Pacific in the battle of Coronel off the coast of Chile.

Chapter XVI

Fighting Revels and Bandits in Haiti

Until 1915 when we Marines came to Haiti, the President of the little black republic did not occupy the most enviable or secure position in the world. From 1911 to 1915 there were seven Presidents of Haiti. Most of them were removed by revolutionary violence or sudden death.

Revolutions followed a definite procedure in Haiti. They always started in the north near the Dominican border so that the rebels could skip over to the sister Republic when the odds were against them. The first battle was invariably fought at Kilometer Post 17, on the railroad to Grande Riviere. Don't ask me why. That's the way it used to happen in Haiti. If the rebels were successful they marched south to Port-au-Prince, the capital. And if the President was wise, he bolted with the treasury before the rebel army reached the outskirts of town.

Just before I arrived in Haiti, the President was Vilbrun Guillaume Sam,* a rampaging bandit leader who had long into the rebels. We didn't think they were so close. They fired first. And then the scrap started.

*Jean Vilbrun Guillaume Sam; President of Haiti from 4 March to 27 July 1915.

It was the funniest fight I ever saw. Those damn Marines were baying like bloodhounds all through the bushes.

"Here comes one;" bang, bang, I'd hear, as they hunted down the Cacos.

"And hell, here's another." Bang, bang.

I kept blowing my whistle, and the bugler kept sounding "To the rear," and "Cease firing," but the men were in their element and nothing could stop them. Those undressed Marines went right on shooting at the Haitians.

It was after dark when we gathered up eight native wounded but none of our men was hurt. It was something of a shock to the rebels to have Marines in underwear suddenly pounce down on them with blood curdling yells. The Cacos fully expected us to wait around and call a conference over the burning of the railroad.

The next morning at four o'clock I started out with fifty men in hot pursuit of the Cacos. They fled in front of us through bushes and across fields. We could have picked them off easily one by one, but we made them shoot first.

They soon lost their appetite for firing. All they wanted was to get away and they ran along like antelopes, keeping us on the jump for eleven miles until we came to the thatched hut hamlet of Poteau.

The little village was alive with Cacos, running around and making feverish preparations to evacuate. At our approach they scampered out of town with a party of fifty mounted men at their heels. We pushed hurriedly along after them.

I asked several strong-lunged huskies near the head of my column to shout for General Rameau. The lusty chorus attracted the General's attention and he stopped his horse. With two of my privates I walked over to him. He was a wizened up Negro, a sour-looking, vicious little devil, and he screwed up his face maliciously as he looked down at me.

"You get off that horse," I said, "and stand on the ground as I'm doing."

He muttered something under his breath, and I jerked him out of the saddle. This was more humiliating to him than defeat in battle. His prestige with his men was destroyed, and he was no longer the great general.

"Look here," I told him, "you can't go on burning railroads. You'll have to sign an agreement to lay down your arms."

The horse episode really finished him, and he surrendered. We sent him down to Port-au-Prince for safe keeping.

Rameau was out of the way, but other Caco leaders were buzzing around with their bands, stirring up plenty of trouble in the mountains.

While I was still in Gonaives, Colonel Waller radioed me to return at once to Cape Haitien, where the revolt was becoming serious. The Cacos had ambushed and shot eight or ten of our men.

That started things. A lot of north Haiti was burned before we got through.

Old and tried Marines, who could stand any hardship without grumbling—most of them are buried in France now—were selected for an expedition into the mountains against the Cacos. We didn't have enough pack mules to carry our supplies up the steep trails, so I thought we'd better take a group of natives as cargadores.

"Round up some strong able-bodied men," I told a sergeant, "and we'll pay them to come with us."

"They've all gone to church."

"All right, wait for them as they come out."

The whole male population of the town, which apparently got wind of my little plan, had flocked in a body to high mass. They kept craning their necks around apprehensively at the sergeant, who stood with his rifle, like a statue, at the entrance. The service was over, but the congregation remained glued to the pews.

Colonel Waller happened to stroll by and saw the sergeant.

"Who put you at the door of the church? What are you doing here?"

"Getting volunteers, Colonel, to carry baggage."

"The hell you are. I don't see them volunteering. Smedley," he called to me, "did you station the sergeant here?"

"Yes, sir."

"Well, you can't force the natives to be your pack mules."

"I'm not going to force them to do anything, Colonel. They're going to volunteer."

"Volunteer, hell. You let 'em alone."

In spite of Waller's scruples, the baggage had to be carried. The sergeant hid in the bushes across from the church, and as the congregation poured out, he asked for volunteers. The natives looked at his rifle and—they volunteered.

We were all set to go when Waller sent for me. "Smedley," he tried to look severe, "did you enlist the missionary's apiary caretaker?"

"I don't know, sir."

"Well, the missionary tells me you did. You'll have to lend him a Marine to look after his bees."

Marines don't like to tend bees, so I turned the beekeeper loose. But the sergeant was not to be outwitted. He locked the missionary in his house. Before he could get out we were off to the mountains with the bee expert. He was so tall and thin that the men called him String Beans.

A few miles from town the Cacos tried to ambush us. When they opened fire, we gave them a good dose in return. String Beans was following behind me with a box of ammunition on his head. At the first crack of the rifles, he collapsed. He sank to the ground like an accordion, with the ammunition still balanced on his head.

But String Beans soon preferred his new job to the bees. The carriers were well fed, and we paid them ten cents a day. They exulted in being on the winning side; for they all had grudges to settle against the Cacos.

It was slow traveling. Every little while we had to stop and put to rout the Cacos, who crouched in ambush as we pushed through the tangle of scrub.

We hiked for miles through the mountains, cleaning out nests of bandits. We breakfasted before we broke camp, carried cans of salmon and hardtack in our pockets, and, if we were lucky, ate hot corned beef hash for supper. On forced marches we often lived on oranges, which could be had for the picking in Haiti.

We always knew which way the bandits were going by the orange peels. They left one continuous peeling along their trail. If the first peels were moist and the next were drier, we knew the Cacos had approached us and turned off. If the first peels were dry, the bandits were some distance ahead of us. We got so expert that we could almost smell the rascals.

But we couldn't seem to root them all out. They were still coming down to the lowlands to prey on the peaceful farmers. We learned that somewhere in the heart of the mountain country was a fort known as Capois. A powerful band of Cacos, using Capois as a secure and unapproachable base, sallied forth on their predatory excursions. If we were to restore peace to the countryside, we had to find the fort and destroy the band.

Cole, my Colonel, reported to Waller that six battalions —three thousand men—would be required to clean out the mountain region between Cape Haitien and Fort Liberté It was an area sixty by twenty miles, with five-thousand-foot mountains. To the trained military mind, a big army movement was necessary to get at the Cacos hiding somewhere in that untouched wilderness. But Waller didn't have three thousand men. There were only twenty-five hundred Marines in all of Haiti.

Cole was a fine officer but inclined to be over-educated. If you have too much education, you are acutely conscious of the risks you run and are afraid to act. Cole attended every naval and military college in the United States. I never went to any military school, and so perhaps I wasn't trained to know danger when I saw it. At that time many of us in the Corps were called the uneducated. We did all the bush work and never had time to go to school.

It was my opinion that an elaborate military expedition against the Cacos was nonsense. I radioed Colonel Waller that if he would allot me two hundred dollars to buy pack animals I'd find the fort and stamp out the bandits.

The dear old fellow promptly sent me one of his typical messages: "Money allotted. Go to it."

Twenty-seven of us—all old-timers—mounted ponies to hit off into the mountains to find Fort Capois. We had a dozen pack animals to carry our food and one machine-gun. The officers with me were Captain William P. Upshur, two lieutenants, and Assistant Surgeon J. T. Borden, the battalion doctor. Upshur, one of my closest friends, who came of a distinguished Virginia family with fighting traditions, was always so solemn and serious that we called him the "Deacon." I have always admired and loved him.

The First Sergeant of our little detachment was Dan Daly, the "fightingest man" I ever knew in the Marine Corps. Daly had won a Congressional Medal of Honor during the Boxer rebellion in China. When the relief column in which I was marching reached Peking, everyone was talking of Fighting Dan Daly. And in France in 1918, he captured a German machine-gun nest single-handed and risked his life again and again to bring in wounded Marines from No Man's Land. America gave him the Distinguished Service Cross and France awarded him the Medaille Militaire.

Daly is retired now. A year or so ago, we wrote and asked him to put on his old uniform and medals and join the Marines in the Armistice Day celebration in Philadelphia.

"Aw, hell," he wrote, "my fighting days are over. I'm too old to stand the trip. I couldn't march a mile and I ain't going to ride in an open car like a visiting fireman."

Dan is right. His fighting days are over, but they were far from over in Haiti. He had already spent twenty-five of his forty-five years in the Corps. His hair was grey even then, and he looked a little like Lon Chaney. He was smooth faced, with skin like leather. Hard-boiled as the devil, but fine clear through. He was my top sergeant in Haiti. I admired his courage and modesty and became very much attached to him.

Ripley, of "Believe It or Not" fame, once said I was the only person awarded two Congressional medals. That is not true. So far as I know, four men share this distinction, and I'm proud to state that three of them are Marines. Dan Daly received two Congressional medals. He was given the second medal for his gallantry in Haiti on this very expedition into the mountains.

Well, our little party headed in high spirits for the mountains on the Caco hunt. For the first fifty-four hours we were so zealous that we didn't stop for sleep. We scoured more than one hundred miles of rough, unbroken country without finding a trace of the Cacos. But we knew that they couldn't be far away because they were committing depredations in our rear. For once the orange peel trail was missing.

On our third morning as we were jogging along a river bank, we met a hideous, ungainly brute. He must have been the ugliest native in Haiti. His arms hung clumsily to his knees and he looked like an ape. We grabbed him and through our interpreter asked where the Cacos were hiding. He chose to know nothing.

"I'll give you five dollars in Haitian money if you lead us to the Cacos," I offered. "And if you don't, I'll shoot you."

"All right, I'll take you," he gibbered to the interpreter.

He swung us back across the river and turned into the mountains several miles east of the slopes we had just searched. The river bottom was so choked with high grass that we could never have found the trail without the guide.

At three in the afternoon we stopped to rest and eat our lunch at a little stream bubbling crystal clear over the rocks. The ape-guide dragged the interpreter over to me.

"You come with me. I'll show you the Cacos now."

Through an opening in the valley the guide pointed to a mountain about a mile away, towering one thousand feet above us. The cone-shaped peak was circled with rough stone walls and trenches. Every detail was outlined distinctly in the afternoon sunlight. Through my field glasses I saw men crawling over the ramparts and the thatched roofs of the huts inside the walls.

Here it was right in front of us, Fort Capois, the Caco stronghold. To have that damned fort dangling close, like a toothsome bait, was certainly tantalizing. But twenty-seven men couldn't tackle the peak. I had to go back for reinforcements.

I began to be suspicious of our guide. I was certain that the Cacos had received some signal from the ape man or had caught a glimpse of us below. It was a safe bet they would jump us at night.

Our map, which we discovered later was valueless, showed the little town of Valliere, about five miles from where we thought we were. But our thoughts were vague. The only certainty was that we were lost in the mountains of Haiti. My one desire was to get moving and strike out in the direction of the town. If a large native force swooped down on us we could at least barricade ourselves in the church.

We pushed steadily on for several hours through a drizzling rain that had commenced falling with no sign of Valliere. About seven-thirty we stopped short at the edge of a canyon. The rain was lashing across our faces and it was pitch dark. We had to feel our way, slipping and sliding along the trail. The roar of the river two hundred feet below was scarcely music to our ears.

I had a magnificent horse, Tom Dick, named after my two-year-old son. Whenever we were climbing particularly steep trails, we tied the other horses in a long line behind him. Tom Dick would plant his legs firmly on the most dangerous footholds to keep the horses behind him from losing their balance and crashing down the mountainside.

The canyon trail to the river was almost a perpendicular drop. Although Tom Dick's hoofs were worn to the quick and his feet were sore and lame, I had to place him at the head of the column. He was game, all right. He picked his confident way down the trail. Every man led his own horse and held the tail of the horse in front of him. We knotted white handkerchiefs around our necks so that we wouldn't shoot one another in the dark if the Cacos treated us to a surprise party.

The river, swollen by the rains, tore through the narrow canyon. But Tom Dick plunged into the black, swift current and swam across, with the other horses following.

I climbed up the bank first with my orderly, Sam Gross. Suddenly I heard the men in the river shouting that someone had lost his grip on a horse's tail, and the column was broken. I gave Gross my pocket flash and told him to guide the men to shore. Tom Dick had felt his way up the only ledge of bank that wasn't sheerly perpendicular.

Just as Gross was flashing his light at the river bank, the Cacos jumped us. Rifles seemed to crack out from the sky, from below, from all sides. Firing broke out all around us.

The ape man, we learned later, had been sent to trap us. He had signaled to his friends and had then led us down to the river where the Cacos were waiting for us.

We were in a nasty mess, but for some reason I felt strangely exhilarated. I turned to Doctor Borden who had just crawled up the bank and said, "Isn't this great?"

"Great, hell! We're all going to be killed."

The horses were neighing their distress and plunging wildly in the water. A dozen were hit, but the seasoned old Marines lay flat on the horses' backs. Little Gross stood on the bank flashing his light until all the men were out of the river. Our men were safe but twelve of our horses were lost.

There was no place in the hollow to put up a defense. It was still raining and too dark to see three feet ahead of us.

We crawled along on our hands and knees, pulling our horses after us, until we reached the high land, where it was more open. At least we were free from the firing until we could catch our breath and look around, since the Cacos as yet had not followed us out of the river bottom.

Poking around with my flash I stumbled on a shallow pool. We shoved our trembling horses into the little pond and formed a circle around it.

"Better set up the machine-gun, Daly," I said.

"It was lost in the river, sir."

"Well, we'll do the best we can without it."

Daly didn't answer. Instead, he quietly disappeared without my knowledge. We were at least a mile from the place where we had crossed the river.

In an hour Daly returned. "I've set up the machine-gun, Major."

With the bandits continually shooting at him, he swam around in the river until he found the machine-gun on a dead horse near the bank. He coolly and deliberately strapped the gun on his back, picked up the ammunition and climbed up to rejoin us.

I wouldn't have had the courage to do it. Remember, he went back on his own initiative without a hint or suggestion from me. For this amazing stunt I recommended him for the Medal of Honor. And that's how Fighting Dan Daly got his second Congressional medal.

It was lucky we had the machine-gun, because the Cacos, twenty to our one, were now swarming in the bushes around us. From my bush-whacking experience in the Philippines and Central America, I knew it was safer to keep moving than to remain in one spot. Hardly would I swing my little detachment a few yards to the right or left, when a howling mass of natives would dash by us and slash through the bushes with knives and bayonets. It was a hell of a night. We kept moving and the bandits kept rushing the place where we had been sheltered the moment before.

The Cacos tried to chill our hearts by blowing incessantly on their conch shells. They called out to us, and our interpreter explained that they intended to chop us into small pieces when they caught us. Everybody's hands were cold and clammy. I rubbed mine to warm them and then reached out in the dark for the nearest hand to give and receive a little courage. All the men were praying. Even hard-boiled Marines pray when they feel helplessly snared in a death trap.

I had divided our detachment into three squads. Just before daylight I crawled around to each squad.

"Just go for those devils as soon as it's light. Move straight forward and shoot everyone you see."

At daylight we knocked hell out of them. The natives who had surrounded us during the night were now firing from a little fort on a hill three or four hundred yards away. This, we were told later, was Fort Dipitie. We carried the fort at a run. You never heard such a damned racket. We killed about seventy-five Cacos and the rest took to the bushes. But the Marines went wild after their devilish night and hunted the Cacos down like pigs. We destroyed the little fort and the thatched huts around it. By this time the Cacos who valued their skins had all disappeared.

Then we sat down to dress our wounds and take stock. We had practically nothing to eat. The pack train was lost and all the food had been washed down the river. But all twenty-seven of us were very much alive and had fortunately come off with only one man wounded.

We figured out that the river which had led us into so many difficulties was the Grande Riviere and that if we followed it far enough we would reach the sea.

Wearily we set out on empty stomachs. The Cacos whom we had not wiped out scampered along the high bank and sniped at us all day, but it was futile to climb after them. The little devils were as annoying as gnats. They cut down trees on the trail ahead of us to hinder our progress. But they respected us now and always vanished before we could take a shot at them.

The ape man was still with us. When the attack began the night before, he was afraid he would be killed if he tried to make his escape. In the morning when he saw we were winning, he must have decided that he liked us better than his former playmates. He stayed glued to our sides. We couldn't drive him away. We used him as an extra orderly. His name was Antoine, and he was faithful after his one and only betrayal of us.

We kept close to the river all day. The men were too tired even to cuss. Just before dark we came to a canyon with straight smooth walls of rock four hundred feet high. A narrow trail, cutting around the edge of the steep embankment, led through the canyon. It was only six feet above the river.

As we started into the canyon, there was a sudden cloudburst. Torrents of rain—a regular Biblical deluge—swept furiously through the gorge. There we were—lashed and half-blinded by biting gusts of rain, on a slippery, treacherous trail, with the roaring, turbulent river rapidly swelling toward us. The river rose about twelve feet in twenty minutes.

We stretched up the cliff and clutched frantically at the roots of trees and dwarf bushes growing between the rocks. Several of our horses were swept into the torrent, but we couldn't save them. Good old Tom Dick stood on his hind legs, with his front legs pawing up the bank. Every few minutes a man slid headlong into the torrent, and we had to form a human chain to haul him back.

I rested for a moment against the branch of a gnarled little tree, hanging there, half dead with fatigue. We hadn't slept for three or four days. I grew more and more drowsy. The roar of the river seemed fainter. My head nodded, my eyes closed, and I relaxed my tense grip on the branch. I woke up bobbing and whirling around in the angry current. Gross, my ever reliable orderly, pulled me out of the water.

I had hardly been pushed up the rock to safety, when another man tumbled into the rushing waters. "Deacon" Upshur stripped off his clothes and jumped in to the rescue. When he came out he found that his clothes had been washed away. We had to wrap our naked Captain of Marines in a mosquito net until we returned to civilization.

The water fell as quickly as it had risen. The flood served one good purpose. The natives, convinced that we had all been drowned, ceased to annoy us.

Early the next morning we pushed on, wet, bedraggled and exhausted. Before noon we came to the town of Valliere, forty miles from the place indicated on my map.

A friendly, hospitable French priest filled our empty stomachs with delicious, steaming hot food. The whole gang of us then lay down in the plaza with our horses and went to sleep. We were so tired that we didn't care if the natives killed us or not.

When I woke up at dark, I realized that we couldn't remain in an exposed position in the plaza. The priest fed us a hearty supper, and then we took possession of one of the houses belonging to the church, where we could defend ourselves against a surprise attack. But the natives were quiet. If they had been so inclined they could have wiped us out before, when we were asleep in the plaza.

We had our bearings again. A thirty mile trail led over the mountains to Fort Liberté, on the north coast of Haiti near the Dominican border, where my battalion headquarters were now located. At three in the morning we left Valliere, which will always be linked in my mind with a kind French padre and a very unreliable map and tramped into Fort Liberté in the late afternoon.

Colonel Waller was delighted that we had found Fort Capois and gave me permission to go back with a sufficient force to clean out all the Cacos and put a definite end to their raids.

The actual capture of Capois seemed an anticlimax after our hair-breath escapes and misadventures in the search for the fort.

We trekked forty miles to the little town of Ste. Suzanne, way up in the mountains, where we established field headquarters.

From Ste. Suzanne I led our forces through the tangled underbrush and across the valley toward Capois. I instructed Captain Chandler Campbell, with his two companies, to attack the mountain from one side, while I went up the other side with three companies of Marines. We also had two companies of sailors, whom I left below to guard our stores and pack train.

At three thirty in the morning, we marched through the bushes to the foot of the mountain and deployed in a long skirmish line. Campbell's men reached Fort Capois first. While we were climbing our side of the hill, we could hear them firing. But we found the fort deserted. The Cacos took to their heels and disappeared into the bushes at our approach. The fort was ours without anyone being hurt on either side.

We stationed a small garrison of Marines at Fort Capois and returned to Ste. Suzanne, which we used as our base. Every day we went out over mountains and valleys, hunting down Cacos. We took several rebel strongholds and except for a stray, elusive little gang here and there, we practically cleared the north country of bandits.

CHAPTER XVII

The Storming of Black Mountain and the Capture of Fort Riviere

IN 1931, I BROADCAST THE STORY OF THE TAKING OF Fort Riviere in Haiti. When I came to the part where Sergeant Ross Iams said, "Oh, hell, I'm going through," I was cut off the air for using "obscene and indecent" language. Apparently, the radio people didn't know Marines.

But that wasn't all. The next day the newspapers carried an interview with Monsieur Dantes Bellegarde, the Haitian Minister to the United States. The Haitian Minister insisted that no such fort as Riviere had ever existed. After considerable battledoring back and forth the Haitian Minister admitted that there was a slight misunderstanding—that he and many other Haitians had never happened to hear of Fort Riviere—but none the less he left the impression that Fort Riviere was the creation of a fevered and overworked imagination. However, I was awarded the Haitian Medal of Honor by President Dartiguenave for its capture.

Well, back in 1915, the Marines thought Fort Riviere was real enough and they displayed abundant heroism in storming it. Until then the fortress had been regarded as impregnable. It was the last stronghold of the Haitian rebels. The Capture of Fort Riviere was the final act in stamping out the Caco insurrection in north Haiti.

When we came out of the mountains after the campaign against Fort Capois, we reported to Colonel Cole, who was stationed at the town of Grande Riviere.

I was very tired. Cole's porch looked inviting, and I slung myself into his comfortable hammock and dozed off. I was awakened by a buzz of voices. A conference was taking place in the room off the porch.

Several of Cole's officers had just returned with a couple of companies from a reconnoitering trip to Fort Riviere. Having explored the place, they almost agreed with the natives who believed the fort was unassailable.

It was an old bastion fort with thick walls of brick and stone, built in the latter part of the eighteenth century during the French occupation. The fortress stood on the peak of Montagne Noire, four thousand feet above the sea, midway between four towns, Grande Riviere, Dondon, San Rafael and Bahon. Fort Riviere was approached by three trails, each a twenty-mile march—one from San Rafael, another from Dondon and the third from a point on the railroad midway between Grande Riviere and Bahon. On three sides the masonry of the wall joined the rock of the mountain, thus forming a steep precipice into the valley. On the fourth side a gentle slope led to the sally-port.

"We'll need a regiment with a strong artillery battery to take Riviere," I heard one of the officers telling Cole.

This sounded interesting. I didn't want any more sleep. I slipped out of the hammock and joined the conference.

"All this talk about the difficulty of taking the fort is nonsense," I broke in. "Colonel, if you let me pick one hundred men from the eight hundred you have here, I feel that we can capture the place at once without wasting more words."

Cole frequently scoffed at my ideas as impractical, but we were just back from a successful expedition which he had labelled next to impossible at the outset. This time he decided he'd let me have my way.

I formed four companies of twenty-four men each— three companies of Marines and one of sailors. The Marines were the cream of the Corps and the sailors were a splendid crowd. They had been serving with the Marines for two months and from them had learned a lot of the tricks of bush warfare. They were even wearing Marine uniforms. And they'd stopped shooting each other as they had at Vera Cruz and later in Port-au-Prince; also, they had no senior "know it all" naval officer playing soldier.

The next day—November 16—I stationed two companies of Marines at the Main trail between Grande Riviere and Bahon, the company of sailors at Dondon, and a third company of Marines at San Rafael. The orders to the company commanders were to start up the three trails in time to reach positions as close to the fort as possible by seven-thirty in the morning. The men were to remain under cover until I gave the signal to charge.

That night I spent with the company at San Rafael. The Captain was W. W. Low. I had been an usher at his wedding. He was afterwards killed during the Santo Domingo revolution. The lieutenants were John Marston and George Stowell. Marston has long been my close friend and associate. He has the knack of doing everything well.

The San Rafael trail was rough and poorly marked. It was a slow, difficult climb in the dark. I trudged along in the lead, stumbling over stones and hoisting myself up rocky ledges. As the ascent became steeper a private dashed to my side. "Man sick in the rear, sir." I halted the column until the private reported that the man could now go on. This happened several times. It was exasperating, but a sick man couldn't be left behind on the trail.

Later, I said to the captain, "Who was that sick man who kept holding us up?"

It was Stowell, the second lieutenant. He wasn't sick, but the good old chap was so fat that he had to stop every few minutes to get a second wind.

As we were climbing through the woods at dawn, we met several women with gay bandanna turbans coming down the trail from the fort. This was a pretty definite indication that the Cacos had seen us and intended to put up a fight, since they always sent their women away before a battle.

At seven in the morning we stopped near the edge of the woods. We were close to the top now. Between the woods and the fort, which was about one hundred feet higher, the slope was covered with rocks and provided no shelter from a single bush or tree.

It was a nasty job to tackle. The fort, two hundred feet square, with bastions at the corners, towered threatening and uncompromising above us. The walls, following the contour of the ground, varied in height from fifteen to thirty feet. The original loopholes were blocked up, but the embrasures indenting the rim of the walls offered perfect lookouts from which to riddle an invading force. The fort looked deserted, but I was familiar with the native trick of seeming invisible and I was taking no chances in advancing recklessly.

It had been agreed that if the other companies could not advance to the attack because of the steepness of the ascent, they were to lie flat in their positions and fire on the fort to occupy the attention of the defenders.

At seven-thirty I blew my whistle. The other companies answered the signal to let me know they were in position, but I saw at once that they couldn't advance because the approach from the other three sides was almost perpendicular.

There were twenty-seven of us—three officers and twenty-four picked men who lived for a good scrap and were tough customers for an enemy to fool with. I knew we could take the fort.

I detailed Marston, who was in charge of our two machine-guns, to follow us, as we leaped from rock to rock. I told him to shoot every native head that appeared above the wall. Then I divided the company and one-half advanced, while the other half fired to protect the forward movement. Marston remained among the rocks about a hundred yards from the fort and with the steady cracking of his machine-guns, he kept the bandits down inside the fort.

I was with the section of the company that made the final rush. The last spurt up the rocks was exciting. The Caco bullets rattled all around us. When we reached the wall, we discovered that the original entrance—the old sally-port—had been closed with stones and brick.

Cautiously we skirted the walls to look for an opening. On our side of the fort we found the Caco entrance—a drain four feet high and three feet wide extending back for fifteen feet into the interior.

Stowell, the fat lieutenant, poked his head into the dark passage. Bang, came a bullet. Stowell fell back and rolled over and over like a rubber ball down the mountain. I thought at first, he had been shot, but he was merely startled by the prompt reply to his curiosity and lost his footing.

The opening to the drain was partially blocked by a brick ledge behind which a native rifleman had been lying. At our approach he jumped up and fled, half-turning to send stray shots through the tunnel without bothering to take accurate aim.

We were flattened against the wall so that the Caco defenders couldn't shoot down on us without exposing themselves to the fire of Marston's machine-guns. We were quite safe where we were, but we couldn't remain in that position forever.

I was sticking tight as glue to the wall one side of the drain opening. Across from me on the other side of the drain was Sergeant Iams, with my orderly Samuel Gross next to him.

I knew that the only way to get into the fort was through that hole. I it was who had brought the crowd up there. I it was who had bragged how easy it would be to take the fort. So now it was up to me to lead the procession. A stream of bullets was crashing through the passage. I simply didn't have the courage to poke my head into the drain, although I might have worked myself up to the infernal plunge, if I had been given time—a long time.

I had never experienced a keener desire to be someplace else. I was writhing inside with indecision. I glanced across at Iams. My misery and an unconscious, helpless pleading must have been written all over my face.

Iams took one look at me and then said, "Oh, hell, I'm going through."

Before I could stop him, he had jumped into the hole. Gross was a gallant little fellow. I tried to follow, but Gross shoved ahead of me and beat me to it. I was third in the single file that started to crawl through the drain.

The big bandit who had bolted from the opening when we first arrived, now fired right into our faces from the inner end of the passage. I was all right, but I was certain that Iams or Gross must have been hit.

"Hurt, boys?" I called out anxiously.

"No, we're O. K., Major," they chorused.

We were almost completely blocking the hole. It seemed incredible that the rebel's bullet should have gone wild.

Iams was creeping forward with his rifle across his chest, pulling the trigger with his left thumb without daring to take time to bring the gun to his shoulder.

Before the guard at the hole could reload and fire again, Iams pushed through the opening and shot him. He was a brawny Negro giant, stripped to the waist, with prize-fighter's muscles. He reeled, flung up his arms and fell back dead.

Gross and I, close at Iams' heels, emerged into the fort. Sixty or seventy half-naked madmen, howling and leaping, pounced down on us. Gross and Iams killed the two leaders, who were cheering their men forward. At the same time a strapping Negro made a frenzied rush for me. I fired at him with my automatic but missed. Just as he was bringing down a heavy club on my head, Gross aimed his rifle and finished him.

It seemed an eternity that we three were alone in this den of wild Cacos, but it probably wasn't more than a few seconds before the rest of the company began to pop out of the hole like corks out of bottles.

Cacos and Marines scrambled together. The bandits in their panic reverted to the primitive. They threw away their loaded guns and grabbed swords and clubs, rocks and bricks, which were no match for bullets and bayonets. Those who were not killed jumped over the ramparts and were taken prisoners. The other three companies now began hopping over the wall and helped us to haul out the natives who were hiding in the casements and vaults.

The rebel commander, Josefette, at one time a cabinet officer, was killed in the fighting. I can still see him, sprawled out on the ground in his high hat and frock coat, with a big brass watch chain across his waistcoat. He was a pathetic picture.

The fight within the fort lasted only fifteen minutes. The futile efforts of the natives to oppose trained white soldiers impressed me as tragic. As soon as they lost their heads, they picked up useless, aboriginal weapons. If they had only realized the advantage of their position, they could have shot us like rats as we crawled one by one, out of the drain.

Fort Riviere, the last stronghold of the Cacos, was now in our hands.

When we started back, after we had cleaned out the fort, we old Marines were tired, too doggone tired to want to celebrate our victory with anything but sleep. As for me, I was worn ragged, and became suddenly aware of my badly swollen ankle which I had sprained on the climb and forgotten in the excitement. From ten o'clock the night of November 17 until we returned to San Rafael, fifty four hours later, we were continually on the jump. We had covered nearly sixty miles on foot up and down those blasted mountains.

At San Rafael, where we rested for a day, we assured the peaceful natives that they could return to work on their farms without fear of being molested by the bandits. The Caco power was broken, and the revolution was over.

When President Dartiguenave had first heard that I was leading an expedition against Riviere, he had sent me word that he would give me the finest horse in the West Indies if I captured the fort. I now telegraphed him: "Have captured Fort Riviere. Where is my horse?"

He presented me with a magnificent silvery-tan horse, a high-bred stallion, named Dessalines after the famous old Haitian who massacred the pioneer French residents and made himself emperor of the country. Dessalines used to carry me fifty miles a day over the mountains without sweating. He had only one fault. He would throw his stifle joint. I think the rascal did it purposely whenever he wanted a two weeks' vacation. Dessalines, now twenty-one years old, is still on the cavalry farm in Haiti playing polo.

The three of us, Iams, Gross and I, were each given the Congressional Medal for the Fort Riviere stunt. Iams came up through the ranks and was commissioned during the World War. He is now a captain of Marines. As for Gross, shortly after his gallant action at Fort Riviere, he developed epilepsy. When the attacks became more frequent he was sent to a veterans' hospital. I lost track of him for twelve years.

In 1930 I was speaking in Coatesville, Pennsylvania. I was telling my audience, some of whom were from the big veterans' hospital near the town, that a sergeant and a private of Marines had taken all the risk in the capture of Fort Riviere and that I always wondered what had become of the private. After the talk who should come on the stage with his hospital attendant but little Gross. He was partially paralyzed and looked very ill. The attendant had not even known that Gross had won a Medal of Honor. I gave Gross my button.

Chapter XVIII

High Jinks in Haiti

IN DECEMBER 1915, I WENT DOWN TO Port-au-Prince to organize the gendarmerie. After the American intervention the Haitian army with its three hundred generals and a thousand or so privates was disbanded, and Haiti agreed to establish a native constabulary with an officer of the United States Marine Corps as commander in chief.

I had just been raised to a lieutenant colonel in the Corps, but my new position as commander of the Haitian gendarmerie carried with it the imposing rank of major general. The colonels of the gendarmerie were captains in the Marine Corps; the majors were first lieutenants; the captains, second lieutenants; the first lieutenants, top sergeants.

It's not easy to build up an efficient organization out of a population speaking a language you don't know and with customs you don't understand. But Colonel Waller, with his usual generosity, contributed the pick of the Marines.

I have never found their equal anywhere in the United States service. Many of them soon learned to speak Creole fluently with their men and they worked like Trojans to lick the gendarmerie into shape. One hundred and twenty Marines were detailed to officer a force of twenty-six hundred Haitians.

The native gendarmes were good soldiers, too. Their most difficult job was to learn to keep shoes on their enormous feet. Out on the trail they often slung their shoes over the muzzles of their rifles. But they wore their footgear with pride, when they had an audience, and walked with a swagger, those black soldiers. With shoes and buttons shining and hats cocked over one eye, they strutted along the street and basked in the admiring glances of strapping Negro women.

A few months after the new treaty between Haiti and the United States was ratified in February 1916, the gendarmerie was sufficiently drilled and disciplined to take over the whole policing of the republic.

Article Ten of the treaty provided for the creation and maintenance of the Haitian gendarmerie under American officers, but I had gone ahead with the work of organization even before the treaty was formally adopted.

We struggled over the gendarmerie agreement for three months. The Haitians wanted the gendarmerie under their control. Since we were to be responsible for the police force, we naturally wanted it under our control.

Dartiguenave, the President of Haiti, had a dizzy time trying both to please us and his political adherents. At last he sanctioned our plan—anyway, he pretended to approve. We sent a copy to our Department of State, since the document was to be signed at Washington. But Dartiguenave, as I soon learned, was sending his Minister in Washington instructions contrary to his promise to me. The Department of State notified me that the Haitian Minister refused to sign the agreement.

I had come to have a great liking for Dartiguenave. I knew he was an old rogue, but only in politics, not in his personal associations. He was about sixty years old, mulatto in coloring, and when he lifted his great bulk around, he looked like a good-natured hippo. He had unfailing dignity and the urbanity and education of a cultured white man. Dartiguenave would talk to me in French and I would answer in English. Usually we understood each other, but if our conversation was important we had an interpreter.

When I learned that the gendarmerie contract was held up in Washington, I got in touch with Dartiguenave. He told me to come to the palace early in the morning—about half past five—before his colleagues appeared on the scene and he would cable his minister to accept the agreement.

I wrote a long cablegram in English and together we translated it into French. The President insisted on sending it in code. His code man was right at his elbow. I suspected some monkey business, and I sent one of my lieutenants to the cable office to bribe an employee to give him the code cipher and a copy of the code message.

The President and I had written three hundred words. In the code message, there were four. Translated, they read:

"Butler put pressure on me. Have him relieved at once and ordered back to the United States."

I stormed back to the President's office.

"Does this represent the cable we wrote?" I demanded, waving the paper at him.

"Mais oui."

"It does not. This is what it says," and I read him the deciphered message.

"Oh, a terrible mistake. My code man has deceived me."

"Then dismiss him."

"I can't. He has seventeen children. But I'll straighten everything out, General. It's a great, a very great mistake." The old reprobate tore at his hair in anguish.

In a short time, my lieutenant brought me a copy of the second cable that had been dispatched.

It said: "Butler knows I sent the other message. Be careful not to have him detached at once."

I pushed this under the President's nose. He could see that I was rapidly losing my patience.

"Oh, again it is a mistake," he said, throwing up his hands in melodramatic despair. "I can trust nobody."

"If that's the case, Mr. President, let's go down ourselves and send the message in straight French."

Most amiably he urged me to do it myself. I filed the original message and then waited at the cable office to see what would happen next. In fifteen minutes an aide from the President bustled in and filed another message. I secured a copy.

This time the President had cabled: "Pay no attention to message just sent. Butler made me do it."

I streaked back to the President. "Did you send this?" He collapsed in his chair. In a mournful tone, half surrender and half resignation, he suggested, "Let's start all over, General."

After much pulling and tugging, the agreement was signed. Dartiguenave told me that he had intended to stand by me in the beginning, but his Minister of Foreign Relations raised a frightful rumpus and forced him to send the code messages.

Shortly after the ratification of the treaty, the question of revising the Haitian constitution came up. Several provisions in the new treaty with the United States conflicted with the old constitution. In addition, no foreigner could hold land in Haiti unless he was a citizen of Haiti and he couldn't be a citizen unless he married a Haitian. That ruled us out.

Our government submitted the rough draft of a constitution which would be consistent with the treaty. The President and his cabinet pretended to approve it but in the meantime the Chamber of Deputies and the Senate framed a constitution of their own in which they ignored the gendarmerie arrangement and restated the prohibition against the alien ownership of land.

The American Minister, A. Bailly-Blanchard,* sent me an urgent summons to come to his house one morning. I found Admiral Anderson and Colonel Cole, my regimental commander, in conference with him. Bailly-Blanchard read me a cable he had just received from the State Department, which said that the proposed constitution was unfriendly to us and that we could not approve it. He was requested to take measures to prevent its passage.

*Arthur Bailly-Blanchard (1855-1925), American ambassador to Haiti 1914-1921. Butler's description of the Yankee diplomat is accurate. He was a popular, dapper, well-connected 'Man about Town' type and a master negotiator.

Following image: Bailly-Blanchard in 1920.

"Something must be done about this at once," Cole observed. "But Anderson is a naval officer and I'm a Marine officer in the American service. We can't butt in. You're the only one who can act, Butler. You're a Haitian officer."

The National Assembly was holding a hot session. The deputies were so hostile to what they regarded as American interference and dictation that they were stumbling all over themselves to push through the three required readings of the objectionable constitution at one setting and pass it over our heads.

When I returned from the American Minister's, the Minister of Finance, Dr. Edmund Hereaux, called on me with the Minister of the Interior, Monsieur

Cham. Dr. Hereaux was a scholar and a gentleman. He was friendly to the Americans and well-liked by his own people.

"The National Assembly will pass their constitution by noon," Dr. Hereaux hastened to inform me. "And at one o'clock they will proceed to impeach the President on the ground that he has violated the existing constitution. They want to get him out of the way because he is friendly to Americans."

I can hear Hereaux yet: "The President, he do not want to be impeached. He said to me: "You tell General Butler to take the gendarmerie and dissolve the National Assembly"

The three of us hurried to the palace. We were streaking up the steps three at a time to the President's private apartment on the second floor, when his aide, very dazzling in bright red trousers, a poisonous green coat and shining high boots stopped us importantly. "The President is very sick."

The door of His Excellency's bedroom was slightly open. I knew he was listening. I pushed my foot into the crack and looked in. The President was flattened against the door.

"I am very sick," he said mournfully, quickly clasping his head.

"Maybe you are, but we have work to do here," I warned him. "In two hours that constitution will be passed unless you break up the legislature."

"I have no influence," he cried, wringing his hands. "They are all against me. You do it."

"I can't do anything unless you give me a written order," I insisted.

Finally, he agreed to dissolve the assembly if I could bring all the cabinet ministers to him. The cabinet consisted of the President and five members. Two were already present. One member, I knew, was in Cape Haitien, two hundred miles away. The President was stalling for time. He wanted something done, but he wanted me to be the goat.

Finally, the President said, "If you get the other two members who are here in Port-au-Prince I will sign."

I went out on the balcony and called to my chauffeur, Haitian Corporal Ducatrel, waiting below, to collect the two cabinet ministers. In a few minutes he returned. He was driving with one hand and with the other he was clutching the neck of a lively minister struggling to jump out of the Ford. He was very fat and very black and a little ridiculous with his brass-headed cane, bursting tight cutaway and silk hat several sizes too small. But he had a vote and we needed him. In less than a half hour my chauffeur returned with the other gentleman of the cabinet, who had been hiding in a stable.

I had directed a Marine officer to take fifty gendarmes to the assembly and watch the proceedings. He kept telephoning me the latest bulletins from the law-making front. Every time I was called out to the telephone I locked the door behind me to prevent the timid cabinet from vanishing.

Finally, the Marine officer was urgent. "They've passed three hundred and twenty out of the three hundred and sixty articles. They are shoving them through ten at a time. It will be all over in a half hour unless you do something at once."

I rushed back to the state bedroom where the President and his four cabinet members were pacing up and down uneasily. They were still hoping they could wriggle out of committing themselves in black and white. I told the President what was happening in the assembly. He had to act now without delay. The Haitian cabinet was sweating blood. They were all holding their heads at the thought of facing the indignation of their political associates. But without a word they put their names to the decree dissolving their congress. Their signatures were so small that one needed a magnifying glass to read them.

"Mr. President," I said, "according to your procedure, a cabinet minister must read this to the assembly."

"None of the cabinet would dare face the delegates with this decree," he replied. "You'll have to take it."

The minute I appeared in the door of the legislative chamber, I was greeted with loud and prolonged hissing. The gendarmes out of loyalty for me began cocking their rifles. They were a little bewildered when I ordered them to put down their arms, because under previous regimes, soldiers went to the National Assembly with the expectation of shooting somebody.

Through an interpreter I announced that I had a message from the President. More hissing. More banging of rifles. I handed the decree to the presiding officer. But instead of reading it he launched into a tirade of abuse against me and all Americans.

The hall was in an uproar. Tables and chairs were upset, deputies were shouting and surging forward. I had to calm down the gendarmes who were clicking their rifles again. Finally, the presiding officer rang the dinner bell he used for a gavel and reluctantly read the presidential decree. He then declared that the assembly was dissolved and directed that the chamber be cleared. The gendarmes followed the unwilling legislators into the street and locked the door.

On the way out of the hall, the presiding officer came toward me. He was waving the decree wildly, too upset to know what he was doing.

"General, I'm angry," he remarked to me.

"You're not as angry as you're going to be before you get any more government money," I retorted.

As he brushed past me, I grabbed the fluttering, loosely held paper and put it in my pocket. That document is now in the files of the United States Senate.

After I left Haiti President Dartiguenave wrote a long memorial, calling upon President Harding to remove the Marines and liberate the Haitian people. He accused me of dissolving the national government without authority and by force of arms. The memorial, published widely, stirred up a hell of a commotion and put me in the limelight as the principal witness.

Our Senate—this happened in 1921—appointed an investigating committee of which Senator Medill McCormick of Illinois was chairman. A lawyer representing the National Association for the Advancement of Colored People asked me upon what authority I had dissolved the Haitian congress.

"The President himself dissolved the Congress," I answered. "I merely carried his decree of dissolution to the assembly."

My opponents tried to prove that the President's message existed only in my imagination. I goaded them on into such a ridiculous position that the strength of their case rested solely on the existence of the paper.

Finally, I said, "Mr. Chairman, here it is."

Even then the Haitian witnesses claimed that my document was a forgery, but I made them compare the signatures with others by the same men accepted as genuine. The Haitians had to admit that the signatures were identical.

"Mr. Chairman," I said, "I should like to read you the last paragraph of this document: 'Therefore, in order to encourage agriculture and to stabilize the currency, I, Philippe Sudre Dartiguenave, President of the Republic of Haiti, do hereby dissolve the assembly of Haiti.' "

Senator McCormick simply collapsed with mirth. "I can't stand it any longer," he said. "That's good, to encourage agriculture!"

The old presiding officer was at the hearing. When I told how I had taken the paper out of his hand, his expression said plainly, "So that's where the damned thing went." In his excitement over the breaking up of the assembly he had never known how the paper disappeared.

I heard that with Dartiguenave's memorial also came a confidential letter to President Harding in which the Haitian President urged that no attention be paid to the memorial—it was a political gesture—and for God's sake not to take the Marines out of Haiti.

The morning after the dissolution of the National Assembly, a Haitian attached to the gendarmerie, a most intelligent fellow educated in England, came into my office. He was employed under the treaty as official interpreter and he wrote all my French letters. At a later date he achieved high office in Haiti, in fact is a perennial presidential candidate.

"Now that the assembly is dissolved, its legislative functions have been taken over by the President and his cabinet," my Haitian friend explained. "The President has two votes, each of the five cabinet members, one. Those seven votes are required to put through any legislation. Well, the Minister of Education and Cults has just resigned. We can't pass any laws until we get a new cabinet officer."

"Do you know a good man for the job?" I asked.

"I do not. The cabinet is most unpopular just now. The Minister of Education resigned because insults were hurled at him in a cafe last night for his part in dissolving the legislature."

I told him to find somebody for the vacant cabinet seat. In a couple of hours, he walked into the office with a comic supplement. He was wearing a shiny frock coat at least thirty years old, grey striped trousers, tan shoes and a red necktie. He was proudly sporting yellow gloves, an old-fashioned stove-pipe hat and a gold-headed cane. He looked for all the world like one of Primrose and West's minstrels.

"This is the new Minister of Education and Cults."

"I'm glad to meet him. What's his name?"

"Paul."

"Every cabinet minister must have two names. What's his last name?"

"I don't know."

"Can't you ask him?"

The interpreter asked. The new Minister of Education and Cults emitted some guttural sounds.

"What language is this?" I asked.

"That's Creole. He can't speak French. He's never been educated."

"Well, what's his name?"

"I can't quite make out."

"Tell him to write it."

"He can't write."

"I must say this is a fine fellow to have for the Minister of Education and Cults."

"He's the best we can get, General. No one else will take the job. And we must have him for the votes."

"But are you sure he wants it?" I asked.

"Oh, yes, and he's very popular with the people. It will be a fine appointment and help create good feeling between the Haitians and the Americans."

"All right, but for God's sake, get his name."

Together they worked out the name phonetically and wrote down the nearest approximation to the unintelligible gutturals.

"You're sure he wants to serve?" I repeated.

"I'll tell him he gets five hundred a month. Watch him."

Paul's mouth just watered and he nodded his head emphatically. According to my Haitian friend he had never had more than ten dollars at a time in his life.

"He wants to be sworn in this minute," said my Haitian employee.

"Fine. What do we do next?"

"The proper procedure is to present him to the President, so that the President can appoint him."

My Haitian assistant had a most attractive personality with a rare sense of humor. He was enjoying the new minister as hugely as I was.

"Yes, indeed," he chuckled. "We must present Paul to the President. He ought to know his own cabinet minister."

"I think Colonel Cole should know the new cabinet officer, too," I said, as we started out in my little Ford.

At Marine headquarters I found Cole in an anxious mood.

"We're having great difficulty, Butler," he complained. "We have no quorum in the cabinet. The Minister of Education and Cults has resigned."

"Oh, that's all fixed up. I have a new minister outside."

My Haitian friend brought in our Primrose and West minstrel and introduced him with great formality. Cole spouted an eloquent speech in his best Naval Academy French. Minister Paul looked dazed and blinked rapidly. Cole turned to me.

"What's the matter with him? What did I say?"

"That's just what the new minister is wondering."

"What's wrong?"

"He can't speak French."

"What's his name?"

"Paul."

"Paul what?"

"Where the hell is that piece of paper?" I asked my interpreter. He and Paul had to retire to figure out the name again. Cole was puzzled by these antics.

"You say he is a good man?"

"An excellent man. He'll make a splendid minister." The three of us escorted Minister Paul to the palace. The President was very busy. He was standing in his reception room surrounded by the senators and other officials who had lost their jobs the day before. The perspiration was streaming down his face as he tried to explain what had happened. We waited in the bedroom until the President came with the appointment papers, which he handed to Paul. The inevitable sweet champagne without ice was brought in. We drank to the President of the United States, the President of Haiti and the new Minister of Education and Cults.

After these formal ceremonies were concluded I said to Cole, "We might leave these two great statesmen together. This is their political honeymoon, as it were."

We went downstairs, engrossed in a discussion of the Haitian situation. As Cole stepped into his car he stumbled over a pair of legs. It was the new cabinet minister whom we thought we had left in conference with the President. He had managed to make his escape ahead of us. "Here, Butler, you take him."

We bundled him into my little Ford.

I asked my interpreter to tell the Minister of Education and Cults: "We are sorry we can't give you the permanent use of this car, but we'll take you where you wish to go now." And I asked the interpreter to suggest that the minister return soon to the palace and remind him that the cabinet was to meet at one thirty.

Paul didn't want to go back to the palace.

"Doesn't he care to take part in the affairs of state?"

"No, he says he has nothing in common with the President."

"Well, where would he like to go now?"

"To the paymaster's office. He wants to draw a half day's pay."

Paul lasted two weeks. One day I asked my Haitian subordinate where he had unearthed the Minister of Education and Cults.

"That rascal was my barber. He had been owing me fifty dollars for five years. The only way I could get it out of him was to put him in the cabinet."

Commanding the gendarmerie required versatility. My duties seemed to include everything from filling a cabinet vacancy to buying and equipping a navy.

The new Haitian-American treaty provided for a coast guard to patrol the coast and prevent smuggling. At our request the Navy Department purchased four deep-sea going sailboats with auxiliary engines and sent them down to Haiti. The ships were rechristened the Republic, the Independence, the Liberté and the Haiti. The Navy Department lent us American sailors until Haitians could be trained to man the ships. Unfortunately, only two or three of the bluejackets had had actual experience before the mast.

The Republic was the first of the tiny fleet with masts hoisted, ready for her initial cruise. We decided to send her on a two weeks' trip around the coast, with stops at every little port so that the taxpayers might see their infant navy.

One summer afternoon in 1916 the President and his cabinet followed by the national band and half of Port-au-Prince paraded to the navy yard to give the Republic a brilliant send-off. The commander of the ship was a chief boatswain in the United States Navy, an accomplished sailor named Norcutt. The Republic shoved gaily off from the dock on her maiden voyage with the band playing and everybody cheering. Early next morning she was due at the little port of St. Marc, about sixty-five miles away.

When I received no report from the ship by ten o'clock the next morning I was alarmed. I called up the gendarmerie posts along the coast, but the Republic had not been sighted.

That night Norcutt telephoned me. He said that they had sailed comfortably along the coast the preceding night. In the morning when he was eating breakfast the engineer, an American sailor, burst into his cabin and yelled that the ship was on fire. It seemed that there was something wrong with the carburetor, and the fool engineer had struck a match to examine it.

Norcutt and the crew scarcely had time to jump overboard. They swam three miles to the beach, then walked fifteen miles in their bare feet through the brambles to the nearest telephone. The ship went down in three hundred feet of water. And that was the end of the Republic.

It was now my painful duty to inform the President of this great naval disaster. At the palace I found the President in session with his cabinet.

"Mr. President," I said, "I very much regret to announce that a terrible catastrophe has overtaken our navy." And I related what had happened.

The President, Dr. Hereaux and another minister who spoke English burst into loud roars of laughter. I thought perhaps they were laughing in derision at our incompetence to run a navy.

"What's the joke, Dr. Hereaux?" I asked.

"Oh," he said, "Haiti's last navy cost more than half a million dollars and so far, this one has cost only thirty-five thousand. We are happy to get off so cheaply."

And Dr. Hereaux proceeded to tell me the story of the first Haitian navy.

Several years before, fifty thousand dollars was appropriated to send a commission to Europe to buy a navy. In six months the gentlemen on the commission needed an additional twenty-five thousand to continue their search. At the end of the year they reported that they had found a fine battleship. It was an old wooden frigate in the Austrian* navy. It had no engines, but the handsome antique guns looked most effective. The commission recommended its acquisition for the reasonable sum of four hundred thousand dollars. The purchase was approved. The commission bought the old tub and then sent their home government an estimate for fifty thousand dollars to hire a special crew to bring the frigate to Haiti. This extra sum was promptly sent to Europe. The obsolete Austrian battleship, equipped with pianos and stocked with good wines, took four months to reach Haiti. In this time the commission contrived to run up additional expenses amounting to forty thousand dollars.

*Austria's navy branched-off in the 1850s from the massive Kriegsmarine or navy of the Austro-Hungarian empire. The Imperial and Royal War Navy or Kaiserlich und Königlich in German was known as the K.u.K or Kuk Kriegsmarine.

Following image: Kuk Maria Theresia, c.1898-1900.

The old frigate, with all sails set, was very impressive and picturesque as it floated into the harbor of Port-au-Prince. It captured the imagination and enthusiasm of the Haitians. The Austrian crew was notified that Haitian admirals and captains would now be appointed to take over the management of their own navy. The Austrians had no desire to relinquish their soft jobs, with parties every night and liquor flowing abundantly. They took the frigate out in the bay, loaded the guns and threatened to destroy the city. The Haitian government appealed to a British man of war anchored at Port-au-Prince to capture the ship and put the mutinous Austrians on the beach. It cost Haiti fifty thousand dollars to hire a tramp steamer to take the Austrian crew back to Europe.

For two or three years the Haitian navy lay tied to the dock, and the Haitian admirals displayed their brilliant uniforms at the many state receptions held on board. Finally, the President ordered his navy to set sail and put down a revolution which had broken out in north Haiti. More than three quarters of a million dollars had been spent on the frigate and he was determined to use it, even though the revolution was in the mountains. The cruise of the frigate was brief. The ship, in running on a sand bar in the harbor, gashed a big hole in its hull. There the old wreck remained, blocking the channel, a menace to navigation. The government after some years paid twenty-five thousand dollars to have its navy removed.

"So, you see," explained Hereaux, "we have reason to laugh. This wreck cost thirty-five thousand dollars instead of three quarters of a million. We don't even have to spend money for dredging. I congratulate you on getting rid of the ship at such little cost."

The cabinet ministers probably wondered how expensive the rest of their navy would be before it, too, was destroyed, but the other three ships were trimly put in shape and were soon sailing proudly around the coast.

In the winter of 1917 the President urged me to take a cruise around the island to inspect lighthouses. Colonel Percy Archer and Major John Marston went with me on the Independence, the largest of the remaining ships.

On the second day out, we sailed along the Bay of Gonaives past numerous little inlets which had been used by the pirates of the Spanish Main to hide their booty. The ship was speeding quietly on its course under a steady breeze. It was a hot afternoon. Drowsy and tranquil after a good dinner, I lay reading in my cabin. Archer and Marston were lounging in steamer chairs on deck.

Through the hatch I heard Marston say to Archer, "Percy, you don't care much for this cruising, do you?"

"No, I don't."

"I love the sea. I come by it naturally. One of my ancestors was a lieutenant of Captain Kidd. There's pirate blood in me. I like to feel the waves crashing over the decks."

I fell asleep listening to Marston's rhapsody. I was awakened by a pitching and tossing, a groaning and creaking that sounded as if our little ship was going to tear apart. We were caught in a frightful storm in the Windward Passage between Haiti and Cuba. I poked my head out of my cabin door in time to see the pirate's descendant limply dragging himself down the ladder. He was green, woebegone and too sick to lift his head. Water poured down the hatch and the waves swept mountain high over the deck. We were blown way out to sea. We begged Marston for the honor of Captain Kidd's ghost, to come on deck and save us. He was in no mood to be teased.

About midnight the wind changed and we made for shore, where we spent two or three days mending our sails. When we started out again, a strong gale immediately tore away the sails once more. We had to return to shore and put out under gasoline. It took us ten days to accomplish the two hundred miles to Cape Haitien, where Archer and Marston deserted and traveled home by land. "Captain Kidd," in spite of his great love for the sea, decided that he preferred mule-back on mountain roads to a life on the ocean wave.

The Haitian navy gradually disappeared from the scene. One time when the Liberté was rounding the southern point of the island it ran aground and split in two. The Independence valiantly cruised around for three or four years until it had the misfortune to blow up at the dock in Guantanamo, Cuba. The last of the fleet, the Haiti, was finally sold. Once more Haiti had no navy and no heavy responsibilities on the high seas.

Chapter XIX

On Tour with the President of Haiti

THE BIG MARINE EVENT IN THE FALL OF 1916 was the dinner celebrating Waller's promotion to the rank of brigadier general. Four of us officers living on the mountain slope above Port-au-Prince planned to stage the dinner on the terrace among the poinsettias, orange trees and palms. But it began to rain, and we had to take our garden party indoors. There were fifty guests—the President with the Cabinet and other high dignitaries of Haiti and our own American officers and representatives.

We spread ourselves to prepare a gala evening. We wanted to show special honor to good old Waller, our commanding officer in Haiti, to whom we were all devoted. We arranged to have a brigadier general's salute of eleven guns fired from the fort by the gendarmerie, and a flag with a brigadier general's star was to float down over Waller as the salute boomed out.

It was almost midnight before the first gun went off. Everybody leaped to attention. The flag floated slowly down and the band broke into "Hail to the Chief." After an interminable period, another gun boomed, and we all stiffened to salute. Another long wait. A third gun. Then dead silence.

Three guns in the middle of the night is the old Haitian signal that a revolution has broken out. The good people in Port-au-Prince were on the verge of nervous prostration. I hurried down to the fort to find out what had become of our salute. The powder, it appeared, had been dampened by the rain, and the soldiers were warming it in frying pans between each gun.

"Well, warm up enough powder for all the guns and finish the salute in proper style," I ordered.

They managed to send off two more guns and then the firing stopped for good. But by the time five guns had been fired, however, everybody was the worse for wear. No one could remember how many guns belonged to a brigadier general, anyway.

A corporal, who had been a bartender before he became a Marine, was vigorously shaking cocktails, which were being passed around in large tin cups. The President of Haiti was juggling a cigar between his lips while he held a glass of champagne in one hand and a glass of beer in the other. Bailly-Blanchard, the American Minister, a fine old fellow, who before he came to Haiti had been so long at the American Embassy in Paris that he talked English with a French accent, was circulating happily among the guests. Clutching his silk hat and his highball under one arm he shook hands with democratic warmth. When he put on his hat, the highball poured down his face in slapstick movie style.

A colonel of Marines became chummy with the corporal bartender, who was reciting "The Face on the Barroom Floor."

"This man is a military genius! What is his rank?" the colonel asked me.

When I told him, he said earnestly, "That's an outrage. He ought to be a captain. Do something for him."

They went off arm in arm to a corner, where the corporal tried to teach the colonel "Gunga Din."

The popular 1890 poem about an Indian soldier by Rudyard Kipling

A certain unpopular naval officer who had not been invited to the celebration wrote a letter reporting the dinner as a disgraceful affair, accompanied by firing which alarmed the whole city. The State Department referred the letter to General Waller, who by that time had left Haiti and was on duty in the United States. He said that he was the guest of honor at the dinner which had been given by the gendarmerie.

The complaint was then sent to me and I was ordered to make an explanation. My good friend the Haitian President wrote to the American government that the gendarmerie was under his command, that the dinner was given by his direction and that he was solely responsible for it. The State Department may have thought it had me trapped, but it was mistaken.

The next social event on the Marine calendar was the gendarmerie ball, which we gave for the naval officers when the fleet under the command of Admiral Mayo came to Haiti during the winter. We borrowed the new presidential palace, which was in process of construction, took the roof off the gendarmerie barracks and laid it in the unfinished ballroom as a floor for the dance.

Mrs. Butler received the guests with the President, who was a delightful host. All the attractive girls in Haiti were invited to the ball. When the American officers came in, they shied a little from the dusky belles; but, as the evening wore on, their shyness entirely wore off. At three o'clock in the morning it was almost impossible to break up the ball. None of the Navy wanted to go home. The courtyard of the new palace presented a strange spectacle in the glaring and telltale light of a Haitian day. Fifteen officers in full-dress uniforms were sprawling in a row on the grass and snoring like a trombone band. For a long time, everything in Haiti dated from the gendarmerie ball.

The Minister of the Interior was one of the guests. His colleagues found it difficult to work with him. The day after the ball, Doctor Hereaux informed me: "The Minister of the Interior no longer a member of the Cabinet. The President have dismiss him."

"What did he do?"

"The President say he is too immoral to be in the Cabinet."

"But what did he do?"

"At the ball he was found with a woman on the roof, one say."

"Well, was he?"

"No, but they say he was."

"What sort of nonsense is this?" I asked.

"The President say he was found there. In our country, if the President say anything is so, then it is truth."

The Minister was dismissed, but to placate him, the Cabinet had him made President of the National Assembly.

Through our close association over a period of almost two years, I formed a very genuine affection for President Dartiguenave. I knew he was an old political crook. I remember one of his expenditures from the government treasury, a sixteen hundred dollar payment to have the hole in a carpet mended. But in spite of his weakness for the public funds—a weakness which he shared with many American politicians—I liked him just the same. He was hospitable and warm-hearted and went to endless trouble to do a kindness for a friend.

Before Dartiguenave became President, he sat in the Haitian Senate for sixteen years without once returning to his home town in the south. He was afraid to make the trip. In the old days when Haitian politicians attained an official position in Port-au-Prince they stayed in the capital, where they felt comparatively secure.

Now that the Cacos had all been subdued in the north, Dartiguenave began to experience pangs of homesickness. He asked me in the spring of 1917, to accompany him to his native town, about sixty miles along the coast.

I borrowed the big navy tug for this sentimental voyage. The Cabinet in high silk hats and a crowd of distinguished citizens in cutaways came to the dock to present their bon voyage compliments to the President. Into the tug piled His Excellency, the Minister of the Interior, the President's brother, his brother's wife, their two corpulent daughters and the President's aides—colorful colored gentlemen in red coats, green trousers, black boots and French field marshal caps.

As soon as we shoved off, the gendarmerie band which was perched in the bow played the Haitian anthem and swung into a lively medley on the brasses. The music seemed to stimulate the Haitian appetites; for almost immediately the food began to circulate. It was mostly sardines—hundreds of cans of sardines—with crackers and melted butter in tins, all washed down in gallons of warm sweet champagne.

For the first twenty miles, in the lee of Gonave Island, the water was as smooth as glass. Except for the champagne, we might have been a Sunday school picnic floating tranquilly down the Potomac. Then the tug poked her nose into the open sea and began to pitch with a vengeance. The gay holiday mood of the crowded little deck changed swiftly and dramatically. Everybody was seasick.

The President's sister-in-law, an enormous colored woman, turned almost white in her misery. The President's brother in a galloping forward movement of the tug slid down the deck to me.

"The President's sister-in-law, she is verray seek," he said.

He never referred to the lady as his wife, always as "the President's sister-in-law."

"She must be removed from the public gaze. We must put her in a room."

"All right. Put her in one."

"The General must help me."

Since I was being paid two hundred and fifty dollars a month extra for being a Haitian general, I decided that it was my duty to be neighborly. We picked her up, but she was like a loose bag of meal. Puffing and snorting, we lifted her through the nearest door, which happened to lead into the paint locker. We laid her on the table where the paints were mixed. The little hole was stuffy and smelly. I beat it. Husband and wife should commune alone in such a disaster, I thought. I had hardly recovered my breath when friend husband was back again, anxiously pulling at my arm.

"The President's sister-in-law, she is still verray seek. We must remove her stays."

"All right, remove 'em."

"She is too beeg. Alone I cannot."

"That's too bad. But I'm not going to help you take off your wife's corsets. Enough is enough."

God knows the job of being a Haitian general had plenty of queer slants to it, but I drew the line at this intimate domestic service.

The lurching tug, carrying the seasick government of Haiti, finally reached the President's native port. A crazy little boat bobbed over the waves toward us. A coal-black man in frock coat and high silk hat was standing in the middle of the boat, vigorously gesturing with one hand and holding in the other a long scroll from which he was sputtering Creole. The swell from the tug rocked the boat, and he fell overboard, silk hat first. A couple of bluejackets hauled the gasping, half-drowned ebony gentleman on the tug. One of the President's aides told me the dripping elocutionist was the Mayor, presenting his speech of welcome.

The Mayor's official barge was a dugout with an outboard motor. At the prow was erected a huge "Vive Dartiguenave" sign, which made the boat top-heavy. The President refused to get into our own big motor sailor. His fellow townsmen had honored him, he said, by sending out this boat, and he was determined to go ashore in it. Moreover, he implored me to go with him.

Although I thought it was suicidal to venture in the open roadstead in the flimsy shell, I climbed in with two of the aides.

We reached the dock without mishap. A tremendous crowd greeted us with a typical movie welcome. Every fifty yards was an arch where we had to stop and shake hands with a delegation of prominent citizens and school children. The thermometer was rapidly rising beyond the hundred mark, and perspiration was rolling in rivers down my neck. It took us three hours to navigate through the town and drag ourselves up a steep hill to a red house with yellow shutters—temporarily converted into the official guest residence.

Sticky and unwashed, we had to change immediately into our best uniforms and go to church. In Haiti, the church was particularly favored as a pleasant place to murder a president. I was the general of the gendarmerie and it was my job to stick close to the President and see that he wasn't assassinated. High mass in America is one thing, but in a Haitian church with a thousand natives on a hot day—well, that's something else. And the services lasted until dark.

At the guest house we were regaled with a typical Haitian banquet, heaping portions of terrible food, washed down with native rum and warm champagne. After spending the evening bowing and scraping, shaking hands with local politicians and patting children on the head, I was ready for any kind of bed. But there appeared to be a shortage of beds.

The President and I ended by sharing a bedroom. He insisted on my taking the one bed, and he piled some mattresses on the floor for himself. I should go straight to sleep, he said. He was going downstairs to talk to his old friends.

In a little while the door opened. In came the President, wearing a straw hat on the back of his head and a long cotton nightshirt, fastened tight around the neck with a drawstring. He was carrying a tray with the usual warm champagne, sardines and crackers. He made me drink two quarts of champagne and kept urging me to eat more sardines. There we sat until one o'clock—I in my pajamas and the President of Haiti, very big and black in his white nightshirt, munching that pernicious midnight snack. I was deucedly ill afterwards, but His Excellency lay down on the floor and snored like a hippo.

I spent most of my time between official duties in hunting around the house for water to wash my face and hands. It was as scarce as diamonds. On the evening of the second sizzling hot day I was desperate. I took aside the new Minister of Foreign Relations, Louis Borno, who subsequently became president after Dartiguenave.

"Look here, Mr. Borno. I've got to have a bath. Isn't there some place in this town where I can find a little water?"

"Ah, a fine idea. I think all the party should have a bath. I shall arrange it."

The next morning, clad in bathrobe and slippers and carrying a towel, I went downstairs, where I found the President and his aides in nightshirts and silk hats, already assembled at the door. The procession formed, and the bath brigade started down the hill into the village. All the townspeople collected to cheer the President on the way to his bath. We had to stop and shake hands with everybody. It took a half hour to go a half mile.

Suddenly the President broke away from his admirers and turned into a cabinet-maker's shop. In single file we followed him through the shop into the backyard, which was half filled with a concrete contraption eight feet square and three feet high. Some steps led to a narrow wooden door in the high wooden fence inclosing the structure. The concrete platform was indented with a hollow, six feet square. This was the tub, which contained about two feet of water.

"Where does this water come from, Mr. Borno?" I asked.

"It was carried from the creek with great labor and prepared especially for the President."

"You first, General," said the President.

"No, it is fitting that the President bathe first."

"No, no, you first," he urged.

The President's party looked on with great interest while I undressed, plunged into the water and soaped myself. I was no sooner out than the whole crowd threw off their nightshirts and jumped into the tub together. Being the commanding general of the gendarmerie had given me one valuable privilege—the first chance at the bath water.

That night a leading citizen gave a dance for us in his ballroom, which was about twenty feet square. Part of the gendarmerie band was squeezed into one end of the room. Everybody in town who was not invited jammed around the house to look through the windows, which were all closed. The guests lined up against the wall and watched me open the ball with the President's sister-in-law, who didn't weigh an ounce less than two hundred pounds. Circulating in Haitian society was also part of the job of successfully directing the gendarmerie.

The next day we were leaving. Although the sea was kicking up angry, frothing whitecaps, the President, unwilling to offend the home folks, insisted on returning to the tug in the suicidal dugout. The President and his two fat nieces sat forward, I sat in the stern and the Minister of the Interior sat back to back with me, dangling his feet over the water.

We made feverish efforts to get close to the guardrail of the tug, but the two boats were see-sawing up and down beside each other in the heavy sea. In one of these passes the guard-rail hit the "Vive Dartiguenave" sign, and over we went.

The President of the Republic had to be saved, at all events. Clutching the guard-rail with one hand I grabbed him by the neck and held fast to him until the crew of the tug could hoist him on board. While I was occupied in rescuing the government, one of the fat government nieces let out an unearthly shriek and pounced on me from the rear. I was hanging desperately on the rail, and she was hanging on me, clawing my back and screaming at the top of her lungs. The sailors in the tug, laughing to split their sides, reached down with a hook and lifted off the champion female heavyweight. We were all hauled on board, but it was one of those cases where the Marines had not landed and did not have the situation well in hand.

The next time the President and I went traveling, I invited him on a tour to inspect the new road we were building over the mountains. The gendarmerie had charge of the building and repairing of roads. The Haitian customs, which were under American control, guaranteed us for this purpose ten thousand dollars a month—not a large sum, considering that there wasn't a mile of decent road in Haiti. I started the construction of a five hundred mile road system so that the Haitians could simplify their transportation problem and travel easily by automobile. I thought if the President could see what we were doing, he would offer a contribution to the work from the government funds. Incidentally, I wanted to show our government at home that the Haitians appreciated our efforts sufficiently to volunteer some assistance, even if only a small amount.

We set out on one of the yachts of the Haitian navy for Gonaives, an overnight trip. The gendarmes all turned out in the morning to meet the ship, holding a great parade and fancy drill in honor of the President.

We had sent two automobiles to Gonaives, a Ford roadster and a truck. The President sat beside me in the roadster and his Cabinet followed behind us in the truck. The back of the Ford was filled with ice and champagne to drink toasts to the new road. Before we had gone twenty-five miles the ice melted. As usual we drank the champagne warm.

As we traveled in state along the road, all the workmen, who had been carefully coached beforehand, lined up to present their picks and shovels, just as soldiers present arms. The President was greatly impressed by the pick and shovel drill, especially with a quart of champagne inside of him. He promised to give me four thousand dollars. I had some champagne inside me, too, and on the strength of that I agreed to finish the road in six weeks and take him on a trip across Haiti.

Back in Port-au-Prince in a more sober and frugal mood, the President hated to part with the money. But he kept his promise and therefore I kept mine. The mountain road was finished by January 1, 1918. Every time a new road was opened, I took His Excellency out in great style— whizzing along in a Ford, waving an enormous Haitian flag and carrying the President's coat of arms. He always displayed a lively enthusiasm for the roads, which he felt would be a lasting benefit to his country.

Before I left Haiti, I built four hundred and seventy miles of road. Under Haitian law the people who lived along a road had to work on it or pay a tax. I found that they were willing to work if they could have their voodoo dances on Saturday nights. Although the voodoo dances had been prohibited, I permitted them to carry on with their drums and snake symbols and closed my eyes to the Saturday jamborees.

Voodoo practices were so deeply woven into the island customs and superstitions that it was almost impossible to enforce regulations against them, anyway, unless flagrant violations were brought into the open. The natives maintained great secrecy about everything connected with voodoo and shielded their voodoo priests, out of fear, if for no other reason. Although the educated people of Haiti scoffed at voodooism, I observed that they all crossed themselves when they went into a voodoo temple. Even the President was afraid of voodooism. He never failed to make some sign when we passed a voodoo priest's house, which was always marked with certain recognizable symbols.

Once voodoo threw its shadow across my threshold. As soon as peace was definitely achieved in Haiti, Mrs. Butler came with the three children. We lived on the terraced mountain slope above Port-au-Prince in a big comfortable house with wide verandas and a pleasant, shaded garden. My daughter Ethel—we still called her "Snooks"—was about ten then, a little girl with long yellow pigtails. She could chatter French and Creole like a native. Tom Dick, the youngest, talked Creole as soon as he did English.

Antoine, the Caco ape man who had remained with me ever since my first trip into the mountains in pursuit of the rebels, was the children's faithful slave. Whenever I had to go away on an inspection trip, Antoine guarded the whole family. He slept on a couch on the front porch and refused to move until I returned. The servants even had to bring him his food. Antoine always rode on his pony behind Snooks and Smedley Junior when they left in the morning for the French school which they attended with the native children.

One day Mrs. Butler telephoned to me at gendarmerie headquarters that Antoine was on the rampage. She said he had tied a harmless looking Haitian to a tree in our back garden and was cocking and uncocking his rifle. Sam our butler told her that Antoine was going to shoot the man and in Sam's opinion the man ought to be shot.

"Tell them to postpone the execution until I get there," I advised my wife.

I took as interpreter, my Haitian friend, the secretary of the gendarmerie, and streaked up to the house. We arrived just as Antoine was announcing in Creole: "Five minutes more and I'll shoot you." His victim, shouting and begging, wriggled helplessly against the tree.

After the secretary finished his investigation he said shortly, "The man deserves to be shot."

The children, I was told, had met this Haitian on the way back from school. As Snooks rode past him, he had reached up and pinched her little bare leg. Antoine had immediately bolted after the Haitian, knocked him senseless, thrown him over the pommel of his saddle and then tied him to the tree in our garden.

"But that's not reason enough for shooting a man," I said.

The secretary went on to explain that the act had a sinister voodoo meaning. The Haitian, gaudily dressed and saturated with perfumes, was a voodoo representative. By pinching Snooks' leg, he marked her for an indescribable death. The supposition was that she would be whisked away by voodoo spirits and meet a horrible end. The natives understood all this mumbo jumbo. Unless severe measures were taken, the secretary said, Snooks would have to be guarded constantly.

We carted the man off to headquarters. The Haitians didn't have my inclination to consider the crime of little importance. They sentenced the voodoo expert to life imprisonment.

Except for this incident, none of the family was annoyed in Haiti. As for me, I traveled all over Haiti without a gun, after the first Caco uprisings were stamped out. I was, and have been ever since, very fond of the Haitian people, and it was my ambition to make Haiti a first-class black man's country. I felt a definite and personal responsibility for its development because of my position at the head of the gendarmerie. We built a network of telegraph lines as well as roads. Under the direction of the gendarmerie we established a postal service and a country school system and restored and put in shape the lighthouses and channel buoys. In short, we launched a program of rejuvenation for the country, which was hopelessly run down as a result of revolutions, which had occurred almost annually for twenty-five years.

I was enthusiastic about my work in Haiti, but my thoughts were persistently with the Marines who had gone overseas. From the time the United States entered the World War I had been steadily and unceasingly making applications to be transferred to duty in France. All my applications were denied. It was a set of false teeth and not the Navy Department that finally brought me back to the United States, in March 1918. I had to come home to get some bridge work done.

Sailing into New York I had my first glimpse of the war—a camouflaged transport loaded with five thousand men pulling out to sea. I felt that I belonged with them, on my way to the front.

I shivered with the cold in New York and, after three years in the tropics, I found myself without an overcoat. I put on the only warm clothing I had—a light yellow flannel uniform that had once been made as a sample for test purposes. It blended with my complexion, which had turned a dark tan under the Haitian sun.

In the smoking compartment of the train going to Philadelphia the man opposite kept eyeing me closely. Finally, he offered me a cigar and asked, "What nationality are you?"

I just laughed.

"Well," he persisted, "what army do you belong to, anyway?"

"The Haitian army."

He turned to his companion. "I told you he wasn't a white man."

As soon as possible, I began my scrap to get to France I prevailed on the Navy Department to detach me from Haitian service. But I didn't go to France. I was sent to the Marine base established when we entered the war at Quantico, Virginia, on the Potomac, thirty miles south of Washington.

CHAPTER XX

Fighting the Mud at Brest

AT QUANTICO, WHICH WAS THEN LITTLE MORE THAN a filthy swamp, I set to work to train a regiment of raw but willing Marines for the front. I'll never forget my dismal and sickening sense of futility as I stood on the station platform and watched my men pulling out for France without me.

I was at outs with Marine headquarters because I opposed elevating the Commandant of the Corps to the rank of lieutenant general so long as the soldiers were getting no extra reward for doing the heavy work in the trenches. For this honest expression of opinion, headquarters decided that I could stay home.

It was a tough break, but I swallowed my disappointment and started to train another regiment—the Thirteenth. Josephus Daniels, Jr., joined this regiment and literally dragged us overseas. Both Secretary and Mrs. Daniels felt that Josephus should go to the front. It would never do for the son of the Secretary of the Navy to stay in the United States. So, it was not my military record but young Josephus Daniels that finally got me to France.

It was about this time that I came to know and appreciate Mr. Daniels. He was a great and courageous public official and one of the two real Secretaries of the Navy during my third of a century of contact with the Navy Department. Our Secretaries have generally been figureheads, run entirely by Admirals, but not so with Josephus Daniels—he was boss of the Navy and had enough brains to know what it was all about.

Thirteen, my lucky number, had turned up again. I nicknamed the Thirteenth Marines the Hoodoo Regiment and obtained thirteen black cats for mascots. We left Quantico on Friday the thirteenth in seven train sections, each with thirteen cars. I sat in seat thirteen in the parlor car. Thirteen had never betrayed me before. I was confident that we were headed straight for the front.

When we were two days out at sea, the "flu" hit us. There were twelve hundred cases in the regiment and more than one hundred deaths before we reached France. Some of my favorite officers died. I was sick, too.

We landed at Brest September 24, 1918. I stood on the bridge of the lighter that was to take us ashore and looked down on the men. Their white, drawn faces were pitiful. As we were casting off I called out, "Do you suppose you could sing?"

With that, the whole crowd burst into "Sweet Adeline." In the early morning quiet of the harbor, the singing echoed and re-echoed around the docks. The crews of two of our transports anchored nearby poured out of the fire rooms and lined the rails to cheer us as we went in. The only time I ever witnessed a similar demonstration was during the fighting at Vera Cruz. When the First Regiment of Marines went ashore, the entire British fleet, commanded by Admiral Craddock, cheered our men as they rowed past in their small boats.

We marched up the hill to Camp Pontanezen, where American troops wallowed in ooze until they were moved up the line, and we were assigned two choice residential plots of mud. Acres and acres of mud flats with dripping, dejected khaki-colored tents. Beyond, a cheerless steel sea half hidden in fog. Shivering cold, bleak, death-stricken: a hell of a place.

Spinal meningitis had broken out among my men, and we were all quarantined within the mud walls bounding our section. We had no shelter except the pup tents we carried on our backs. We didn't have enough firewood for cooking and had no wood at all to keep us warm. The continuous, steady downpour turned our mud plots into ponds. Every evening I assembled my three thousand Marines for a song fest. I was the world's worst choral leader, but I succeeded in keeping up the spirits of the regiment.

Locked in the mud with no place to go and nothing to do, we waited day after day for orders to move into the fighting zone. Finally, at the end of two weeks, I received a telegram stating that General Pershing had assigned me to the command of Camp Pontanezen.

I was promoted to be a brigadier general and at the same time was handed this wretched job at Brest, which was as far from the Front as it was possible for me to be without jumping into the ocean.

For twenty years I had worked hard to prepare myself for a big war which I felt would come during my lifetime. It nearly broke my heart that I wasn't allowed to go to the front. To sit in the rear and run this dirty mudhole was the first in a series of jolts that finally destroyed my enthusiasm for soldiering. Since then, a number of experiences have proved to me that opportunities are almost always given in the United States service to men with political or personal influence. A man's record is rarely considered.

The Army antagonism toward the Marines contributed, naturally, to my failure to reach the front. Although ninety-seven per cent of my men were expert riflemen and sharpshooters, troops that hardly knew which end of the gun to shoot were sent to the trenches. My crack regiment was broken up and distributed to do manual labor and guard duty.

I always felt that the command at Brest was wished on me because it was a lemon. The camp had been a disgrace ever since the A. E. F. first landed at Brest, and when the influenza epidemic swept over France it became a pest trap. One officer after another had been put in command and gone his way without effecting any improvement. The camp had been mismanaged with gross incompetency. When the people at home found out about conditions at Brest there was bound to be a national scandal. Undoubtedly, those in charge of operations overseas preferred a Marine to shoulder the blame rather than one of their own officers. But I will say that in the whole thirty-three years of my service, I have never been so well treated, even by my own Corps, as I was by the Army during the period of construction and when my job was done. The Army commanders acknowledged their debt to me in papers of appreciation and awarded me their distinguished service medal— the Navy did, also—for my work at Brest. They were good enough to say that by my reorganization and administration of the camp, I had pulled them out of a mean predicament. All the same, cleaning up a concentration camp was not soldiering. The job could have been handled by any enterprising hotel-keeper or circus manager.

Of course, Brest was a disagreeable anti-climax to my years of active campaigning, but I was deeply stirred by the plight of our boys who were dumped in that mud-hole on their arrival in France. I rolled up my sleeves and dug in, determined to make it as decent and comfortable a place as possible.

There were, at that moment, sixty-five thousand men in the camp. You can imagine the mess and confusion with twelve thousand cases of influenza and no doctors in many of the outfits.

I took command at two o'clock in the afternoon. At four o'clock the base headquarters in Brest telephoned that the Leviathan had just come in with ten thousand men on board. Four thousand had the "flu," and I was to put them in the camp hospital. We had a small collection of buildings called a hospital, already filled to its capacity of two hundred and fifty—and twelve thousand men were lying sick in the mud.

Our total transportation that day amounted to nine trucks and two horse-drawn ambulances. With these I was expected to carry four thousand helpless men the four miles from the docks to the camp.

My first act as camp commander was to release my own regiment from quarantine and send it down to the docks. Between five in the afternoon and midnight the regiment made two round trips and carried all the sick men on improvised stretchers to the camp. My Navy friends on the destroyers in the harbor contributed thousands of blankets and tents. We repaired all the old French rolling kitchens and started to feed everybody. For two days and nights my regiment went along the rows of desperately sick men, giving them hot soup and coffee and warm blankets wherever they happened to be lying. We made roaring bonfires out of wood for which we had to pay seventy-five dollars a cord. I waded through acres of mud, running from group to group to speed the work and to encourage the invalids.

Our regimental band of sixty pieces was a knockout. It was composed of Italians, musical to the fingertips, who had been recruited and trained by a band leader, whose name was Felix Ferdinando. His father had been leader of the Royal Band of Italy. Felix, in addition to being a highly gifted leader, had the guts of a real soldier. He marched his Italians up and down the hill day and night. They played, until their drums were soggy, to give courage to those poor devils flattened out by the epidemic. I soon had more than thirty regimental bands in different sections of the camp, playing jazz, one-steps, stirring military marches, in continuous shifts. The doughboys, miserable as they were, were soon shuffling their feet in the mud to keep time to the lively airs.

The day I took command we had two hundred and fifty deaths. I selected the medical officer of my regiment, Captain Chambers of the Navy Medical Corps, to take control of the situation. Hardly stopping to eat or sleep, he threw himself heart and soul into the fight against the epidemic. In two weeks his skill and energetic drive proved so effective that the deaths were negligible.

Camp Pontanezen occupied a historic site. The old Pontanezen barracks had been used by Napoleon's troops, but they accommodated only fifteen hundred, and sixty thousand doughboys couldn't rest their bones on history— and mud.

I wanted spacious tents with floors and comfortable beds. I planned to erect a semi-permanent camp and run it like a big hotel. Down at the docks were vast storehouses filled with all sorts of supplies that we needed, but I realized I'd have to pull wires with a vengeance to get them.

General James G. Harbord, commander of the Services of Supply at Tours and his competent chief of the quartermaster division, Henry Smithers, shoved aside the cumbersome machinery for making requisitions to rush me the materials to build the camp.

General Harbord was one of the greatest officers and soldiers, if not the greatest, our country has had since the Civil War. If he had been a West Point graduate he would undoubtedly have been appointed Chief of Staff of the Army. Harbord was broad-minded and able—a man who wanted results and had the courage to shoulder the responsibility for the necessary disregard of regulations. After serving under him a few days I discovered that he would back me in everything that would relieve the suffering of the soldiers. I broke regulations all the time, and Harbord approved my acts. When I ran one million dollars ahead of my ration allowance because I was feeding the troops in camp four and five times a day, the quartermaster department stirred up a mighty battle of words on paper. I appealed to Harbord, who said firmly, "Keep on feeding 'em." I never enjoyed service under anybody as much as I did under that man.

My immediate superior was General Eli A. Helmick, commander of Base Section No. 5, which extended up and down the coast on both sides of Brest. Helmick, like his life-long friend, Harbord, was a man of courage and initiative who saw things in a big way. The two of them stood by me in recon-structing the camp.

Piled in the warehouses were eighty thousand sections of duckboard, made to be laid on the bottom of trenches. I wanted them for sidewalks, so the men wouldn't have to wade through the eternal mud.

I submitted request after request for the material, but in this particular case even Harbord and Smithers didn't seem able to cut the red tape that had frozen our system to a standstill. The old-time army quartermaster in charge of the warehouses was afraid he would be court-martialed at the end of the war if a duckboard was missing.

Finally, I got sick and tired of waiting. Helmick was away, so that I was temporarily in command of that section of France. One afternoon I marched down to the docks with seven thousand men and burst into the warehouses. As long as we were invading the sacred premises, I thought we might as well make a clean sweep. We needed shovels, axes, picks and kettles as well as duckboards.

Late in the afternoon the strangest column that ever marched through France trudged along on its way up the hill. Some of the men heaped pots and pans on the duckboards and carried them like stretchers. Others thrust the handles of picks and shovels between the rungs of the duckboards, which they lifted over their shoulders. I snatched a pick and shovel, and, ordering my automobile to follow slowly, fell in at the rear of the column.

A half mile from the docks the road passed under a railroad culvert. A soldier was leaning against the wall with his duckboard beside him.

"What's the matter?" I asked. "Can't you carry your duckboard?"

In the dark, with a drizzling mist of rain, the boy didn't recognize me as an officer.

"I'm no damned pack mule," he sputtered. "I enlisted to fight, not to carry chicken coops. I'll be damned if I will."

"You're perfectly right. It's an outrage to make you do this. How old are you?"

He was a Michigan boy—age, twenty-one; height, six feet one; weight, one hundred and ninety pounds.

"Well, I'm nearly forty and weigh only one hundred and forty, but I'll give you a hand," I told him.

I shouldered his duckboard and my pick and shovel and stumbled for-ward, bent nearly double under the unaccustomed load. I looked back, and my soldier was still propped against the culvert.

"You enlisted to march, anyway, didn't you?" I said. "I agree that you are a free born American citizen, as you say, but I hope it's not unreasonable to expect you to walk. Soldiers have to walk, you know."

He had no idea who I was and didn't give a damn, but, grumbling and protesting, he fell into step beside me. As we started up the hill, several soldiers who knew me gathered around us and guyed the life out of the boy for letting a general carry his pack. He begged me to give the duckboard back to him.

"I should say not," I refused firmly. "You're not strong enough." This brought loud cheers and horse laughs from the crowd.

Duckboards were piled in front of every little bouvet on the road up the long hill. I would separate the soldiers from the cognac, restore them to their duckboards and climb on. I was pretty tired myself when I came to a heap of duckboards almost blocking the entrance of the last estaminet near the top of the hill. Staggering under my load, I walked into the bar. I had no mark on my blouse to indicate my rank. A husky private, very red and noisy, was reaching out his hand for another glass.

"What the hell are you doing here?" I demanded sternly.

"What the hell is it to you?" he bellowed, gulping down his drink.

"Butler's not far away. You'd better beat it," I warned him. He came out with twenty doughboys at his heels.

At the entrance to the camp one of my own M. P.'s was on guard. I was marching in the light of my automobile, which was crawling behind me. The M. P. jerked me roughly by the arm.

"Here, soldier, you're blocking traffic. Get t'ell out of the road and let the General's car go by."

"That's my car."

"How do you get that way? Who the devil are you? If that's your car, why don't you ride in it? Get down in the ditch and let that car by or I'll show you who you are." Just then the sergeant chauffeur, stopping the automobile, leaned toward me and said, "Well, General, what do we do now?"

"I don't know, sergeant. I seem to be arrested."

When I was in the wash-house the next morning, the privates splashing in the row of basins on the other side of the tin partition were discussing the duckboard episode. I heard one of them say, "I'll be damned if any goddam shrimp of a general can carry up more duckboards than I can."

All day long streams of enthusiastic volunteers swarmed down to the docks to fetch duckboards. Everybody at the camp became duckboard-conscious. The men painted duckboards on the trucks, duckboards on rosettes decorating the horses' harnesses. General Pershing authorized us to wear a white duckboard on a red background as a shoulder mark. Some clever newspapermen in the Eighth Infantry brought out a newspaper called The Duckboard. I was called 'General Duckboard.' From now on I could do anything with the men. When a back-breaking job had to be pushed through quickly all I needed to say was "Come on you, birds," and the soldiers ate up the work like gluttons. As one private expressed the morale and spirit of the camp, "I'd cross hell on a slat if Butler gave the word." That duckboard story built the camp.

Those who don't like statistics can skip this part, but I think a few figures will give punch to a picture of what was the largest A. E. F. camp in France. Remember, we started with nothing but mud. Before we finished, the camp, built in 15 sections, each holding 7,000 men, covered 1,700 acres. There were 100 cooks in each of our 15 kitchens, each of which could feed 7,500 men an hour. In our warm, comfortable tents we had 106,000 bunks, with mattresses, sheets, pillow cases and blankets. We burned 250 cords of wood a day in 11,500 stoves. We had 75 miles of boardwalks, 35 miles of stovepipes, 15 electric light plants and a water system which provided 3,000,000 gallons a day. We could give baths and fresh clothing to 4,000 men an hour. We had a big delousing plant, 2 laundries and 32 steam sterilizers. We used to sterilize 200,000 blankets a day. The original 9 trucks were increased to 900. We had hospitals, sewers and paved streets.

When the Armistice came, we had to reverse our machinery. Brest, America's great port of entry, became a mammoth evacuation camp. Our organization was running so smoothly that we could make any number of changes in personnel daily. On our biggest day we had 38,000 changes. Twenty-six thousand men were put aboard ships, 2,000 men came off ships and 10,000 men arrived from the line. Every man was deloused, bathed, freshly dressed and equipped within twenty hours.

Fifteen thousand army troops were stationed permanently at the camp to facilitate the movements of the incoming and outgoing soldiers. It required fourteen hundred clerks at headquarters just to take care of the records. I have never worked with a more splendid group than the three hundred and sixty men on my staff. Lieutenant Ray A. Robinson, "Torchy" to me, and Josephus Daniels, Jr., who was one of my aides, and I were the only Marines. The others were all Army officers.

One machine gun battalion of Marines stationed at Pontanezen lived across the road from my shack. Major Hal Turnage who commanded them, who has always been one of my ideal American fighting men, served through Haiti with my outfit. Of course, I loved Torchy and Joe like sons, but I want to pay a justly deserved tribute to some Army officers whose friendship I gathered at that time and who made the camp a success. Colonel Morris M. Keck; commanding the fine old 8th Infantry; Colonel A. H. Holderness, my Chief of Staff, and Colonel Louis Sherer, second in Command, both cavalrymen, stood by me in affectionate readiness to carry out my every wish and spare me all the knocks. God made all these lovable and able friends and has since taken away dear old "Dutchy" Sherer. There were many others who did great work, in fact, there was not a bum on that staff. I have never known their equals and without them there would have been no camp.

The first time General Pershing came to the camp, he seemed determined to find fault and I fully expected to be relieved of my command. He left without saying goodbye to me, although he made a point of shaking hands most ceremoniously with the orderly. During 1919 Pershing visited us every month. On one occasion, to impress him with the efficiency of our kitchens, we fed eleven thousand, two hundred and fifty men and four hundred and fifty officers from one kitchen in forty-nine minutes.

We were continually annoyed by all kinds of inspectors, mostly G.H.Q. colonels wearing spurs and using Brest, even though out of the way, as an excuse to visit Paris. A refrigerator colonel, distressed to find our men cutting the meat with axes, recommended that we put stoves in our refrigerator to melt the meat. A guardhouse colonel discovered that our guardhouses were damp—in a place where it rained ninety-five per cent of the time. After earnestly advising weather stripping, he went blithely on his way to Paris. A drainage colonel gloomily surveyed the camp from a dry position on a board, so that he wouldn't ruin his clean spurs, and then informed me that mud was entirely a matter of drainage.

When these pests returned to G.H.Q. at Chaumont, they reported my levity and contempt for authority. I had no patience with them. It was irritating to be bothered by such a pack when my men were working twenty-four hours a day, week in and week out. General Harbord appreciated the situation and finally arranged that we were not to be disturbed except by real staff officers who came to help us.

One day Mary Roberts Rinehart, armed with credentials from the Secretary of War, appeared in a pouring rain. Not only is she one of the most attractive and fascinating women I've ever met, but she has brains and the understanding of a man of big caliber. She put on rubber boots and a raincoat and tramped all over the camp. She crawled into tents, ate our meals, poked into everything and asked sensible questions. Her report to the War Department went a long way toward stopping the abuse that had been heaped on us.

My old friend Secretary Daniels also came to Brest. He ate in the kitchens, talked to the men and lived in one of their tents. After three or four days of intensive inspection he cabled President Wilson a highly appreciative endorsement of the camp.

General Helmick at one time inspected the camp without my knowledge. Ignorant of his visit, I went on a tour of inspection a few minutes after he left. I found one of my youngsters looking very dejected. He was a lieutenant of engineers running one of the big kitchens.

"What's the matter, my boy? You act as if you'd lost your last friend."

"General Helmick was just here, sir, and bawled me out for not saving the meat bones to make suet."

Helmick had stormed through the kitchens, sharply finding fault because the cooks were not boiling the bones to make suet. The kitchens were each feeding four or five meals a day to six thousand men. It was all the cooks could do to prepare the food and keep the kitchens spotlessly clean without trying to salvage the bones. I was furious. I got the Chief of Staff on the telephone.

Right here I want to take off my hat to Colonel Asa L. Singleton, this Chief of Staff. He was not only a thoroughly equipped soldier man but a human being. Has no superiors that I have met.

"If the General has any complaint with the camp," I said, "tell him to pick on me and not on a young lieutenant who is doing his level best."

The Chief of Staff tried to calm me down, but the next time I saw General Helmick, I brought up the subject. I thought he was a little hard-boiled in his attitude. I finally worked myself up into such a state over the suet that I asked to be detached. The Chief of Staff called me up to tell me that the General was very much worried and asked me to withdraw my application.

An hour later Helmick came into my office. "What's this all about, anyway?"

Without any preliminaries we went into the battle of the suet. I lost my temper, pounded on the desk and told Helmick what I thought of him for jumping on a boy. The General sat calmly in his chair and looked at me without a trace of annoyance.

When I had run down, as all hot-tempered people do, he said, "Now, Smedley, I'll talk. I've let you abuse me, your commander, for two reasons. First, because you've been of such tremendous value to my organization, and second, because I know I didn't do the right thing by that boy. I realize also that you've worked yourself into a state of nervous collapse to make the camp a success. I know you don't mean what you're saying. I never permit myself to be aroused by a tired man's utterances, when that tired man is a good man."

"General, by God, you are some Commander," I choked out.

Helmick never did things by halves. He insisted on going with me to the boy and he made a handsome apology before all the cooks and mess men in the kitchen. The youngsters running the kitchens had become embittered and indifferent. Helmick's generous act restored the morale of the camp. And Helmick taught me a lesson that I'll never forget. When a man snaps at me because he is tired from doing my work, I grin and take it.

Helmick and many other commanding officers in the A.E.F. sent me tributes for overcoming the difficulties at Brest and successfully building up a great evacuation camp. The soldiers who came through from the front appreciated our efforts to make them comfortable. Even now hundreds of ex-soldiers bob up in different parts of the country and speak to me in a friendly way about their experiences at Brest.

Before I left France, I spent two weeks visiting the battlefields. It was a curious experience for a soldier who had smelt his first gunpowder in the Spanish-American War.

On my return to Brest one midnight, I was met at the station by a group of the staff, headed by my able friend, Colonel A. H. Holderness of the cavalry. As we approached the camp the fire companies blew their sirens and a battery of big French guns sent off a brigadier general's salute. Near the shack where the headquarters staff lived, a great arch had been erected in my honor. The Red Cross girls of the camp had filled my room with flowers. Fifteen of the staff officers gave me a reception which lasted until three in the morning.

In August 1919, I sailed home with my brigade, which was mustered out at Norfolk.

After a few weeks' leave I was ordered to Quantico as second in command under General Lejeune, one of the outstanding soldiers of our time. He was appointed Commandant of the Marine Corps in 1920. He blocked every movement to reduce the Marine Corps to an inferior position, which would take away the little independence we enjoyed. The nine years of his service as Commandant are a superb record of his achievement for the Corps.

When General Lejeune left to take up his new duties in Washington I became the commander at Quantico. After the Armistice the temporary shacks were gradually replaced with permanent buildings. It was my ambition to convert a wartime camp into a beautiful Marine post. But it was difficult to secure appropriations. I had to use my twenty-five hundred Marines as carpenters and plumbers. I succeeded in arousing their enthusiasm so that I had the whole outfit working as day laborers at fever heat. We quarried rocks for building and even went into the Potomac to salvage piles and bolts from old shipways.

It was at this time that the Marines' most distinguished World War officer came to Quantico, —Captain Roy Hunt. His record for courage and ability has since been an inspiration to me as has his loyal and unselfish friendship.

Quantico's mascot was Jiggs, the bulldog celebrated in Marine circles. I purchased him in 1921 from the athletic funds, and he was the best bulldog money could buy. The idea of having a bulldog as a Marine mascot occurred to me during the war when the Germans called us Teufel Hunds—devil dogs.

Some of our new recruits did not live up to their name of devil dogs, however, when we were holding maneuvers in September 1921. We were having a three day sham battle reproducing the Civil War Battle of the Wilderness between Grant and Lee, where Grant said: "I propose to fight it out on this line if it takes all summer."

It took us two days to march the twenty-seven miles to Fredericksburg. On the third day we set out on a seventeen mile march toward the Wilderness. Leading my horse, I was walking at the head of a long column with Colonel Tommy Holcomb, my Chief of Staff and bosom friend of twenty-five years. We had gone ten miles when a motorcycle orderly streaked up to report that twenty men, complaining that it was too hot to march, had fallen out as we left the camp site.

I went back to the rear in the side car of the motorcycle. Lying under the trees were the twenty privates, eating ice-cream cones with some girls. I had no marks on my uniform to identify me. Besides a number of new men had been brought in from other posts for the maneuvers, and they did not all recognize me. I asked the smallest man why he had fallen out. He was all in. As a matter of fact, he hadn't even begun marching. I knew there was only one way to get the man moving.

"Give me your pack and your rifle and belt, and I'll carry them." His equipment in addition to my own totaled seventy-five pounds.

The whole crowd protested violently that they couldn't march.

"You're going to march this seventeen miles whether you like it or not. If I can do it, you can. Come on, let's go."

I formed them in a column and away we started. They looked very glum and sour, but I whistled unconcernedly and they were soon whistling and singing, too. We marched fifty minutes with ten minute rests, when I made them take off their shoes and air their feet. On the road ahead of us I saw men who had fallen out, nimbly jumping to their feet and running to catch up with the column. Word had gone out that the Old Man was marching the stragglers in.

By noon we had covered eight or nine miles, and I said it was time to eat. The privates had already eaten their lunches and drunk all their water. They sat down in the shade with me and watched me eat. One of the men who had been in Quantico only two days spoke up, "Are you an officer?"

"You've been obeying me as one, haven't you?"

"Yes, you act like an officer."

Another private chimed in, "Don't be a damned fool. That's the General."

"Gee, you ain't the General, are you?"

"Why don't you think so?"

"I never heard of a general carrying a knapsack. Generals don't march."

While we were discussing the walking peculiarities of generals, a party of distinguished guests from Washington drove up on their way to the camp. They stopped to ask the way. And where could they find General Butler? Was he at the head of the column?

"Sure," said one of the men in the car, "he'll be up there on a horse, while these boys have to walk."

"Sure," I agreed, "all the officers are up in front."

The privates looked as if they would burst. I thoroughly enjoyed the situation. After that we had a good time together. One of the boys said he couldn't march a step farther, and I dropped back with him.

"Where are you from?" I asked.

"Minnesota."

"Didn't you ever walk up there?"

"Yes, but I'm tired."

"Son, I'm more than twenty years older than you, but we're going to do this together."

We kept on. I was playing out myself, and my pack began to hurt. I was more than forty years old and the others were youngsters. The men competed with one another to take my pack away from me, but I refused to give it up. I wanted to show them that they could force themselves to do things that would be necessary in war.

When we reached camp after dark, I was worn out. I had to take restoratives for my heart, and my feet were so swollen that I couldn't wear shoes for several days. But in all the hikes we took later, the word passed around Quantico that there was no use trying to fall out. "The Old Man will make you hike." I never again had to prove my capacity to march with my men.

We staged any number of darned good maneuvers but they were diluted peace time battles, just play-acting after all. And garrison routine at Quantico year in and year out is not exactly exciting. I was itching for a scrap—action—something with snap to it.

Then out of a clear sky came the Philadelphia offer. Philadelphia opened up interesting possibilities—and a new type of war for a Marine.

Chapter XXI

A Devil Dog in the City of Brotherly Love

WHEN I WAS INVITED, URGED AND IMPLORED to serve as director of the Department of Public Safety of Philadelphia, I was innocent enough to believe that the administration intended to carry out its pledges to clean up the city—to wage ruthless war on crime and vice and to enforce prohibition.

Before I was handed my hat and shown the door, I knew better. I was hired as a smoke screen. The politicians were buying the reputation I had earned in twenty-six years' service as a Marine. I was to make a loud noise, put on a brass hat, stage parades, chase the bandits off the streets—and let vice and rum run their hidden course.

Philadelphia had been overrun with gangsters. Pickpockets, bootleggers, dope peddlers fearlessly plied their trades. Liquor places, gambling joints, white slave dumps, disorderly houses, were wide open. The boldest holdups were pulled off in broad daylight. The city was in the clutches of every form of lawlessness.

The good people of Philadelphia inaugurated one of their periodic reform waves. W. Freeland Kendrick was elected Mayor on a reform platform to clean up the city and make the streets safe for the people. That was a very popular campaign plank—to make the streets safe!

Kendrick announced in his campaign speeches that he would get a real live general to make the city safe—a general who could not be bought, bullied or bluffed—to divorce the police from crime and politics. When he was elected the newspapers clamored, "Where is your general?"

He looked over the available stock of generals. I was the only one eligible. None of the others was a resident of Pennsylvania, which was required of an appointee by law. Kendrick didn't know me. Undoubtedly, I was pictured as a white-haired, red-faced, side-whiskered old boy who would be docile and "reasonable" and grateful for my salary.

A friend of Kendrick's telephoned me at Quantico in November 1923, that the Mayor-elect wanted to see me. Since I was going to a football game in New York, I stopped off in Philadelphia on my way back. The meeting was arranged with considerable secrecy in a room at the Bellevue-Stratford Hotel. I was accompanied by my lifelong friend, General Cyrus Radford—the gentlest, finest character I have ever known. Kendrick enlarged on the crime conditions in Philadelphia, on the banditry that held sway and the poison liquor that was killing scores and wound up by offering me the post of Director of Public Safety.

I told him that I wasn't interested, that the organization controlling Philadelphia would never permit the police to be separated from politics. He continued to plead with me. I expressed the conviction that the two big political bosses of Philadelphia, Congressman William S. Vare and Charles B. Hall, President of City Council, would block any honest effort at reform. Kendrick suavely answered all my arguments. He displayed a sincere desire to have the mess cleaned up and complete confidence in my ability to handle the situation. He guaranteed that I would not be handicapped by any interference.

"Don't say no," he begged. "Think it over and write to me."

Several days later I wrote him that I would not resign my commission in the Marine Corps for any position. President Coolidge would have to be willing for me to accept the offer and grant me the necessary leave of absence. If Kendrick would give me a free hand in the conduct of the department, and the President approved, I would be willing to reorganize and command the police force of Philadelphia.

Thereupon, Kendrick, with a delegation of Pennsylvania politicians, including the two United States Senators and "Bill" Vare, descended upon President Coolidge to plead for my services. I was notified by the Secretary of the Navy that an application for one year's leave would be approved by the White House.

As soon as the President's consent was made public, attempts were made, even before I assumed office, to influence me in the selection of immediate subordinates. Mayor Kendrick pressed me to dismiss the Superintendent of Police, William B. Mills. I never regretted that I didn't act. Mills was an excellent police officer, a man I'm glad to include among my friends.

Then the big boss "Bill" Vare made an appointment to see me. He told me how eager he was to see me make good.

The corpulent Congressman leaned over mysteriously and half whispered in my ear that there was only one honest policeman in Philadelphia. He recommended his honest policeman, Lieutenant John J. Carlin, as Superintendent. I explained politely but firmly that I had no intention of removing the present Superintendent unless I had strong cause. Our meeting was amicable enough, but I never saw Vare again. As for Carlin, I soon demoted him and put him in the traffic division, having found him unfit to handle his station duties. After I left Philadelphia, he was exposed in connection with the graft scandals.

I was sworn in as Director on January 7, 1924. I already had some idea of what I was up against. In preliminary tours of the city, I found few policemen on the streets—a handful of fat lazy fellows, leaning against doorways and swinging their clubs while speakeasies, disorderly houses and gambling dives were openly breaking the law before their eyes.

I called the police force together and told them I was willing to forgive past indiscretions, but from now on loyalty, honesty and efficiency would be demanded. The police were ordered to clean up the city within forty-eight hours. "Clean up or get out" was the slogan. I knew it would be impossible to clean up the Philadelphia cesspool even with model police in that period, but I issued the order so that I might learn which police officers were loyal and would make an effort to carry out my instructions.

The war against crime and vice was on.

It was one continuous drive. Speakeasies, gambling dens, haunts of crooks and the underworld, all were raided. The police raided 480 places in the first week—more than had been visited in several months the previous year. But the police didn't believe I was really in earnest. They thought I was putting on a spectacular show to hoodwink the people. They soon began to let up on their activity.

I had to prove to them that I meant business. At all hours of the day and night I cruised through the tenderloin and made surprise visits at station houses. The lieutenant in charge would frequently tell me his district didn't need cleaning up. I would go outside and find half a dozen saloons operating within a block of the station house. I demoted and suspended many lieutenants, sergeants and policemen. I learned that the law unfortunately did not give me power to dismiss them.

The determined drive of my first month in office caused the underworld to sit up and take notice. There was a general exodus of crooks, gamblers and other undesirable citizens.

It did not take me long to realize that I could not remove the police from politics and control them as a disciplined army in the war against crime and vice without adopting heroic measures. The police districts had the same boundaries as the political sub-divisions—the wards. The police lieutenant in command of each district was under the thumb of the ward leader and took orders from him rather than from the Director of Public Safety. Of course, if the ward leader happened to be at outs with the administration in power, a police lieutenant "loyal" to the political machine was assigned to the district until the ward leader was forced to capitulate to the administration.

There were forty-two police stations. A careful study revealed that eighteen could be eliminated and save the city annually hundreds of thousands of dollars. I worked out a plan to divide up the districts so that each station covered two or more wards. Instead of one lieutenant, a captain and two lieutenants selected from different sections of the city and of different political affiliations were to be placed in charge of each station. This arrangement would prevent the possibility of control by the ward boss.

The announcement before the end of my first year that the redistricting plan would be put into effect immediately acted like a bomb shell. The ward politicians hated me before, but how they did hate me now!

"Can prohibition be enforced?" was the question I was asked most frequently during my stay in Philadelphia.

My work in Philadelphia made me a prohibitionist. In my time I have been a drinking man—not a "booze hound," but a moderate drinker who could take it or leave it. I awakened to the fact that disregard of one law would prove a real menace by breeding disrespect for all law. Moreover, I began to realize that liquor never did anyone much good and that it can be productive of definite harm. Liquor is undoubtedly at the root of ninety per cent of our crime today.

To enforce any unpopular law you must have, first of all, honest and conscientious public officials, honest police, vigorously directed, and interested courts and district attorneys, determined to mete out justice. Judge Harry S. McDevitt was the only Judge who stood squarely and unflinchingly by me.

In Philadelphia under my regime, the police raided three or four thousand speakeasies. In one year more than ten thousand liquor violators were arrested. But what happened? The grand juries returned less than two thousand true bills and of the whole ten thousand only three hundred were convicted.

In spite of this lack of cooperation, I persisted in the war. The political bosses grew savage when I descended upon saloons under their special patronage or those in which they had some financial interest. They tried in every underhand way to undermine and oust me, but I went blithely on. I conducted a campaign against the breweries and succeeded in padlocking the most flagrant offenders. The others were watched so closely that one by one they began to shut down. When I left Philadelphia, not a single illegal brewery was operating.

I had been appointed, presumably, to enforce the laws and I intended to enforce the laws without compromise, no matter how unpopular I became in the process or how many efforts were made to obstruct my efforts. Perhaps my direct, blunt methods were too drastic for Philadelphia.

From the beginning the newspapers ridiculed me. They published everything I did and ate and wore and elaborated on my talks with each policeman until they disgusted everybody with the columns and columns of over-publicity. They insisted on treating me like a queer animal from the circus. My chance remarks were twisted and distorted to paint me in the worst light.

Before I was dismissed from office, however, about fifty of the minor officials and correspondents of the newspapers became my loyal friends, but they had no influence in shaping the editorial point of view.

The Mayor had a versatile tongue and spouted eloquent orations from public platforms on his determination to carry out his campaign pledges for vigorous and impartial law enforcement. While he never interfered with me in small scraps, he never supported me in a real crisis. He dodged responsibility and sat on the fence, ready to jump either way. Law enforcement was all right so long as it did not annoy his political, social and financial friends. The

Mayor fairly bristled with memberships in fraternal organizations. The rich and powerful were not to be disturbed. So far as the Mayor was concerned, I could fight a lone battle whenever a serious issue was involved. Our relations were frequently strained to the cracking point.

At one time when the politicians who had elected the Mayor were pressing him to throw me out, he declared, "I had the guts to bring General Butler to Philadelphia, and I have the guts to fire him." This aroused the citizenry. An indignant mass meeting was held, demanding my retention. Mayor Kendrick, feeling the public pulse, decided it would not be wise to dismiss me and effected a reconciliation.

Any number of times I was threatened by important citizens who insisted on having unusual privileges. On one occasion a prominent banker's car, parked across a trolley track, was blocking traffic. The chauffeur arrogantly refused to obey the policeman's order to move the car. In the ensuing scuffle, the policeman beat up the chauffeur. That afternoon the Mayor sent me an urgent summons to come to his office. The banker and his chauffeur were pouring out their woes. The Mayor insisted that I punish the policeman.

"I'll look into it," I replied. "If the policeman is guilty, I'll punish him as I see fit."

An investigation disclosed that the policeman was in the right, and I promoted him. The banker never forgave me and became my bitter enemy.

The whole history of my two years in Philadelphia is filled with similar incidents of people approving my work until it interfered with their own violation of the law.

A delegation of ministers visited me to insist that I prohibit Sunday baseball. The Pennsylvania law forbade professional sport on Sunday. But, I explained, if they wished me to stop every little amateur game of baseball on Sunday, then I would also close the golf courses in the city. This brought down on my head the wrath of a leading Philadelphia churchman, who accused me of not being a Christian.

On one of my early morning tours of inspection I found all the police in a certain district loafing in the station house and the lieutenant in command lying down in his room. I reduced the lieutenant to a patrolman for grossly neglecting his duty. The next day two councilmen and a ward leader stormed into my office and demanded that I restore the policeman to his former rank. If I didn't, they threatened, they would know the reason why. I ordered them out of my office. My refusal to knuckle under won me the enmity of the councilmen.

Thus, the Mayor, the councils, the political bosses, the churches, the banks and the newspapers ranged themselves against me. The influential groups refused to lift a finger to help. My foolish notion that the laws of our country applied to rich and poor alike accounted for the growing feeling of antipathy toward me. In the two years I spent in Philadelphia, except for visits to the homes of my relatives, I had only five invitations to private houses.

By the end of 1924, I had been cussed, discussed, boycotted, lied about, lied to, strung up and reviled. Several times I was on the point of resigning. The only reason why I continued in my unpopular and uncomfortable position was to see what the hell was going to happen next.

About this time, I was told that one of the men controlling the brewery racket had stated that the Philadelphia brewers had made an agreement with the Republican State Campaign Committee that I was to be withdrawn by the Federal administration and returned to duty in the Marine Corps. The brewers were to pay the campaign fund two dollars for each barrel of high powered beer that they were permitted to manufacture and distribute. It was at least a compliment to me that the payment was contingent upon my recall.

Toward the end of my second year the Mayor kept urging me to stay on through his administration. When I left, his troubles would begin, he said. But the President refused to extend my leave, and in September, after a visit to Washington, I announced publicly that I had been assigned to command the Marine post at San Diego from the first of the year.

The Mayor then stated to the newspaper world: "I should be deeply grateful for any plan that will enable' me to retain General Butler as Director of Public Safety for the remainder of my term."

A "Keep Butler" movement now gained popular momentum. The Mayor declared "General Butler's presence here as Director of Public Safety during the Sesquicentennial is absolutely necessary."

At a "Keep Butler" mass meeting the end of October, the Mayor was the principal speaker. In the course of his address he said: "To announce that General Butler is to leave his post here would be tantamount to inviting an army of criminals to Philadelphia. There is nothing more important to the welfare of the citizens than the retention of General Butler."

When President Coolidge was again approached, he still considered it advisable for me to return to the Marine Corps. At my suggestion the Mayor named George W. Elliott, my able assistant director, as my successor.

But the Mayor repeatedly pressed me to remain in Philadelphia even if I had to resign from the Marine Corps. His friends came to tell me of his intense desire to have me continue as Director. I was actually convinced of his sincerity.

In the meantime, something occurred to seal my doom with the Mayor, although I didn't realize it at the time. In December I tried to persuade the Mayor to revoke the dance license of one big Philadelphia hotel and institute padlock proceedings against another for liquor violations. He hesitated to act. He didn't want to antagonize the powerful hotels and the Hotel Association. He let the matter drift for a couple of weeks.

While I was waiting for him to take some action I wrote again to the President asking for an extension of leave. On December 21, I was informed that no further leave would be granted.

I was in a quandary. I wanted to return to the Marines. I also wanted to finish my job in Philadelphia. I had just learned that the Mayor intended to permit one of the big hotels to dance without a license on New Year's Eve. I was enraged. I decided to press the whole hotel situation at once and clear it up before I left. That night I wrote two letters to the Mayor. In the one I pressed for the revocation of the dance license of the Bellevue-Stratford Hotel. In the second I insisted that padlock proceedings against the Ritz-Carlton Hotel should be instituted without further delay.

When I got home that night I couldn't eat. I paced the floor to think out the whole situation. Suddenly it came over me in a flash that I would be wrong to leave Philadelphia in the midst of a scrap. There was much unfinished business. I wanted to show that I, at least, was impartial and did not favor the privileged classes. Success loomed just ahead. I felt, also, that I owed something to the honest policemen who had stood up against all obstacles and pressure. I didn't want them punished by the politicians for their loyalty to me. And in spite of our disagreement about the hotel situation, the Mayor had made it clear that he wanted me.

By midnight my mind was made up. I was going to sacrifice my career in the Marine Corps and stay on the job in Philadelphia. A few minutes later, a newspaper man happened to call me up about some other matter, and I told him of my decision. The next morning the papers carried the story that I had resigned from the Marine Corps to remain in Philadelphia.

Mayor Kendrick sent for me.

"What is all this in the papers about your resigning from the Marine Corps?"

"It's the only way I can stay here. The President won't extend my leave."

"I don't want any resigned generals around me. You ought to go back to the service where you belong. The President doesn't want you here."

"What are you trying to do? Dismiss me from office?" "No, not exactly, but I don't want you as a resigned officer."

"Oh, hell," I said. "I can't talk to such a weak fish." And I walked out. A few hours later I got a letter from the Mayor requesting my resignation. I was dismissed without trial and without hearing. The Mayor issued orders to have a wide open New Year's Eve, since I would be out of town by that time.

After my dismissal, a handful of newspaper friends gave me a little informal midnight dinner. They presented me with a little gift—a small silver token, square. It was square money, they told me, the only kind I would take.

When I left Philadelphia, except for some Marine friends, only one old man in the council and two policemen came to the train to see me off. Even my assistant director, whom I had warmly recommended as my successor, didn't turn up at the station. I obtained my first real insight into the lack of moral courage and the absolute insincerity of people. Both qualities produce the same spineless results.

I discussed the whole experience with my father, then Chairman of the House Committee on Naval Affairs. I had fought to the best of my ability and impaired my health working eighteen and more hours a day. In spite of the raw deal I had received, my father shared my belief that there were still some people who were on the level. He thought it would strengthen my morale to know that the President approved of my effort. I wrote President Coolidge a letter, which my father delivered at the White House. It was reliably reported to me that the White House called up the Philadelphia organization to learn its wish in regard to me. The political crowd directed the President to have nothing to do with me. I received a note from the President's secretary informing me that the President could not see me. "Bill" Vare, the Philadelphia boss, was at the time ranking member of the Appropriations Committee of the House. His henchmen held important positions on committees handling naval affairs.

My friend General Lejeune, Commandant of the Corps, insisted that I withdraw my resignation from the Marines. He was kind enough to say publicly, "I told General Butler that I could not with equanimity contemplate his leaving the Marine Corps. I have the highest regard for General Butler with whom I have served for twenty-seven years and I don't want the Marine Corps to lose him."

My two years' education in city politics taught me that there never was any real intention of enforcing prohibition in Philadelphia. The administration had hired me as a dramatic gesture. As I said in the beginning, I was expected to be a smoke screen to distract the minds of the good people from municipal affairs while the political game continued its operations behind the smoke.

I have no quarrel with the Philadelphia crowd, nor do I feel embittered toward Philadelphia. But anyone who thinks I had a pleasant job as Director of Public Safety is greatly mistaken.

CHAPTER XXII

A Tempest in a Cocktail Glass

SO MANY DISTORTED AND PREJUDICED VERSIONS of the Williams court-martial were published both at the time of the trial and again in 1931, when my connection with the Mussolini affair opened up the whole subject again, that I think it is only fair to myself to give the straight story of what actually did happen.

Most of the newspapers presented me as a double-dyed, teeth-gnashing villain and Williams as a martyr in shining armor sacrificed on the fanatical altar of prohibition.

If I had not already become an unpopular figure in alcoholic circles throughout the country because of my strong stand on prohibition during my two years in Philadelphia, the Williams' court-martial would have slipped by as obscurely as most military trials. As an officer in the service of the government, I was forced to take action. I was literally dragged into a situation which I should have vastly preferred to ignore. Certainly, the publicity was unpleasant both for me and poor Williams.

Well, here are the facts. General knowledge of them can do no one any harm now. You can judge for yourselves.

Admiral Ashley H. Robertson commanded the Eleventh Naval District, which included my little garrison of three hundred men. The Admiral was a naval officer of the highest type and an old friend of mine. When I reported to him, he painted a pretty dark picture of conditions in my command. He said that the post had become a thriving headquarters for bootleggers. The whole garrison, he deplored, was demoralized and needed to be hauled on to the carpet from the top officer down.

Colonel Alexander S. Williams, who commanded the Fourth Regiment of Marines, had been temporarily in charge of the barracks until my arrival. Several times he had been reported drunk at Tia Juana. Robertson hesitated to take action in the matter and invite the criticism that naval officers were always jumping on Marines. He wanted the Marine base cleaned up by a Marine. I had always been on good terms with Williams. He had been my second in command of the gendarmerie in Haiti, and I recommended him as my successor. I certainly didn't want any friction with him.

Williams' first greeting was a trifle sarcastic. "Had a fine time in Philadelphia, didn't you?"

"That depends on what you mean by a fine time," I answered. "The Philadelphia crowd beat me."

"Well," he said belligerently. "I don't believe in this prohibition law and I'll be damned if I obey it."

"All right, 'Ally,' but don't tell me what you're going to do and don't put it up to me. You know as well as I do that we've had a rule against drunkenness in the service regulations for a great many years before the Volstead Act."

(Since 1872 the naval regulations have prescribed that an officer found guilty of drunkenness shall be tried by court-martial. The statute does not forbid an officer to take a drink, but it is definite on drunkenness.)

Not long after this conversation, Mrs. Butler, my daughter and I were invited to a buffet supper at Colonel Williams' house, which was not on the naval reservation, but in Coronado. We were met at the door by Colonel Williams and a maid carrying a large tray of cocktails. I refused to take one.

"Oh, don't be a hypocrite," Williams urged. "You always used to take them."

"I know I used to," I admitted, "but I'm not drinking anymore."

Now I've liked a drink in my time, and I don't feel superior to people who drink. I'm not a prig nor a professional reformer. But I had just come from Philadelphia where I had spent two years enforcing prohibition and knocking the heads off subordinates for getting drunk. It was up to me now to be consistent.

Colonel Williams continued to press cocktails on me. When I shoved them aside, he drained the glasses he brought me as well as his own. The situation was becoming embarrassing. I was Williams' superior officer, but he was my host. Finally, I strolled out on the porch to avoid his persistence. Mrs. Butler joined me and suggested that we go to the Saturday night dance at the Coronado Hotel. I was greatly relieved to get away.

As we drove off, I saw Williams lurch out of the door in his shirt sleeves and stumble headlong into a flower bed. A couple of officers were behind him and picked him up.

"Thank Heavens," I thought, "that's over. His friends will put him to bed and he'll be all right in the morning."

We were standing in an alcove watching the dancers when I was conscious of a commotion behind me. There was Williams who I thought had been safely put to bed an hour before. He was reeling from side to side, giggling, mumbling and glaring at me. The onlookers, highly amused and interested, had drawn aside to give him the center of the stage. I saw at a glance that Williams was very drunk and would fall down and create a more unpleasant scene unless he made a speedy exit.

The two officers with my party acted quickly. They walked briskly over to him, took him by the arms and half carried, half dragged him out of the hotel through the main corridor, where the guests swarmed to view the exhibition of a Marine officer staggering and swaying in his cups for the public entertainment and scorn.

Mrs. Butler and I left immediately and returned to our quarters. All day Sunday I worried about the episode. I didn't want to take steps against Williams, but he had forced me into a devilish position. If he had only stayed quietly at home I could have ignored his conduct. But I couldn't ignore his performance at the hotel. Since I had become a commanding officer, I had never failed to try by court-martial an officer who publicly disgraced himself and the Marine Corps.

However, we were both Admiral Robertson's subordinates. Before taking any action, I went Monday morning to Robertson's office to get his advice.

"I know why you're here, Smedley," he peered at me over his desk.

"What do you want to do about it?"

"There's nothing to do but court-martial him. We can't permit officers to behave in this fashion."

"Admiral, will you prefer the charges, or shall I?"

"He is under your immediate command," Robertson replied. "You prepare the papers and send them to me, and I'll request his trial by general court-martial. This town is wet, and we're going to get a hell of a drubbing out of this. You'll have all the newspapers on your back and you'll get the worst of it after your Philadelphia fight. But remember this, Smedley, I'm with you."

At the barracks I sent for the witnesses. They all admitted frankly that Williams was very drunk in the hotel. I then placed Williams under arrest and at the same time sent him a letter calling upon him for any statement he wished to make and informing him that it was my intention to recommend him for trial by general court-martial.

At the end of thirty-six hours when my action leaked out, the San Diego newspapermen descended on me in a body and told me that a story was being circulated that I had taken a drink with Williams followed by a fight and that I was now trying my host for getting drunk in his own house. The newspapers wanted my version of the story.

"It has never been my habit to try a military case in the press," I explained. "Admiral Robertson has all the papers in the case. If he thinks it advisable, he can make a statement."

"If you don't say something," the reporters persisted, "the other story will be given out."

"I'm not talking, boys, and that's final," I said.

Many newspapers printed this false story and pictured me as a horned toad, a base wretch who outrageously abused hospitality and had no sense of honor. At this point I cannot emphasize too strongly that it was never brought out in the charges that Williams was drunk in his own house. He was tried for drunkenness and conduct unbecoming an officer in a public place.

Before I landed in California, I received an invitation by radio from the San Diego Chamber of Commerce to a luncheon in my honor. The luncheon was scheduled to take place four or five days after Colonel Williams had been placed under arrest.

The morning of the luncheon Admiral Robertson sent for me. He was stamping up and down his office in a boiling rage. A delegation from the Chamber of Commerce had just visited him. They told him they were going to let me walk right into the dining room, find the table set and all the places empty. I was to stand around by myself and wait. No one was to come to the luncheon. They warned the Admiral to stay away so that he would not be humiliated. Robertson was furious.

"I told them I was going and going with you, and I advised them all to be at the luncheon. If not, I'd make recommendations to the Navy Department to move the naval base. The Navy spends twenty-seven million dollars a year in this town, and the town depends on it. I'm not going to let them snub you without putting up a fight."

"Admiral," I said, "I've been insulted by experts and professionals. This is only a bush league out here. Suppose neither of us goes. Then nobody will be snubbed."

"No such thing," he fumed. "I'm going to wear my best blouse and you and I are going together. If our hosts don't show up, there's going to be one hell of a row."

The old man was so angry that his face was crimson and the veins in his forehead were purple and swollen. In his excitement his false teeth kept slipping out of their moorings, making his voice rattle like the wind through a hollow cavern.

I had seen some of my superiors in Washington display so much weakness and flabbiness that I was overwhelmed by the Admiral's moral courage, especially since he was extremely popular with the local people.

When we arrived at the club where the luncheon was to be held, no one was on hand to greet us. In a few minutes one of the members of the Chamber of Commerce happened to saunter in. The sight of the Admiral sitting straight and stern in his best blouse and gold stripes galvanized the committee of one into immediate action. He bolted to the telephone. In fifteen minutes the guests began to arrive and put up a show of cordiality toward the Admiral. Few of them spoke to me. The table was set for twenty-five. About twenty turned up.

Toward the end of the luncheon the President of the Chamber of Commerce rose and said, "I don't know the guest of honor, but I'll read from the Marine Corps newspaper published at his own post." He proceeded to read the little account of my record, which our newspaper had published on my arrival. When he finished he said, curtly, without welcoming me to San Diego, "He may now speak for himself."

With that Admiral Robertson jumped to his feet. "If you won't tell these people about General Butler, I will."

He launched forth into a fine tribute to me and wound up by saying, "You are attempting to make him very uncomfortable in this town, but I want to tell you he is doing you an honor by being willing to live in San Diego." And he turned to me. "Now, Smedley."

I didn't mince matters. I made it clear that they couldn't bluff me and run my post. More powerful interests than they represented had failed to intimidate me. The luncheon broke up with considerable confusion immediately after my remarks. The Admiral and I walked out, arm in arm.

From that moment the group in San Diego that controlled social and public affairs decided to put me in my place.

A few days later the court convened, with Admiral Thomas Washington as president of the court- martial. Three of the witnesses who had given me written statements in addition to their oral ones were so cowed by San Diego opinion that they perjured themselves on the witness stand. They testified that Colonel Williams was not drunk but ill—that he was suffering from a nervous collapse when he staggered into the hotel. Later, one of the officers admitted to me that he had lied. "You don't know the pressure that is being brought to bear on us," he said. He had a wife who enjoyed society and didn't want to be ostracized.

In spite of the false testimony, the bulk of the evidence proved that Colonel Williams was guilty, and he was convicted by a court of admirals and colonels. Williams had a good record as an officer. It was a pity that he forced me to take action against him. As a penalty he was dropped four numbers in grade, relieved from the command of the Fourth Regiment and transferred to San Francisco. That was in April 1926. In October of the same year his car plunged into San Francisco Bay one morning at four o'clock. He was alone in the car and was drowned. An investigating board declared the death was accidental.

So much publicity was given to the court-martial and there was such popular determination to make me the goat that Admiral Robertson issued a vigorous statement during the trial in which he said among other things: "Colonel Williams is tried as a military officer by a military court for a military offense. General Butler will not be on trial, and it is because there appears to be a disposition to regard him as the unofficial defendant that I think it only fair to remind the public that he preferred his charges only after consulting with me and being advised by me to file them."

Not long after the court-martial, a Marine officer and his wife gave a dinner at the country club for Mrs. Butler and me. I have always admired the fearlessness of our hosts. When we arrived at the club tin pans were beaten and my name was jeered, but the disturbance soon subsided. The next day I was told that when the other dinner parties at the club learned that I was coming, they announced their intention of pelting me with eggs and tomatoes and driving me out. However, a retired major general of the Army, who was an early arrival at our dinner, warned the disorderly crowd that he would stand for no nonsense. The hymn of hate simmered down to tin pans and boos. My Marine friend was threatened with dismissal from the club for bringing me as his guest. Needless to say, I was never invited there again.

Everywhere my family was subjected to embarrassment. Whenever a member of the family was seen entering one of the Pantages theaters, my picture would be thrown on the screen for the crowd to hiss their disapproval. Then Colonel Williams' picture would be projected and receive a great ovation. At a social gathering in the home of a senior naval officer my daughter was asked by one of the guests if she was related to that low-lived Butler.

All the time I was in San Diego I was as popular as a skunk at a picnic. I didn't care what San Diego thought of me, but it was a different matter to have my wife and children live in a hostile atmosphere in which they were ridiculed and annoyed.

In fairness it must be said that there were several families in San Diego who were more than kind and friendly to me and mine.

And the crowd that jumped on me were citizens of a town that had the lowest moral standards I've ever encountered. The streets were filled with degenerates preying on the young enlisted men of the navy. In cleaning up the Marine post, I ran across a trail of the most deplorable degeneracy which led to the chief clerk of one of the leading hotels. The hotel clerk and a captain of Marines had been running a joint for the seduction of boys. The Marine officer was court-martialed and sent to prison for twenty years, but the hotel clerk was warned by his friends in time to make his escape. The lowest form of vice was permitted to flourish unchecked. When I took the matter up with the Mayor, he said he couldn't get the police to take any action.

I received hundreds of letters commending my stand in the Williams' court-martial and as many or more abusing me. I was called Smelly Butler and Meddly Butler. One letter addressed me as Smedley Cad Butler; another said I was a yellow dog instead of a devil dog. I was called a skunk, a tin soldier, a swivel chair four-flusher, a bigoted fanatic, a half-baked fool, an ignorant blackguard, an egotistical and fanatical balloon—and just about all the names that aren't in the dictionary.

My friends are always cautioning me to adopt a safe middle course that conciliates people. But I'd rather take a definite stand on a principle or issue which I am convinced is right, even if bricks are thrown at me. I prefer it to sitting on the fence and receiving empty ovations. Popularity is not worth the sacrifice it sometimes exacts. I try to be a fighter, not a politician.

CHAPTER XXIII

Treading Softly in China

ABOUT THE FIRST OF MARCH 1927, they sent me off to take command of the American Marines in China.

I felt a little like Rip Van Winkle. I was returning, after twenty-seven years, to the scenes of my first grilling military experience, when as a nineteen-year old lieutenant I took part in the siege of Tientsin and the famous march to Peking during the Boxer Rebellion.

Once more, China was furnishing plenty of excitement. The country was in the throes of civil war, with the northern and southern armies fighting for the mastery. Chiang Kai-shek, at that time commander-in-chief of the Cantonese armies, had forced a boycott on the British and declared against all foreign imperialism in China. The whole Yangtze valley was in chaos, and the foreign residents were panicky.

I arrived in Shanghai March 25, a day or so after the Nanking outrage, when the Chinese rose against the foreigners, looted and burned their property and killed many of them, including several Americans. Most of the Americans escaped and were taken on gunboats down the river to Shanghai. My aide, Captain "Torchy" Robinson, had already reached Shanghai but joined me at once, and with his fine acute mind and affectionate companionship I was ready for anything. There is no one quite like "Torchy."

More than five thousand Marines were now in Shanghai, Peking and Tientsin. When I arrived, the Fourth Regiment was already in Shanghai—the same regiment of Marines which helped guard the International Settlement in 1932, when the Japanese invaded Shanghai in their astonishing drive against the Chinese—a drive which might be subtitled: 'When Isn't a War a War?' Three thousand men from the Japanese fleet were on shore in 1927, this time to aid in the protection of the Settlement, and eleven hundred more were ready to land at a moment's notice.

There was considerable fighting north of Shanghai proper in the Chapei district, but we refused to be drawn into it. The Chapei district, which the Japanese later pounded to dust, has now become almost a household word—a symbol of how not to gain the good will of the Chinese. Certainly, in 1927, we did not do our job the Japanese way.

The Marines were sent to protect American citizens and their property. If we could not have maintained friendly relations with the Chinese and have accomplished our purpose without fighting, the expedition would have been a failure. We held ourselves in readiness for any emergency and prevented disturbances by patrolling the city. Each district had a truck patrol provided with a machine gun and carrying a non-commissioned officer and eight men who vigilantly toured the streets.

Shanghai was at a nervous pitch. All kinds of baseless and exaggerated rumors were circulating. One member of our staff did nothing but rush around to quiet nervous citizens who had become panicky after the Nanking uprising.

The military representatives of the other nations in Shanghai decided that a punitive expedition should be launched against the Chinese to square the Nanking business.

Our nation was most fortunate in the matter of its Naval Commander-in-Chief at Shanghai, as Admiral Clarence S. Williams was head and shoulders above the average Admiral—in addition to great ability, he possessed a delicious and effective sense of humor coupled with unselfish courage. They came to Admiral Williams, commanding the United States Asiatic fleet and, as senior officer in Shanghai, entitled to preside at any allied conference. They disclosed their plan to go up the Yangtze River and knock down the Nanking forts as a retaliation for the outrages against foreigners.

"Will you join us?" they urged.

"No," said our Admiral, "but I'll be here when you get back."

He was firm in his determination not to disrupt relations with the Chinese.

My knowledge of the Chinese situation was meager. Moreover, it suited my purpose to have no opinion on Chinese politics or on the strength of the various military factions. But I held to the principle that the Chinese had to settle their own form of government and pick out their own rulers. Any attempt to solve the Chinese tangle would have been shadow boxing. All we could do was to see that mutinous Chinese troops didn't get out of hand and shoot Americans. It was up to me to prevent a repetition of the Boxer and Nanking difficulties.

My Marines were behaving splendidly. When they chafed under inaction they polished their equipment and burnished their mess gear until it sparkled in the sun. I even let them nickel plate their bayonets and scabbards although it was against regulations. I was glad to have them out of mischief. The whole brigade spruced up with the ambitious desire to rival the smart and dazzling appearance of the Coldstream Guards, Great Britain's crack regiment, which was also swanking down the streets of Shanghai.

The Marines were under fine control, and I hammered it into their heads that they were to continue to hold themselves in restraint while they remained in China.

In May I went to Peking to see if it was advisable to increase the guard at the American Legation. I was the official guest in Peking of the American Minister, John V. A. MacMurray. His tact and profound understanding of the

Chinese were most helpful to us during our whole stay in China. I found on the Legation Staff at Peking my old companion of Haitian days, F. L. Mayer. He was Counselor of the Legation and, unlike many State Department representatives I have met, Freddy has plenty of independent courage to act on his own initiative. I have not always had much use for diplomats but MacMurray and Mayer are refreshingly different.

The rival Chinese armies were battling continually in North China, and many of the troops were undisciplined and ready to break loose and go on the rampage to loot and kill unarmed civilians. I found the situation so much more critical in the North than in the Shanghai district that I decided to move the Marines to Tientsin.

We disembarked four thousand officers and men for Tientsin at Taku Bar and transported them in lighters up the Pei Ho, the same river on which old Wirt McCreary, flying an admiral's flag made out of a blue flannel shirt, operated his junk fleet in 1900.

Once more I was living over the stirring events of the Boxer uprising. When my wife joined me, I tried to show her all the places that recalled my Boxer experiences, although Tientsin was so changed that it was difficult to find some of the old landmarks. The city had quadrupled in size, and the foreign concessions had increased tenfold since the famous siege.

Mrs. Butler and I stayed in a little hotel next to the godown where the Marines had been quartered during the Boxer fighting. Back in 1900, the hotel was an amusement building. It was here that I had been carried when I was wounded in the leg during the siege. With the help of the proprietor I located the exact spot where my cot had stood. Mrs. Butler and I had our table placed there. Near the railroad station was the old engine house which we had defended against hordes of Boxers. I pointed out the joss-house porch, where I had sat with Colonel Meade and General Liscum the day before Liscum was killed holding the colors of his regiment.

We named our billets in Tientsin after the men and officers killed in 1900 during the Boxer fighting, but I continually lectured the men that our purpose now was peaceful and that we weren't carrying any chips on our shoulders that might lead to fighting. I was tolerating no clashes with the Chinese people. I warned them that if a Marine so much as laid a hand on a rickshaw coolie he would be court-martialed.

Some of our Marine aviators came up from the Philippines and established an aviation field next to the Standard Oil compound about ten miles from the mouth of the Pei Ho. I frequently flew back and forth between Tientsin and Tangku, and from the air I could look down on the twenty-five miles of railroad along which we had fought so fiercely with the Boxers and crawled inch by inch over streams and broken bridges.

Under the terms of our agreement with the Chinese, we were permitted to fly between Peking and the sea, in a zone four miles wide. Although we were confining our flights to the short stretch between Tientsin and the sea, the Chinese objected to our airplanes. Very politely I explained that the planes were a vital part of our equipment and as much a protection to the Chinese as to the American residents. Every so often the Chinese Minister of Foreign Affairs at Tientsin, through his secretary, lodged a formal protest which I was told not to take to heart. It was only publicity. The little secretary even went so far as to admit that the Chinese felt safer with our airplanes scouting around.

I got along beautifully with the Minister of Foreign Affairs. Few of the Americans knew he could speak English, but when he and I tired of all the red tape and the interpreters we pushed everybody out and had a good intimate talk behind closed doors. He even knew American slang and was a regular fellow.

I must have attended more than twenty interminable Chinese banquets. The first course would be watermelon seeds. By the time I had finished cracking them to pry out the microscopic insides, I was generally exhausted. The second course was liable to be a pinkish white slippery mess, sweet, sticky and unpleasant. Once I asked the interpreter what it was. "Fish lips," he said. With that one of my two aides turned pea green and leaped right through a paper window.

Before my aides went to a Chinese dinner they drank olive oil so that they could consume unlimited quantities of alcohol. They drank the Chinese generals right under the table. The next day the Chinese commander would send formal apologies to me, not because his generals got drunk at the banquet, but because they couldn't compete with my two aides in holding their liquor.

At dinner one night I sat next to a most attractive Chinese woman, a Mrs. Lu, who spoke perfect English.

"You are a Marine, I see," she opened the conversation. "My father and I have always felt greatly indebted to a Marine lieutenant who in 1900 got us transportation down the river from Tientsin. In fact, he carried me to the boat. I was three years old."

"Do you remember his name?" I asked.

"I think my father said it was Buckley."

"There was no Buckley in the Marines then. His name was Butler," and I introduced myself. Laughing I added, "I well remember carrying you. You considered me a hateful 'foreign devil' and shrieked lustily, struggling every inch of the way."

During the siege of Tientsin, long ago, the Marines had been quartered in the godown of the China Merchants Steam Navigation Company. The secretary of the company, a cultured Chinese merchant who had graduated from Andover and spoke fluent English, lived across the street. One day he rushed over to the godown where I was on duty as a lieutenant and said a shell had just crashed through his roof. Could I give his family transportation down the river to safety? I had only fifteen minutes to get them on board one of our boats. The little girl of three was now my dinner partner. She had been educated abroad, and her husband was a Harvard graduate.

The northern army was not making any gains. Peking was still under martial law, and we could hear the firing from the battles outside the city. We Marines just sat tight. The Chinese by this time were inspired with a wholesome respect for us and decided to keep their battles at some distance.

There was not an hour day or night when our Marines were not prepared to leave at once for Peking or any place in North China. Our motor trucks, equipped with machine guns, gas masks, ammunition and rations for a self-supporting foray of ten days, were always ready to move like a fire company at a moment's notice. Our plan for rescue, if necessity arose, included sending the motor trucks to Peking, seizing the Temple of Heaven where we would collect the Americans until we could evacuate them by truck and airplane to Tientsin and the coast. In case of an uprising against foreigners, we had arranged to shelter in Tientsin the several thousand Americans in the northern area. We had provided cots, rations, food for babies, medical supplies. After what had happened at Nanking, we had to be prepared for any emergency.

The Japanese also had their troops in Tientsin. They were commanded by Lieutenant General Takata, a highly intelligent and efficient officer. We were a little suspicious of the Japanese intentions in North China. Even then it seemed to me that Japan was only waiting for a favorable opportunity to gain complete control of Manchuria.

In my conversations with Takata I always gave evasive answers to his pointed hints for direct information. He adopted the usual Japanese tactics of flattery and told me what a great soldier I was. "Apple sauce," I told him. With great difficulty I succeeded in making him understand what it meant. After that whenever I saw him he pointed his finger at me and said, "Apple sauce." The Japanese entertained us and we in turn entertained them. We always talked a lot of social flubdub, but neither side knew what the other was really thinking.

The Chinese children expressed their approval by sticking up their thumbs and calling "Ding how." If they didn't like something they said, "Boo how" with thumbs down. The Marines were in such good standing around Tientsin that the children put up their thumbs and shouted "Ding how" every time they saw an American in uniform.

The day before Christmas, 1927, we had our first and only real fighting in China. It was a battle with fire. The plant of the Standard Oil Company in Tientsin caught fire and ignited a million pounds of candle grease. Nine minutes after the alarm sounded we had a battalion of Marines at the spot. I went along to direct the fire brigade. At last I discovered that my two years' stay in the City of Brotherly Love was of some value. I had learned something about fighting fires as Director of Public Safety in Philadelphia.

I found two big warehouses blazing. Twenty feet away was another warehouse filled with gasoline. Nearby were six three-million gallon oil tanks. If they exploded the destruction and disaster would have been terrific. I sent a hurry call for a thousand more Marines.

By the middle of the afternoon we had two thousand Marines fighting like—well, like Marines. They built a fire wall sixteen feet high, of earth, empty drums, iron doors and other non-inflammable material, between the burning warehouses and the stores of gasoline. They labored like heroes to remove cases of oil and tins of gasoline from the adjoining buildings. By night the fire was under control. One hundred and fifty men continued to fight the fire, however, and one hundred guarded the gasoline and oil piled in the open all over that part of China.

Three o'clock Christmas morning the main drain of the plant blew up, and a giant stream of burning oil spouted forth and spread over the river. The Marines spent Christmas Day building a bulkhead around the mouth of the drain. At midnight an ice jam came down the river with the ebb tide and carried away part of the bulkhead. The river was covered again with burning oil—and the blaze was just across from the foreign concessions. The oil burned fiercely on the river all the next day. It was four days before the fire was put out. It was a million dollar loss, but the Standard Oil Company said the Marines saved them four millions more.

During 1928 I went in for road building. A heavy rain washed out the bridge on the motor highway between Tientsin and Peking. I sent our Marine engineers to rebuild the bridge out of scrap lumber salvaged from abandoned billets. The Chinese officials were amazed at the speed with which the work was completed and delighted to have the bridge. Without it the road was useless.

The road was nothing but a trail anyway, and I now had the bright idea that it would be a good plan to rebuild the Peking-Tientsin motor road.

Our engineers were most enthusiastic. We sent out artillery tractors and homemade road drags and five hundred Marines to put the first sixteen miles in good condition.

This was not soldiering, but it was a good way to keep friendly with the Chinese. I used regular American ballyhoo. The Chinese generals, Colonel Miller, my remarkably able Chief of Staff, and I had our pictures taken as we turned the first shovels of earth. The Chinese officials got a great kick out of riding on the tractors. It was a familiar sight to meet a Marine driving up the road with a fat old Chinese in a little round hat and long silk coat sitting beside him and grinning from ear to ear.

At the official opening of the road, I was invited to a luncheon with one hundred distinguished guests including the Governor of the province. It was quite a celebration. General Fu Tso-yi reviewed the Marines and I reviewed his troops.

A small town across the river couldn't establish contact with Tientsin when the bridge was washed out. The new bridge and the new road meant that the people in this little town could get their produce easily to the Tientsin market.

According to ancient Chinese custom, a Blessing Umbrella is bestowed on a great public benefactor, but only with the unanimous vote of the residents of a town or district. The town felt that I had done them an enormous service and presented me with one of these umbrellas. I have been told that no foreigner either in Tientsin or Peking has ever before been honored with one of these umbrellas. They are gorgeous affairs and are carried in official processions. Chinese who have had the honor of being awarded an umbrella in the past have usually been buried with it.

Curiously enough, before I left China I received a second Umbrella of Ten Thousand Blessings. One afternoon I was driving toward the Tientsin suburb of Boxertown where we had been keeping a detail of Marines on duty at the Standard Oil plant since the big fire out there. Boxertown was Boxer Village, in 1900, the scene of some of our fiercest fighting with the Chinese just before we entered Tientsin. The little mud village had expanded enormously. It was now one of the outlying suburbs of the city, with a population of more than forty thousand.

As I drove along the bumpy old roads into a narrow street, I met men, women and children, much agitated, running past me with bundles on their backs. A raiding column of the opposing Chinese army was advancing to loot the suburb. The engine of my car, with the muffler off, was making an infernal racket. The approaching raiders thought my exhaust was a machine gun popping. When some of them saw my car blocking the narrow street, they believed I had an army back of me. They beat it, along with the rest of the column, and the suburb was saved from a bandit brigade of looters.

Boxertown hailed me as its deliverer. I protested that I had nothing to do with the retreat of the enemy. But the Chinese insisted I had saved them, whether intentionally or not, and voted me a Blessing Umbrella.

The elders of the town in their long ceremonial gowns marched through the streets to my headquarters to make the formal presentation. The umbrella was a magnificent canopy of red satin, with small silk streamers, bearing the names of two hundred elders of Boxertown. Two banners came with the umbrella. One said, "Your kindness is always in the minds of the people." On the other was an inscription in Chinese characters, "General Butler loves China as he loves America."

After their flowery and poetic address, I gave a little speech in which I said that time certainly effected great changes. The last time I was in their town, twenty-eight years before, I marched up the railroad track and from every house came the cracking of guns. Three of us were killed then, and nine wounded. We took to our heels and ran away as fast as we could. Now I said, this very town was conferring its greatest honor on me.

At this point five of the old men, standing with their hands up their sleeves, smiled a little. I turned to the interpreter who was translating my remarks. "Have I said anything to offend them?"

He went over to investigate and came back laughing. "Those old men were in the crowd of Boxers that shot you up in 1900."

In January 1929, I had my orders to withdraw the Marines. When the Marines were leaving Tientsin, great electric signs were erected, flashing China's last word to us: "Goodbye and Good Luck, Marines."

The Chinese have a proverb, "He who treads softly goes far."

Chapter XXIV

My Damned Follies at Quantico

I WAS BACK AT MY OLD STAMPING GROUND, Quantico, as commanding officer of the Marine base, when, on July 5, 1929, I was promoted to be a major general, filling the vacancy caused by the death of General Eli K. Cole. I was forty-eight—the youngest major general ever to have been in the Marine Corps.

I flung myself heart and soul into the task of creating a model post. The Chief of Staff was my friend of many years, Jim Meade. The little town of Quantico had been loading up my Marines with bootleg poison. Before I came at least seventy men were in the brig for drunkenness every pay day. I boycotted the town, and the merchants drove out the bootleggers in double quick time. They didn't want to lose the Marines as customers, their chief source of revenue. When the town was dried up, I led a parade down the main street, with our bands playing. Legitimate business was briskly resumed.

Everything about the post was spick and span. The men were responsive and cooperative. Bayonets shone like silver, machine guns were almost manicured. A legend floated about the barracks that Old Gimlet Eye could tell in the dark if a private had really polished his buttons or rubbed them carelessly with a dirty rag. The garrison was as disciplined and well-trained a body of men as one could find in peace time.

But I was destined to have little satisfaction out of my new rank or the sprucing up of Quantico. My desk superiors apparently enjoyed the sport of pin pricking. Petty irritations, like mosquito bites, can be infuriating—and also significant.

I made a speech in Pittsburgh in which I intimated that our government had used strong arm methods to elect the President of Nicaragua when I was there with the Marines in 1912. The Secretary of the Navy, Charles Francis Adams, sent for me to administer a stiff reprimand. He impressed upon me that he was acting at the direct personal order of the President of the United States.

I told him: "This is the first time in my service of thirty-two years that I've ever been hauled on the carpet and treated like an unruly schoolboy. I haven't always approved of the actions of the administration, but I've always faithfully carried out my instructions. If I'm not behaving well it is because I'm not accustomed to reprimands, and you can't expect me to turn my cheek meekly for official slaps."

"I think this will be all," he replied curtly. "I don't ever want to see you here again."

"You never will, if I can help it," I snapped, and walked out of his office.

After the death of General Neville Marine Corps headquarters leaned over backward to snub me. My aide was detached without my having been given any notice. It's not customary to take away a general officer's private aide without first consulting the general. Then I was not appointed to the Marine Corps selection board, although I had always previously been a member. This rebuff was followed by a letter from the Commandant of the Corps in which he suggested that I make fewer speeches—my post was not in good shape because I was away too much. I laid the Commandant's letter next to the most recent official report of the inspector, which commended Quantico as the finest post in the United States.

The Secretary of the Navy came down to Quantico in July 1930. Secretary Adams never liked me and our duel of words over my Pittsburgh speech hadn't improved our relations. However, I was glad of the opportunity to show him that the Marine base was efficiently run.

With a certain amount of pride, I took him over the barracks and parade grounds. His only comment was that Quantico was the most expensive place in the United States for training men. We held what I thought was a very handsome review in our dress uniforms. My crack regiments outdid themselves in his honor. He observed drily that he had seen the naval cadets march, implying that the Marines did not carry themselves as well as the midshipmen. Our air squadron gave a beautiful performance. I asked him how he liked it. "Humph," he snorted. "I've seen navy fliers."

At the partially completed stadium which I had started in 1921 with the volunteer labor of the men and with cement contributed by cement companies of the eastern states, the Secretary stopped long enough to point out, "That's one of your damned follies."

And again, at the club house which we were building without expense to the government, using stone quarried on the post and lumber cut on the spot, he grumbled, "And there's another of your follies."

I couldn't resist telling him a story about General Grant. When Grant was President he proposed to appoint Robert Ingersoll to the Court of St. James. "But," a friend remonstrated, "he doesn't believe in the Bible." Grant replied, "Oh, that's just Ingersoll. He doesn't believe in the Bible because he didn't write it himself."

The Secretary nettled me throughout his visit with petty fault finding. While he was inspecting the airplane squadron, he picked up a blade of grass. Hunting all around the wing of one of the airplanes, he found a tiny hole, pushed in the blade of grass and said triumphantly, "You ought to attend to this."

He upbraided me for filling in the last swamp area at Quantico to enlarge the landing field.

"Why do you want a large landing field?" he complained.

"So that our planes can land without difficulty."

"Well, I don't see what the Marines are doing with airplanes, anyway," he said. "The Navy can do all the flying for the Marine Corps. And we don't need a flying field here to protect Washington. We're not going to have any more wars."

He was so disagreeable and so unappreciative of the effort we were making to please him on the occasion of his visit that I couldn't help showing my irritation. After he left, I told some of my friends a story to illustrate his attitude.

A preacher making the rounds of his parish stopped one day at a farmhouse for dinner. The farmer's wife heaped her table with good things.

"Won't you try some of this beef?" she urged. "I raised and butchered the animal myself."

"I don't like beef," he remarked contemptuously.

When she persuaded him to taste some of her delicious sugar-cured ham he turned up his nose. He spurned in turn her chicken, her garden grown vegetables and her damson plum preserves.

At this point the little son of the family, who was watching through a crack in the kitchen door, called in a stage whisper, "Say, Mom, maybe the old buzzard will suck an egg."

This story, which later got back to the Secretary's ears, was not exactly helpful to my interests in the Corps.

When General Lejeune retired in 1929 to become Superintendent of the Virginia Military Institute, General Neville was appointed Commandant of the Corps. Shortly before Secretary Adams' visit to Quantico in the summer of 1930, my dear old friend Neville had dropped dead. Lejeune, Neville and I, the three musketeers of the Marines, had served together in countless campaigns. The Corps seemed different without them.

I was now the senior ranking officer in the Marine Corps —the next in line for Commandant. But neither my rank nor my record was considered. One staff admiral blustered out that he'd be damned before he'd see me Commandant. In no time, he said, I would be trying to run the navy. Probably plenty more was said behind closed doors.

Although I was a major general and the senior officer, the selecting board went half way down the list and picked out a brigadier general. With the recommendation of Secretary Adams, Brigadier General Ben H. Fuller was appointed Commandant.

It had broken old General Waller's heart not to be made Commandant when he was in line for it. I remembered how I had seen him at the last—paralyzed—a sorry end for the magnificent fighting man he had been. I refused to be crushed like that. Right then, with almost half my life before me, I made up my mind to retire from the Marine Corps. Contrary to reports, my decision to leave the active list of the Corps had nothing to do with the Mussolini incident.

CHAPTER XXV

The Mussolini Incident

I HAD JUST RECEIVED AN OFFICIAL NAVY DEPARTMENT DOCUMENT, "The U. S. Navy in Peacetime," in which I was praised for the tact and diplomacy with which I had handled the situation in China. My eye lighted on this:

"Probably no finer example of successful arbitration by American Officers has been demonstrated in recent years than the peace-making achievements that crowned General Butler's efforts in China in 1927 and 1928."

When I had hardly finished reading the paragraph, I was notified that the Navy Department had ordered me under arrest and was court-martialing me.

Even now I cannot look back calmly on this uncalled for episode. It was pretty stiff to be knocked over the head with a court-martial toward the end of my service career, without a previous blemish on my record. Moreover, the whole performance was conducted with deliberate brutality. I was handed a loaded "pineapple" with the insulting compliments of the state and navy departments. But the thrust intended to disgrace me and shove me into oblivion acted as a boomerang on those who were howling for my scalp. Most of the newspapers saw through the farce and sided with me. Before the case had gone very far, the administration repented that it had ever started anything.

The storm broke about my head because of a speech in which I repeated a story I had been told concerning Signor Mussolini. A week later the ball started rolling. I received a letter from the Secretary of the Navy directing me to state whether I had made the remarks attributed to me. If not, what had I said? I answered the letter without reserve.

My letter was received at the Navy Department about half past nine in the morning, January 29. At ten-twenty four A. M. that day my telephone in Quantico rang. It was General Myers, assistant to the Commandant of Marines, telling me that the Commandant in Washington wished to speak to me. Immediately General Fuller was speaking on the wire.

"General Butler, you are hereby placed under arrest to await trial by general court-martial. You will turn over your command to your next senior, General Berkeley, and you will be restricted to the limits of your post. The Secretary of the Navy wishes you to know that this action is taken by the direct personal order of the President of the United States."

I was placed under arrest in accordance with provisions of the Articles for the Government of the Navy.

Charge One: "Conduct to the prejudice of good order and discipline."

Charge Two: "Conduct unbecoming an officer and a gentleman."

In the service we always called these the Old Mother Hubbard charges: they cover everything.

I notified Brigadier General Randolph C. Berkeley that I was under arrest. He came at once to my house but refused to receive my sword—an act of true courtesy, which touched me deeply. Of course, my flag was hauled down. For the first time in thirty-three years of service I was a prisoner. The manner of my arrest added to the humiliation. I am the only General Officer of the United States Service who has been placed under arrest since the Civil War. It was unheard of for an officer of rank to be placed under arrest by telephone. More than that, even the newspapers knew of my humiliation before I did.

General Berkeley at once went to Washington and secured my old friend Major Henry Leonard as military counsel for me. Later Berkeley was ordered to Nicaragua ahead of his turn and I am convinced it was due to this friendly act. Leonard, it will be recalled, was the Marine Lieutenant who lost his arm during the Boxer trouble. He is today one of the ablest lawyers in the United States. No one was better equipped to deal with the crowd that was snarling at me. He and Hon. Roland S. Morris, one of the leading lawyers of the United States, formerly Ambassador to Japan, undertook my defense.

Mr. Daniels, former Secretary of the Navy, and Governor Franklin D. Roosevelt immediately telegraphed that they would appear as witnesses at the trial in my behalf. General Harbord sent word from Bermuda that he would be on hand to testify for me. I also had the support of the majority of ex-service men in the country. The American Legion posts in Philadelphia were the exception.

Within a few days after my arrest, I received notice over the telephone from General Fuller that I was to be tried in Philadelphia. He admitted the difficulty of finding Marine Officers to sit on the court since there were only two officers senior to me in rank and they were both on the retired list. This meant that I would have to be tried by a court of admirals. The only other communication I had from Washington was the official letter confirming my arrest and extending my arrest limits.

According to the original order, I was confined to the post at Quantico. No officer other than one to be tried for a criminal offense had ever before been denied the privilege of extending the limits of his confinement so that he might interview counsel and arrange for his defense. It was nearly a week before such extension was granted me.

I have always believed that had it not been for the storm of public indignation aroused over this point, the extension would not have been granted at all.

On Thursday evening, February 5, at ten o'clock Major Leonard telephoned me to be at his house in Washington, the next morning at eight o'clock.

I was there on the dot to learn the latest developments.

Leonard breezed in about half past nine. He was very cheerful. The night before he had met a representative of the government who stood high in its councils, to discuss ways and means for stopping the trial.

An avalanche of newspaper criticism was descending on the administration. There were indications that the administration was eager to quash the court-martial and thus stop the newspaper storm which was annoying it. But Leonard realized that a delay would increase the criticism and react in our favor. I was banking on the essential fairness of the American people. I wanted the facts to be aired.

Leonard was in full accord with me.

The trial was set for February 16. We were preparing to fight to the end. The time was growing short and we had much to do to prepare our defense and secure witnesses.

That Friday morning Leonard went on to Philadelphia. He was meeting Morris, Lieutenant Colonel Dyer and other members of my counsel to complete the preparations for the trial. I certainly had no idea then that the administration would back down so completely.

I again met Leonard at his house when he returned Saturday morning. All that day he was busy running to conferences and consulting with me.

The first offer received was that I should be detached from my station, reprimanded and placed in a status of awaiting orders indefinitely. This we refused to consider.

The second proposal was that I should be reprimanded and detached from my command, which was also rejected by my counsel. A third time the representative came back to say all would be forgiven if I would write a letter of apology. This was refused.

My counsel finally grew impatient and, with the suggestion that much time was being wasted in unprofitable discussion, indicated that with but one week remaining in which to prepare his case for trial, the matter of whether or not there was to be a trial must be settled at once.

That brought the matter to a head. They asked what our terms were and were told that we would agree to a reprimand, which my own lawyer, Leonard, would write and to the complete restitution of my rank and the privileges to which I was entitled as a Major General.

By Saturday evening our terms were accepted. It was decided that I was to write a letter, which was drafted in conference, emphasizing the already known fact that the meeting at the Contemporary Club where I had spoken was a private, not a public affair. My statement of this circumstance was to furnish the public excuse for dropping the case. I was willing to sign the letter, since there was nothing in it of a back-walking nature. Leonard and I would have preferred to have this letter to

Secretary Adams go by the usual channels through the Commandant of the Marine Corps to the Secretary of the Navy's office. But the Secretary was impatient to rush through a settlement before the Monday newspapers came out, and the letter was handed to him directly on Sunday afternoon, February 8.

Before I handed over my letter, however, I received the official reprimand signed by Secretary Adams. In my letter I expressed regret that my indiscreet remarks had "caused embarrassment to the Government." As soon as Secretary Adams had received it, he released me from arrest and restored me to duty. The next day the Commandant of the Marine Corps was informed that I had been restored to duty.

To have worked for thirty-three years with a spotless record, to have been awarded two medals of honor and sixteen other decorations for service to my country—and then to wind up my career in the Marine Corps by seeing my flag hauled down and being placed under close arrest like a criminal—well, it was a pretty savage blow. But, as I said before, I already had my mind made up to retire from the Corps. This affair merely cemented my decision to get out in to civil life where I could do something for powerless juniors degraded by the autocratic action of their department superiors.

I retired from the Marine Corps on October 1, 1931. It was not easy for me to leave the men. All the life I knew had been bound up in the Corps. But I realized, too, that it was best to retire while I still had time to build another life.

We live on momentum. If you stop going, you are finished. Well, my momentum and enthusiasm will still carry me forward. There's plenty of fight in me yet.

THE END